T0348369

# The
# WAR
## of
# WORDS

# BOOKS BY MOLLY GUPTILL MANNING

NONFICTION

*The Myth of Ephraim Tutt*

*When Books Went to War*

*The War of Words*

# The
# WAR
## of
# WORDS

**HOW AMERICA'S GI JOURNALISTS BATTLED CENSORSHIP**
and **PROPAGANDA** to **HELP WIN WORLD WAR II**

## MOLLY GUPTILL MANNING

**BLACK
STONE**
PUBLISHING

Printed in the United States of America

First edition: 2023
ISBN 979-8-200-96159-7
History / Military / World War II

Version 1

Blackstone Publishing
31 Mistletoe Rd.
Ashland, OR 97520

www.BlackstonePublishing.com

*To those who spread freedom of expression across the world by writing, cartooning, reading, and sharing their stories of war.*

# CONTENTS

Introduction                                          1

Chapter One: The Word Factory                         6

Chapter Two: The Obscenities in Washington           17

Chapter Three: Comma-Flage                           30

Chapter Four: Tear-Stained Pillows                   50

Chapter Five: Hello, Suckers!                        65

Chapter Six: *45th Giornale Militare*                80

Chapter Seven: A Monument to Intolerance             94

Chapter Eight: Don't Send Me In                     115

Chapter Nine: Democracy?                            136

Chapter Ten: Now—Where Were We?                     169

Afterword                                           181

Acknowledgments                                     185

Appendix of Troop Newspapers                        189

Notes                                               203

Selected Bibliography                               243

Index                                               255

# INTRODUCTION

When Dean Chatlain led his unit into battle in southern Tunisia in early 1943, he did not expect the day's events would turn him into a literary celebrity. As the twenty-four-year-old's tank rounded a corner, the Germans scored "a perfect artillery shot" at point-blank range. Flames erupted, shrapnel flew in all directions, and four of Chatlain's crew died instantly. As Chatlain tried to escape the inferno, he realized that he could not run because his left foot was barely attached to his body. Clawing across the ground, Chatlain crawled to a shallow trench, where the tank's only other survivor died in his arms.

Alone, Chatlain lay on the hot sand as his mangled foot tortured him with pain. Worried he would bleed out, Chatlain made a tourniquet with his belt and amputated what remained of his left foot with a jackknife. When German soldiers overran Chatlain's position, they did not bother to take him prisoner. Chatlain did not look like a man who would live through the night. Realizing help might never come, Chatlain's thoughts drifted to his wife, whom he had married only a year before. They had dreams—buying a home, having kids, growing old together. Instead, she would receive a Western Union telegram reporting the death of her husband and their dreams.

The desert grew dark and cold as hours ticked by. The unrelenting percussion of artillery confirmed the battle raged on. Death was taking its time. As he waited for it, Chatlain realized he had a notepad and pen in his breast pocket. He always carried writing supplies. Since his early days in the army, Chatlain wrote poems about his adjustment to the military, capturing feelings that proved universal. "That's what I think," Chatlain's fellow soldiers said when they read his verses. Now, angry that his life was coming to an end, sad for his friends who had just died, and bitter that they would all be reduced to a number in a casualty report, Chatlain let off steam by writing:

What did you do today, my friend,
From morn until the night?
How many times did you complain,
The rationing is too tight?
When are you going to start to do
All the things you say?
A soldier would like to know my friend,
What did you do today?

We met the enemy today
And took his town by storm;
Happy reading it will make
For you tomorrow morn.
You'll read with satisfaction
The brief communique.
We fought, but are you fighting,
What did you do today?

My gunner died in my arms today
I feel his warm blood yet;
Your neighbor's dying boy gave out
A scream I can't forget.
On my right a tank was hit,

A flash and then the fire;
The stench of burning human flesh
Still rises from their pyre.

What did you do today, my friend,
To help us with the task?
Did you work harder and longer—for less,
Or is that too much to ask?
What right have I to ask *you* this
You probably will say;
Maybe now, you'll understand,
You see, I died today.

At some point, the earth grew silent. Chatlain's consciousness came in waves. Medics arrived. Over the next several months, Chatlain was shuttled from one hospital to another. He endured rounds of surgeries; his left leg required amputation at the knee, and seventy-four pieces of shrapnel had to be removed from his body. At long last, when he was honorably discharged from the army in February 1944, he wore a Silver Star and a Purple Heart.

In the meantime, the poem Chatlain had scribbled into a blood-stained notebook began to circulate in periodicals printed expressly for US troops in North Africa, Europe, and the Pacific. It described the feelings of American soldiers around the world: they were doing their part to end the war as quickly as possible, and they wanted those at home to do the same. Troops clipped the poem and mailed it home to share with loved ones, and it became an overnight sensation. From the *San Francisco Examiner* to Vermont's *Burlington Free Press*, the poem appeared in newspapers across the country. Representative James Wadsworth of New York read the poem aloud to his colleagues on the floor of the United States House of Representatives. It was even set to music and broadcast nationally on a star-studded CBS Radio program to inspire the public to buy war bonds on the third anniversary of the attack on Pearl Harbor. Before the war's end, Chatlain became a published author of a book of poems, *With Pen and Sword*.

For years, Chatlain's verse galvanized the nation to do more—work longer hours, volunteer, purchase bonds, ration goods, conserve, and work together. And yet, if it had not been for a troop newspaper program hatched by the army, Chatlain's words—and the thoughts of other soldiers who dared to submit their truths for publication—would never have spread beyond the foxholes in which they were written.

———

History has largely forgotten how US troops fought against propaganda and censorship by carting around publishing supplies and printing newspapers everywhere the military took them. But these newspapers proved to be one of the most powerful weapons of World War II. At a time when freedom of expression was stolen from hundreds of millions of people across Europe, the US Army armed its troops with typewriters so they could fight with words.

By the war's end, over 4,600 unique newspapers were conceived by intrepid GI journalists who battled to document the stories and work of the soldiers around them. Under euphemistic banners like *Tough Sheet* and *Scars and Gripes*, troops submitted comical classified ads ("WANTED: a ride home"), printed irreverent cartoons and comic strips, complained about bad chow and slow mail, and shared melodramatic poems ("When our work on earth is ended, / Then our friends on earth will tell: / 'When they died they went to Heaven, / For they have done their stretch in Hell.'"). On a more serious note, they also used their pens to process the battles they endured, acknowledge the grief they felt for fallen buddies, and document some of the most significant events of the war.

Ingenuity, doggedness, and luck were all required to get each issue into the hands of readers. Adversity reigned. Typewriters broke. Mimeograph machines were always at the rear of a convoy. Their paper got soggy. An officer's ego was bruised. They ran out of ink. And some reporters and artists ran out of time. Death was always lurking.

As challenges mounted, so did the tenacity of GI journalists. It did not matter what contortions a paper had to go through to make it into print. Troop newspapers were printed on the backs of vehicle reports, in chicken coops, and sometimes without *w*'s (the Italian alphabet does not include a *w*). As one editor said, "These papers come out daily, weekly, 'irregularly' . . . and sometimes only by the grace of God." Between interludes of fighting, soldiers developed the sense of bloodhounds when it came to sniffing out printing supplies and facilities. Every time an issue managed to go to print, troops savored every word. Like nothing else, troop newspapers sated the emotional and intellectual needs of the average GI. To see their experiences dignified in print, their names attached to the events that made history, and to have a place to share communal joy and sorrow made troops treasure the printed word.

Troop newspapers took on new meaning as American GIs witnessed the enemy's persistent propaganda and indoctrination efforts. Nazi Germany made sure that civilians in all occupied areas were fed a steady diet of falsehoods designed to keep them docile. And Allied troops were routinely peppered with propaganda leaflets to persuade them to surrender. As American troops encountered Adolf Hitler's weaponization of the written word, they understood that printing their own newspapers was a special act of war. In the face of Hitler's tainted messages designed to stoke fear, hate, and lies, American troops responded by printing newspapers to propagate courage, understanding, and truth. With gusto and verve, GI journalists showed that two could play at this game, and they were hell-bent on winning it.

President Franklin Roosevelt famously dedicated the United States to spreading "Four Freedoms" during World War II, including the freedom of expression everywhere in the world. This is the story of how American troops fought for this freedom by carrying guns *and* typewriters into battle.

# CHAPTER ONE
## THE WORD FACTORY

Were it left to me to decide whether we should have a government without newspapers, or newspapers without a government, I should not hesitate a moment to prefer the latter.

—Thomas Jefferson

How does one persuade an educated and civilized nation to wage a world war and to believe in the superiority of an Aryan race? Adolf Hitler's incredibly effective answer was to control newspapers, the primary media of his time. By requiring one-sided coverage and distortions of the truth, Hitler believed he could achieve the mass hypnosis of the public so they would believe and do whatever he wanted. His experiment began in earnest in the 1930s in Germany and quickly spread around the globe.

Ranking first in the world for the number of newspapers it published and sold, Germany's 3,097 gazettes reached nearly every household every day. Hitler believed that by planting ideas within their pages, he could slowly convert the minds of readers to his way of thinking. The main challenge he faced was securing perfect compliance by all members of the German press. These journalists had a tendency to cherish and demand their independence. To bring them in line, Hitler turned to the law. On October 4, 1933, Germany enacted a comprehensive Editorial Control Law that transformed German journalists from objective fact finders to mere puppets propped on the knee of a ventriloquist Nazi government, conveying whatever messages were whispered to them each day.

The Editorial Control Law touched every corner of the field of journalism. In order to work for a newspaper or periodical in Germany, a person now had to apply for admission to the profession. Each editor had to register with the Reich government, establishing that they were German citizens of Aryan descent who possessed the qualities and training needed for "exerting intellectual influence upon the public." If their application was approved, they would be added to the professional roster of the German press, thereby agreeing to comply with the dictates of the German Ministry of Public Enlightenment and Propaganda. No longer could a journalist criticize the government, question authority, or publish a story that might be embarrassing to the Nazi Party. Under the law, newspapers were expressly forbidden from publishing anything that "tends to weaken the strength of the German Reich, outwardly or inwardly," "offends the honor and dignity of a German," or "misleads" the public. If a publisher or editor fell afoul of these rules, charges of treason would be levied, and a trial would be held before specially created Professional Courts that were charged with safeguarding the editorial profession. A guilty verdict would usually result in the revocation of the defendant's professional license, fines, imprisonment, and the loss of civil rights. Those journalists who could not work under such constraints quit and searched for other work. Most registered and hoped for the best.

Initially, few journalists could have suspected the degree to which the German media would be controlled. However, a robust system of supervision was soon implemented, leaving no doubt that press independence was dead. Perhaps the most onerous form of press management came from the Reich's Press Division, an arm of the German Propaganda Ministry, which hosted daily compulsory press conferences. At these meetings, binding directives were issued to editors on which stories to print and how to finesse them to spread Hitler's desired message. As Hitler explained in *Mein Kampf,* "The receptivity of the great masses is very limited," and thus "all effective propaganda must be limited to a very few points and must harp on these in slogans until the last member of the public understands what you want him to understand." To make his points feel familiar through repetition, a catalog of themes was created, and discrete topics were assigned numerical codes. At the daily press conferences, publishers were told which codes had to be woven into each day's news. The themes with the greatest recurrence rates were "5990 The Jews are to blame" and "8314 The Jews want to destroy Germany." The incessant bombardment of repeated lies caused people to become accustomed to them. Over months and years, their opinions yielded to conform to Hitler's warped ideas. In the words of Alexander Hardy, a US prosecutor for the Nuremberg war crimes trials, Germany's controlled presses created "a complete blackout" on free thought and expression, and Hitler's "word factory" was one of the most effective weapons of the era. This is what Hitler had predicted all along. "With the help of a clever persistent propaganda," he said, "even heaven can be represented to the people as hell, and the most wretched life as paradise."

Having mastered a process to spread anti-Semitism and soften the German public's tolerance for military aggression, Hitler next used German newspapers to build support to invade Poland. The Reich government invented provocative lies about Polish atrocities to inflame emotions. German newspapers were forced to publish the manufactured stories of how the Poles were enslaving, brutalizing, and "exterminating" German citizens. Typical headlines included:

"The Polish Terror Against the Ethnic Germans"
"Intolerable Polish Insults, Hate Filled Incitement Against the German People"
"Slaughter and Mass Murder: A Price of 500 Zloty on the Head of Each Ethnic German"
"Poland's Campaign of Destruction Against Everything German"

As Hitler's lies grew more incredible, he had little concern about their plausibility—it only mattered that some people believed them anyway. On the eve of the Polish invasion, Hitler maintained that "the victor shall not be asked later on whether we told the truth or not."

Because France and Britain were treaty bound to assist Poland, Hitler knew they would be forced into the conflict. After Germany's humiliating defeat to France in World War I, Hitler was especially eager to restore Germany's place on the global stage by razing France at record speed, making its collapse an example to the world. Before breaching their shared land border with tanks or bullets, Hitler aimed to neutralize this target with words. Hitler believed that "psychological dislocation of the adversary through revolutionary propaganda" would be more effective than months of bombing. France thus became a laboratory for Hitler's experiment in mental warfare. Unscrupulous French journalists and newspapers, handsomely bribed by Nazi operatives, seasoned their stories with worries over the vulnerability of the French Army, the certain death of French youth in battle, and the invincibility of Germany. The Nazis hired native French speakers for German-paid broadcasts; they sounded like typical French news programs, but interspersed between commercials and weather reports were casual comments about the futility of war against Germany and how Poland was undeserving of French aid. Adding credence to newspaper and radio reports, thousands of German agents were scattered across France to sow "whispering campaigns" that spread gossip of French inferiority and German might.

Nerves frayed fast under Germany's assault of words. So effective was the Nazis' mental warfare campaign that France's preparation for Germany's promised invasion seemed only to confirm inevitable defeat. As French soldiers dug trenches across stately parks and lawns, it appeared as though the nation was physically cracking into pieces. The threat of attack was so imminent that Parisians roamed the city carrying gas masks at all times. And when the usual Thursday afternoon air raid siren accidentally sounded early, hysteria erupted as many believed the end had come. After months of suspension in a constant state of propaganda-induced paranoia, French resolve was so thoroughly undermined that it took less than six weeks for one of the world's greatest powers, forty million strong, to fall to Germany.

As soon as the Nazis occupied France, they immediately sought control of the French media by seizing French newspapers and confiscating their equipment. French journalists and printers were forced to either disseminate Nazi propaganda and indoctrination or quit and shutter their doors. In response, many French journalists tendered their resignations and secretly banded together to print underground newspapers. Having lost control of their printing presses, publishers had to be creative in finding ways to print. One former publisher used a children's stamp kit and painstakingly pieced together stories letter by letter. Others snuck into padlocked facilities to access dormant professional presses that the Nazis had shut down. Some makeshift newspapers printed no more than fifty copies, while others produced thousands.

Lurking behind blackout curtains and curfews, a surreptitious network of civilian saboteurs, reporters, and printers aimed to "introduc[e] a little sand into the Nazi machinery of occupation" by publishing free words of resistance and truth. This secret army understood the power of the printed word. As one member of the French resistance said, "The very act of setting words up in type invests them with new power, new importance. Print is a sanction, an authority." Underground newspapers became a symbol of freedom across France. They proved that there was a strong undercurrent of dissent and that the French would not simply accept Nazi repressions. As long as they continued to be printed, there was hope that France would not be lost. The Nazis were aware of how powerful these defiant papers were, and penalties for any involvement with these periodicals were well advertised. To be caught creating, distributing, or reading these papers invited a visit from the Gestapo, with violators possibly never to be seen again. Yet the papers continued to be made and read, proving that, for many, the proliferation of free words was worth the risk of death.

———

Well before Hitler invaded Poland or waged his robust mental warfare campaign in France, German agents quietly infiltrated the United States and laid the groundwork to sway public opinion in favor of Nazi Germany. By 1935, the United States was the unwitting host to more than eighteen Nazi-controlled organizations. Adopting patriotic-sounding names like "Crusaders for Americanism" and "American Guards," these Fascist groups spread propaganda that blamed social and economic troubles on the Jews, suggested Roosevelt's New Deal was a "Jewish-Communist" conspiracy to rob Americans of their independence, and painted Roosevelt as a jingoist who was unnecessarily dragging the United States into a foreign conflict.

Once the war began in Poland in 1939, the Nazis earnestly ramped up their activities in the United States by producing pro-German periodicals in English with innocuous titles that hid their true allegiance. For example, the German Library of Information printed a free weekly magazine, *Facts in Review*, which was mailed—unsolicited and free of charge—to an impressively large audience of Americans. The magazine described Germany's military as unsurpassable, published articles sympathizing with the plight of "native Germans," and emphasized the futility of taking any action against Germany.

All these mental warfare activities were funded by Germany's enormous foreign propaganda budget of $134 million per year. The United States, spending an estimated $8 million per year in "defense" against Germany's onslaught of words, was vulnerable. If it mobilized its own newspapers to spread facts and truth, the United States could empower the public to dismiss the manipulated "news" the Nazis were circulating. However, opinion polls showed that in 1939, approximately 93 percent of voters disfavored America's participation in the war and doubted Germany would wage war against the United States. Under these circumstances, it was difficult to warn the public that the United States was already under an invisible attack of words.

But President Franklin Roosevelt understood the particular importance of newspapers in this war, and he tried to delicately caution the public about the mental warfare the nation faced. When he described the United States as an "arsenal of democracy" in a December 1940 fireside chat, he borrowed this term from Herbert S. Houston, who minted this phrase in 1918 to describe the central role that newspapers played in World War I. It was through newspapers, Houston said, that the public understood President Woodrow Wilson's position on the Great War and communicated—through letters to the editor—their support or disapproval of his position. The American press acted as a "great clearing house of public opinion" by communicating the facts and providing a forum where people could participate in their democracy by freely and publicly discussing their candid beliefs. "The free press of America, uncensored and responsible only to the people upon whom it depends for support, has proved itself one of the most effective weapons in the arsenal of democracy," Houston said.

In his January 1941 State of the Union address, Roosevelt expanded on Houston's idea by acknowledging the psychological warfare used by Hitler and then dedicating the United States to spreading and practicing freedom. "The democratic way of life is at this moment being directly assailed in every part of the world—assailed either by arms, or by secret spreading of poisonous propaganda by those who seek to destroy unity and promote discord in nations that are still at peace," he said. Roosevelt knew that Germany targeted minds first, and militaries second. "As men do not live by bread alone, they do not fight by armaments alone," the president said. To be sure, airplanes, tanks, and guns would be the implements of combat, but what would carry one side to victory was an "unshakable belief in the manner of life which they are defending." The best way to keep democracy from destruction was to exercise the liberties it promised and restore the same liberties to nations where they had been stolen. Thus, Roosevelt brazenly dedicated the United States to spreading "four essential human freedoms." It was no coincidence that the first was "freedom of speech and expression—everywhere in the world." What better way for a democracy to wage war against Hitler's controlled presses and propaganda than to herald the dissemination of free words?

But as the time-tested adage goes, "truth is the first casualty of war." Just as Roosevelt promised free expression, he simultaneously deferred to the military's insistence on secrecy regarding all activities pertaining to the preparation for possible war. Leading the way was Secretary of the Navy Frank Knox who, ironically, had worked for years as a journalist and publisher of newspapers between stints as a Rough Rider in 1898 and an officer in World War I. Although Knox's newspaper work earned him a reputation as an anti-corruption "crusader" (one hard-hitting story even inspired someone to take a shotgun to the windows of Knox's newspaper office) and a critic of Roosevelt's New Deal programs (Knox published countless front-page editorials lambasting Roosevelt in the *Chicago Daily News*), he had no plans to extend the freedom he enjoyed as a journalist to the reporters wishing to cover the work of the navy.

Beginning in 1940, Knox instructed all newsrooms to refrain from publishing information about US ship movements, the development of weapons, naval construction projects, and the presence of British ships in American ports. Knox was so greedy for control over press coverage that even when his prohibitions yielded ridiculous results, he did not back down. One such episode occurred in April 1941, when the HMS *Malaya* arrived in New York, groaned through the harbor in broad daylight with a gaping hole in its side from a German torpedo attack, and was moored in Battery Place, just outside the German consulate. British soldiers poured out of the ship and enjoyed days and nights on the town, proudly wearing their uniforms and caps with "Malaya" emblazoned across their foreheads. There was no doubt the British had arrived in New York. Yet Knox demanded that no mention of the *Malaya* be made in local newspapers.

Arthur Sulzberger, the publisher of the *New York Times*, abided by Knox's wishes but privately wrote Knox that withholding news of the *Malaya* seemed asinine. "You admit that it is true that many people can see the ships as they arrive and depart, including enemy agents," Sulzberger said. And yet, Sulzberger continued, Knox took the position that "it seems only sportsmanlike for the American press to refrain from giving this information to Britain's enemies—but you already admit they have it." In response, Knox deflected blame and chided the British: "They sent the damn ship into New York harbor at ten o'clock in the morning," and "on top of that they gave the men shore leave and did not take the trouble to remove the hatband or ensure that they would not do a lot of indiscreet talking when they went ashore." Knox assured Sulzberger that he had "raised all hell about this" and closed rather sinisterly by saying that continued compliance with voluntary censorship would "avoid any necessity for a compulsory one later." In the months that followed, the navy continued to nix newsworthy stories even though the facts were already out in the open.

The December 7, 1941, attack on Pearl Harbor only exacerbated matters. As smoke billowed over the damaged Pacific fleet, the US military declared that all information regarding the strength, location, and movement of troops outside the United States was unpublishable. Stories about the number of ships sunk, planes destroyed, and dead and missing at Pearl Harbor were forbidden—and not for mere days or weeks; months elapsed and still the navy kept quiet. Journalists were flummoxed. "All the suppression or withholding in the world would not raise the ships again," Arthur Krock of the *New York Times* remarked. And there was no question that Japan knew precisely how much damage it had caused. The reason for withholding the facts was transparent: "Knox is merely trying, at the expense of [the press], to protect himself from his colossal failure," Krock said.

Making matters worse, Roosevelt's initial actions after Pearl Harbor seemed to confirm that he supported the strict censorship of the press. Eleven days after declaring war on Japan and Germany, the president signed Executive Order 8985, creating an Office of Censorship. The press feared that such a move would be tantamount to Germany's passage of its 1933 Editorial Control Law. However, the man tasked with heading the Office of Censorship was Byron Price, a lifelong newspaperman who had most recently served as executive news editor and acting general manager of the Associated Press. Balancing journalists' need for independence with the "necessary evil" of wartime censorship, Price denounced compulsory censorship as "the totalitarian way" and instead adopted a voluntary program of "self-regulation." A five-page booklet titled "Codes of Wartime Practices for the American Press" banned only information that directly threatened the nation's security.

Despite Price's flexibility at home, the military still had the upper hand when it came to coverage of overseas action. If war correspondents wanted to provide eyewitness accounts of the early battles in the Pacific (which were largely orchestrated by the navy), they would need to hitch a ride on a naval vessel. Admiral Ernest King, commander in chief of the

United States fleet, loathed the media and resisted correspondents' requests for access to naval engagements. Notorious for his stubbornness, fondness for discipline, and prickly disposition, King was described by his daughter as even-tempered—because he was always in a rage. King was used to having his way, and he insisted on having total control over the navy's news and image. Rosy communiqués were the norm. "Very excellent news has been received," began a 1942 press release. "Highly successful action took place in the vicinity of the Solomon Islands and was accomplished with the loss of but three planes." In reality, *New York Times* correspondent Hanson Baldwin discovered that the US Marines' landing on the Solomons came at the cost of the *Quincy*, *Vincennes*, and *Astoria* cruisers as well as the *Wasp* aircraft carrier and the battleship *North Carolina*. When Baldwin drafted an article telling the truth about the Solomons, navy censors barred Baldwin from publishing it.

The product of all this secrecy was obliviousness. Americans could not understand why millions of young men were being drafted when the war had such one-sided results, always favoring the United States. Furthermore, public-opinion polls revealed that one-third of Americans could not identify a single reason why the nation was at war. And the lack of information only compounded a rising tide of discontent within the military as drafted men failed to understand the purpose of their training or fighting. Ignorance could be as powerful a weapon as enemy propaganda.

Hiding information, preventing the press from disclosing facts, and suffocating free expression—these were not the ways of democracy. Arthur Sulzberger decided to remind the government of this by way of an ultimatum. At a private meeting with government officials, Sulzberger declared that if newspapers were not permitted to print facts about the war, then the *New York Times* would intentionally violate the Code of Censorship. Sulzberger's bold move rattled Washington and produced results. Days before the first anniversary of Pearl Harbor, the navy finally disclosed that 2,343 Americans had died, 1,272 were wounded, 960 were missing in action, 18 vessels were lost, and 177 planes were destroyed on the "date which will live in infamy." Ultimately, the navy, secretly strong-armed by President Roosevelt, promised to be more forth-coming in providing details of its future casualties and battles. Although the navy warned that an avalanche of grim news would hurt the war effort, it had the opposite effect. By bringing civilians into the navy's confidence and telling them the truth about losses and setbacks, civil-ians felt a greater personal stake to do their part to ensure victory. As one editorial stated, "The American people realize as never before that our navy is bound to lose ships . . . [but the disclosure of] bad news . . . gives the people new confidence in their navy and it likewise will spur the effort on the home front."

———

Throughout the war, there was constant tension between democracy's guarantee of freedom of the press and the government's fear that news-papers might publish secret military information that would fall into enemy hands. Distrust ebbed and flowed between the US government and its domestic press.

Surprisingly, even though censorship and military media suppres-sion threatened to choke the newspaper industry, the 1940s beckoned astronomical growth. Thousands of newspapers were hatched during the first few years of the war. Almost all of them came from the most unlikely source: the military. As troop morale sank to disturbingly low levels in 1940, the War Department responded by revitalizing its tra-dition of publishing soldier newspapers to attempt to right the ship.

# CHAPTER TWO
## THE OBSCENITIES IN WASHINGTON

If I were giving advice to the boys who have already been called into the Army and will go away in a few days, I'd sum it all up in this:

"Paint the town red for the rest of your civilian week." . . .

Two weeks from now, you will be thoroughly disgusted with your new job. You will have been herded from place to place, you will have wandered in nakedness and bewilderment through miles of physical examinations, you will look upon privacy and individuality as things you left behind you in a golden civilian society.

—Pvt. Marion Hargrove

They arrived wearing their Sunday best, with suitcases knocking at their knees and butterflies in their stomachs. Days earlier, they were students, factory workers, salesmen, musicians, office clerks, mechanics, and farmers. Now, they were reporting for induction into the United States military. Their range of attitudes toward service could not have been more diverse. For some, there was romance to wearing a uniform, learning to fight, and shipping out to exotic locations to risk it all for love of country. They happily escaped the trappings of their small-town roots and embraced the prospect of being paid to go on the adventure of a lifetime. Others left their jobs and family reluctantly; they were angry and bitter about being drafted. They said begrudging goodbyes, choked back tears, and resentfully did their duty.

After taking their soldier's oath, groups of newbies were shepherded into reception centers. Within minutes, the army managed to steal any sense of privacy or dignity. Orders came to form a line, strip naked, wear a paper identification tag around their necks, undergo physical examinations, and endure a battery of mandatory vaccinations. After tolerating hours of humiliations, they were given an ill-fitting uniform and placed in quarantine.

As troops were routed from reception centers to army posts for basic training, many discovered that the army was not ready to receive them. In late 1940, the 105th Infantry Division arrived at Fort McClellan, Alabama, to discover there was no "fort"—no barracks, no classrooms, no latrines, and not even roads. They slept in tents and relieved themselves in what one man described as "piss cans." Because there were no mess halls, the men ate outside—rain or shine—inescapably near the stench of the makeshift toilets. One soldier assigned to Camp Blanding in Florida described his surroundings as nothing more than "a bare sandy lot of unoccupied land." Even established training facilities experienced growing pains. In February 1941, the 106th Medical Battalion reported to Pennsylvania's Carlisle Barracks; they were flummoxed that they would be spending the winter sleeping in pyramidal tents with seven strangers (after all, they were at Carlisle *Barracks*). While hardened soldiers would live under much worse conditions in combat, enlisted men serving in peacetime bristled at their primitive environs.

Not only were facilities nonexistent, but so were basic supplies—from uniforms to weaponry. The army was forced to improvise by recycling equipment from the Great War, which did not go over well. In the words of one enlistee, the "clothing and equipment we were issued had a certain historical value," with shirts "at least twenty years old," mess kits with "names and '1918' scratched on the aluminum," and ancient "underpants with drawstring arrangements [that caused] clinging, itchy legs." "We looked terrible, and we felt bad," he said. There was also a dearth of armaments. When it was time to gain proficiency with weapons, troops were given dummy mortars made out of stovepipes or wood. Mop handles propped on sawhorses imitated antiaircraft guns. Trucks were labeled TANK, and metal pipes bore signs reading CANNON, so the men knew what to pretend during field exercises. Confidence lagged. In the words of one man from Brooklyn, "[I've] never fired even a .22 in a Coney Island shooting gallery." Pretending that scraps of firewood were firearms seemed futile.

Regardless of the scarcity of supplies, the men had to train. War was spreading overseas faster than a wildfire on a windy day, and it was only a matter of time before America would be dragged into the fray. Unfortunately, with moth-eaten uniforms on their backs and broomsticks in their hands, the importance and urgency of training were imperceptible to most men. Although the army had failed them in outfits and supplies, no concessions were made when it came to physical conditioning. For many, this only added a layer of disgust to the already intolerable experience of becoming a soldier.

Up at 6:00 a.m., greeted by drill sergeants barking orders, the men marched and maneuvered, practiced shooting weapons (real or imaginary), and were assigned dirty jobs constructing, maintaining, and policing camps. From reveille to taps, the average soldier marched ten miles per day and performed all manner of grueling tasks. At the end of these long days, muscles ached and discontent swelled. Though they may have camouflaged outward appearances of unhappiness, these civilian soldiers raged inside. As Private Marion Hargrove explained in his best-selling book, *See Here, Private Hargrove*, within the first few days, each man "will have developed a murderous hatred for at least one sergeant and two corporals," and he will "writhe and fume under what [seems like] brutality and sadism." He wrote, "You'll drill and drill, a little more each day," growing more resentful by the hour. Yet all of this "persecution is deliberate, calculated, systemic," Hargrove said. "It is the Hardening Process." It was refreshing for troops to read Hargrove's words and have their feelings validated. The military took a different approach: "You may be homesick and lonesome for a while," one handbook conceded. "We all were. . . . Grin and bear it like we all did."

At the end of each long day, darkness brought some relief. Lights out provided anonymity; it gave men the privacy and psychological space to grieve the civilian lives they had left behind. "Some guys in basic training cried in their pillows," one serviceman recalled. By the war's end, approximately one in three American males between the ages of eighteen and forty-four would experience the same bewildering initiation into military life.

For those drafted in 1940, a twelve-month cap on their military service promised relief. However, when Congress extended this one-year maximum term in August 1941, a near mutiny broke out. Redacting language that could not be printed, *Time* magazine quoted a soldier's reaction as best it could: "Those obscenity obscenities in Washington! Obscenity the whole obscenity lot of them!" "What the hell are we being kept here for," another soldier-in-training asked, his disgust palpable. Silent protests swept camps. At one, "OHIO" ("Over the Hill in October," one man explained) was carved and scribbled on latrine walls, artillery pieces, and everywhere in between to advertise that mass desertions were planned. "Snasu" ("situation normal: all screwed up") was another outfit's response."

Many men felt lost. They had been dragged into a sea of anonymity whose current drew them through induction, classification, and training. They were forced to wear the same drab uniforms, eat the same food, sleep in the same tents, and meld into the same monotonous mold as the thousands of others at their posts. It was hard to shake the feeling that they were becoming mere cogs in the military's machinery, easily cast aside and replaced should they become maimed or worse. They craved any sign of their uniqueness. Beleaguered by the loss of privacy, material comforts, opportunities to pursue personal interests, and independence, many draftees' discontent ripened into loathing. In the words of one enlistee, "The soldier, especially the conscript, suffers so deeply from contempt and damage to his selfhood, from absurdity and boredom and chickenshit, that some anodyne is necessary."

———

If Congress had only listened to Chief of Staff George Marshall, the army's morale crisis could have been avoided. But Marshall discovered that politicians tended to follow what was politically popular rather than what was necessary.

Sworn in as the chief of staff of the army only hours after the German Army attacked Poland on September 1, 1939, George Marshall was tasked with raising and equipping the army at the same time as President Roosevelt was adopting measures for neutrality. It was an unenviable task. Since World War I, the size of the American Army had dwindled to 174,000 troops. The army's equipment, which was modern in 1919, was now obsolete. "As an army, we were ineffective" and on par with "a third-rate power," Marshall said. Meanwhile, overseas, Germany was attacking with a state-of-the-art, mechanized fighting force that had been years in the making. Marshall knew that he needed to increase the size of his meager army, build an entire air force, purchase contemporary weaponry, and construct training areas to prepare soldiers for warfare. But to do this, Marshall needed congressional approval for a hefty budget. Obtaining it was no easy task.

From 1939 to 1940, Marshall was forced to make countless visits to Capitol Hill to grovel for military funding. Widespread isolationist sentiment caused elected officials to balk when asked to consider a mandatory draft that would shepherd sons and husbands into military service or to approve billions of dollars for the expansion of the armed forces. The reality was the United States would likely be dragged into the war, and the army needed to be prepared. Marshall tried to impress upon politicians the urgency of the army's needs. "I repeat, it is of vital importance that we have modern equipment for this initial protective force . . . ; that we modernize our artillery; [and] that we replace our 34-year-old rifles with more modern weapons," Marshall told Congress in 1939. Marshall's message made little impact. One senator described Marshall's position as "one of the most stupid and outrageous things . . . ever perpetrated on the Congress." Another congressman suggested that Marshall was exaggerating the army's deficiencies, to which the chief of staff could not help but answer, "My relief of mind would be tremendous if we just had too much of something besides patriotism and spirit."

Marshall did not back down. In February 1940, the chief of staff submitted a budget to Congress seeking $850 million to equip 227,000 men in the regular army, 235,000 in the National Guard, and a possible 500,000 troops who were to be called in case of an emergency. Marshall explained that the army needed to provide for a soldier's every need—food, clothing, shelter, bedding, grooming supplies, and medical care. Buildings needed to be constructed to house classrooms, cafeterias, barracks, bathhouses, hospitals, and offices. Plus, Marshall estimated there would be "a lag time of one or two years between the initial order and the delivery of the finished product to the soldier." To Marshall's consternation, in April 1940, the House Appropriations Committee diminished the budget for the armed forces by 10 percent. At a time when Marshall needed to build an air force, Congress allotted him only fifty-seven replacement airplanes. According to his biographer, Forrest Pogue, as Marshall watched Germany's progress across Europe, he became "depressed" and "more deeply troubled than ever by the terrible weakness of his own country."

When France abruptly surrendered to Germany, the shock of Germany's decisive victory rattled some of the complacency out of American politicians and the public. When opinion polls showed that 71 percent of Americans suddenly favored compulsory conscription, politicians received a booster shot of political courage. In September 1940, Congress passed the Selective Training and Service Act, requiring all men between the ages of twenty-one and thirty-six (later raised to forty-four) to register for military service. On October 16, approximately fourteen million Americans registered with local draft boards, and the army prepared for immediate inductions. Initial plans called for thirty thousand recruits reporting for service by November 18; four hundred thousand would be in uniform by the end of February, and eight hundred thousand would enter the armed forces by mid-June. While the draft ensured that Marshall would be able to raise a sizable army, Congress's failure to approve Marshall's full budget promised that men would be drafted before the army had uniforms and supplies. It was a recipe for disaster.

Letters arrived at Marshall's desk each day, reporting that rudimentary necessities were missing at army posts across the country. The

Monterey Reception Center had run out of shoes. The 367th Infantry did not have field manuals. Hospital patients in Louisiana were wilting in the heat because fans and air conditioners had not arrived. Fort Sill's hospital was running out of medical supplies. Field gear never arrived at a number of facilities. And First Lady Eleanor Roosevelt was personally forwarding complaints to Marshall over the army's neglect of Black troops.

As Marshall zipped around army camps trying to do anything to ease supply shortages, an incessant stream of blame targeted him for failing to capably maintain an army. Parents wrote him furious letters. Legislators, whose procrastination had caused this predicament, forwarded complaints from their constituents. And the army's morale problem was aired in national periodicals. *Time* magazine explained that camp life was intolerable because the food was inedible, the monotony of drills and maneuvers bored men to tears, and the whole business seemed unnecessary when the nation had no plans to go to war. Plus, while civilian soldiers in the early stages of training "gladly played that a forked stick and a lath were a machine gun, that two wheels and a wooden barrel were an anti-tank gun; today they are tired of stage properties." With no sense of meaning for their service, many draftees felt trapped in the military with no worthwhile job to do.

*Life* magazine echoed these sentiments. Unlike World War I—when Americans felt a "burning incentive to fight" and proceeded on a clear trajectory of training, shipping out, and fighting in France—the reasons for training in 1940 and 1941 were unclear. "The Army's purposes are confused, many of its soldiers not even understanding why they are being trained." Plus, relentless drills alone did not make great fighters. "Above all, their morale must be kept high. They must be kept happy and busy. They must be given warm places to sleep, good food to eat, adequate pay and comfortable clothes. Also, they must have some recreation," *Life* pleaded.

Marshall knew that uniforms, weaponry, and other supplies would eventually arrive. But they would not improve morale. *Time* and *Life* were right. For an army of civilian soldiers, the army needed to provide civilian comforts. To solve the morale crisis, troops needed recreation and entertainment for their off-duty hours.

———

Before 1941, most officers had chosen military service as a career path, and some had attended elite academies like West Point. As "regular army" men, they had willingly embraced discipline, they naturally felt pride in their uniforms, and many gladly took up the torch to continue a family tradition of service. These officers had no empathy for civilian soldiers who balked at protocol and felt little reverence for the armed services. But the army's chief of staff was different. He had struggled in the classroom, attending an institution that produced only a handful of "regular army" men each year, and he sympathized with those who wilted under military discipline. Just as his background was unconventional, so were Marshall's leadership ideas. Believing happy soldiers were better soldiers, Marshall's military career was marked by experiments in how to bring out the best in those around him. The lessons he learned inspired one of the most comprehensive army recreation programs in history.

His first foray into fostering soldier morale occurred shortly after he was commissioned as a second lieutenant in 1902 and was given command of G Company in the Philippines. Stationed in the remote locale of Mangarin Bay, one man joked that their only visitors were "half of all the world's mosquitoes." Marshall admitted to being "tragically lonely," and he was keenly aware that his men also struggled with isolation coupled with disgruntlement over the litany of menial tasks they were assigned because there was no outside help. Rather than ignore the rising chorus of complaints and discontent, Marshall decided to reward his men for the hard work they did. Secretly, Marshall ordered games, playing cards, checkers, books, and magazines so the troops could enjoy themselves at night. When a transport delivered these supplies, all were deeply moved by the gesture. By showing that he cared and valued his men, Marshall earned their admiration and respect. Marshall recognized that maintaining morale was like trying to clutch a handful of sand; by tightening his grip, he would lose more and retain less.

The role of newspapers in fortifying esprit de corps became obvious to Marshall when he was brought to the front lines of France during World War I. As an operations officer, and later aide-de-camp to General John J. Pershing, Marshall took every opportunity to understand the conditions US troops faced. Riding on horseback through areas where shells were falling, Marshall developed a sincere sympathy for the plight of the infantryman, whom he described as "the poor devil of the Army" who "marches tremendous distances; he is in the mud; he's filthy dirty; he hasn't had a full meal . . . and he fights in a place he has never seen before." These men needed something to boost their spirits as they endured a bitterly cold and wet winter, bore the brunt of constant bombardments, and feared they might never see home again. Marshall thought of Mangarin and believed the Great War's troops would benefit if some sort of recreation was provided to lift their spirits. Sharing Marshall's sentiment was General Pershing, who had the rank and clout to take action.

As commander of the American Expeditionary Forces, when Pershing expressed concern about his troops' fleeting fortitude, the AEF Intelligence Division spearheaded an investigation to find the cause. The resulting study concluded that troops needed newspapers. According to the Intelligence Division, the prevailing consensus among troops was that "The army is doing the best it can by us in everything except giving us the news, and we want that more than anything else." Isolated and lacking proficiency in French, soldiers received no information about the war or events in the United States. They did not understand the value of their service or whether their efforts had any meaningful impact on bringing the war closer to an end. To solve this problem, Pershing wanted to give his men the news they desired, written by GI journalists who understood the niche audience they were writing for.

Giving American troops their own newspapers was not an original idea, as the army enjoyed a long history of having a fourth estate. George Washington successfully petitioned Congress in 1777 for a "small travelling press to follow Headquarters" to keep troops informed and motivated. During the War of 1812, General Andrew Jackson printed a newsletter that explained the issues for which his men were fighting. The Civil War welcomed a host of troop newspapers, including the original army-wide *Stars and Stripes*, as well as papers printed by individual divisions or units. Under Pershing's watch, World War I was a breeding ground for army periodicals, and Marshall had a front-row seat to see what a difference they made in the morale of hundreds of thousands of troops.

Drawing from precedent, General Pershing revived the Civil War's *Stars and Stripes* newspaper in early 1918. Talented newsmen were transferred from divisions across France to the paper's Paris headquarters. Harold Ross, Grantland Rice, Franklin Pierce Adams, Alexander Woollcott, and Stephen Early—to name but a few—toiled over newspaper copy and persnickety printing presses to give American foot soldiers the up-to-date news and amusement they craved. Pershing granted the paper's staff wide leeway to find scoops, print all the newsworthy information they could find, and publish gripes and complaints to acknowledge widespread hardships and build comradery. The staffers understood their audience. In the words of correspondent Alexander Woollcott, the *Stars and Stripes* was by and "for a weary, dirty, cootie-bitten, news-famished, homesick enlisted man in a foul trench." Through honest reporting that always took the side of the GIs, readers found unexpected solace in the *Stars and Stripes*, for it validated their adversities and sorrows while also gently goading them to carry on. The Intelligence Division's unlikely solution to the morale crisis proved to be strong medicine.

To provide more localized news and praise, Pershing also approved the publication of smaller, division-wide newspapers. As Marshall observed, when troops deserved praise for the work they had done, it meant more when it "was made in the presence of those who had shared in the action." When unit newspapers were printed, they recorded every citation and award, reaching a wide audience to share in each triumph. Because they generously included the names of troops, stressed the importance of myriad jobs (from forestry work to trench warfare), and frankly acknowledged the homesickness and gloom many soldiers felt, newspapers became an unexpected source of gratification.

Pershing did not stop with periodicals by and for troops. The Intelligence Division also discovered that troops were eager for periodicals from home. As one American soldier said in a letter to a friend: "I'm out here . . . with krumps bursting on my cocoanut and am going to see it through, . . . [but] if you've got any American newspapers or magazines lying around loose please send them to me, as I am far from California." An American working with the Red Cross in France seconded this sentiment: "The men . . . are pathetically eager for home news, and there is nothing they wish for more than home papers."

To handle some of the reading needs of American troops, the Library War Service was formed by the American Library Association and placed under the direction of the Librarian of Congress. In 1917 and 1918, fundraising and donation drives were launched, and the Carnegie Corporation paid for the construction of library buildings at military installations across the United States. Because troops had an insatiable appetite for the latest news, a wartime postal regulation enabled the public to donate their used newspapers and magazines via mail. By affixing a one-cent stamp on a gently read periodical or gazette, the post office would deliver them to the librarian at the nearest army camp. While the idea was a good one, it resulted in the donation of many out-of-date and unusable magazines and newspapers; they were sold as wastepaper, and the funds collected were then used for magazine subscriptions. While all these efforts were designed to get reading materials into the hands of all troops, they mainly benefited soldiers who had not left the United States.

But Pershing needed materials for his troops in France. Thus, the Library War Service established a headquarters in Paris and undertook the construction of library facilities mainly in rear areas. Popular American magazines were hot commodities overseas, and soon the Library War Service oversaw the shipment of fifteen thousand copies of the *Saturday Evening Post* and five thousand issues of other popular weekly and monthly periodicals to ensure a good selection. This was not nearly enough, but every magazine that reached the trenches was savored and shared. They informed, amused, and served as precious reminders of home.

Marshall watched as the periodicals supplied to troops in World War I energized dispirited soldiers like smelling salts restored the faint. Nothing else came close to fortifying those Americans scattered across Europe who were performing diverse tasks with little understanding of how their roles factored into victory.

As he faced the 1940 morale crisis, Marshall was convinced that the best way to build morale was to give the troops newspapers. But at a time when famous civilian publishers like Arthur Sulzberger struggled under the yoke of censorship, how could low-ranking soldiers fare any better? Fueling Marshall's concern were the navy's frosty attitude toward the press and President Roosevelt's endorsement of the Office of Censorship and propensity to side with the navy. Marshall felt that if he could get the approval of the army's commander in chief, it would go a long way in spearheading the robust army newspaper program that he envisioned.

As it turned out, Roosevelt's fondness for the navy extended to its tradition of supplying sailors with the news. During the first two terms of his presidency, Franklin Roosevelt's favorite escape from Washington was on a presidential cruise. Between 1935 and 1940, Roosevelt sailed on the USS *Farragut, Potomac, Indianapolis, Philadelphia, Tuscaloosa, Augusta,* and *Houston* (the latter ship hosted four presidential cruises in five years). As historian Gaddis Smith stated, during the first eight years of his presidency, Roosevelt spent "more shipboard time than many an active naval officer—averaging close to fifty days a year."

On these weeks-long voyages, Roosevelt aimed to blend in, and he enjoyed feeling the sense of brotherhood that developed as he ate meals with the crew, attended ship-wide church services, watched nightly movies, and became a "shellback." (Sailors who were crossing the equator for the first time—called "pollywogs"—went through a hazing ritual to prove that they "could endure the hardships of a life at sea"; at the end of the rowdy ceremonies, they were crowned shellbacks.) He also learned that many naval ships had a habit of printing shipboard newspapers in peacetime. As an honorary crewmember, Roosevelt was treated to copies of the homespun papers printed during his cruises. These newssheets included articles on the lands being visited, the history of naval rituals (like the equator-crossing ceremony), poetry by the crew, and lively gossip about port-of-call shenanigans. The comradery and connection these newspapers built were felt by all, the president included. Roosevelt and members of his presidential parties were even known to play practical jokes on one another by submitting fictitious and defamatory "scoops" to the editors of ship newspapers and relishing in the uproarious reactions of unsuspecting readers. For example, on one cruise, presidential adviser Harry Hopkins slipped an article to the editor of the USS *Houston*'s newspaper, the *Blue Bonnet*, which claimed that President Roosevelt was being demoted from the office of the president to a government stamp-pasting department. On a later cruise, Roosevelt submitted a scandalous yarn about one of his guests and thoroughly enjoyed watching his unsuspecting friend turn a deep shade of crimson while reading it. Roosevelt cherished the shipboard newspapers from his presidential cruises, saving each one and taking them home.

When Marshall gathered the courage to broach the subject of soldier-made newspapers for troops in the 1940s, he was stunned to receive Roosevelt's wholehearted support for the idea. Roosevelt was aware of the military's morale predicament and understood how troop newspapers could go a long way in solving it. Plus, Roosevelt liked the optics of giving American troops the freedom to print their own newspapers when Nazi Germany stole this freedom from civilians in every country it occupied. If Hitler could weaponize words, the United States would defuse them.

From the early stages of its development, Roosevelt tracked the army's newspaper program with interest and enthusiasm. He made sure the White House was on the mailing list for many troop newssheets. And just like the newspapers on his presidential cruises, Roosevelt could not help but offer his own contributions for publication from time to time.

With Roosevelt as his coconspirator, Marshall returned to the War Department, eager to get typewriters and sketch pads back into the trenches where they belonged.

# CHAPTER THREE
## COMMA-FLAGE

What they really called the paper [the *Leonitic*] was "lunatic." For lunacy was the way we lived and fought the war.

—Gilbert Sandler, navigator, USS *Leonis*

We sailed from an unmentionable port on an unmentionable ship, took an unmentionable course, and arrived at an unmentionable destination on an unmentionable date.

—Corporal Claude Ramsey, *U.S.A.T.*, 1942

In 1942, Marshall announced his plan to revitalize and expand the army's tradition of unit-based troop newspapers. He wanted to make it easy for every detachment that wanted to print its own stories to be able to request publishing supplies and start cranking out their own gazettes. But he also knew that most troops had no background in publishing and would need guidance on what and how to print. So Marshall asked the Special Service Division, which was in charge of all activities pertaining to soldier morale, to figure out the best methods to deliver publishing materials and advice.

Drawing from the knowledge of experts in a variety of fields, the Special Service Division had already developed recreational "field kits" for sports and games, music, radio, theater, movies, and libraries. Each kit was prepackaged in a large crate for easy shipment and was delivered to units upon the request of a commissioned officer or unit chaplain.

One of the most popular kits was the "sports and games" collection, which included everything from footballs and baseball bats to crayons and bingo supplies. Alongside guitars and sheet music, the music kit even contained upright pianos. The motion picture kit contained everything needed to watch a movie anywhere—there was a projector, a portable movie screen, a generator, and a selection of Hollywood films that rotated from one unit to the next.

When Marshall announced his desire for troops to print their own newspapers, the Special Service Division simply created a newspaper field kit that was brimming with printing gear. With an eye toward portable and easy-to-use equipment, mimeograph machines were selected for publishing purposes (rather than professional-style Linotype or offset printing presses). A mimeograph's technology was straightforward: troops essentially engraved their newspaper onto a stencil, the pliable stencil was then wrapped around a rotating drum filled with ink, and with each hand-cranked revolution of the drum, centrifugal force sent ink seeping through the impressions and onto a piece of paper. Accouterments for the machine included packages of stencils, lettering guides, an instruction manual, and ink. Other incidentals for the newspaper kit were Underwood Model II typewriters, typewriter ribbons, correction fluid, type cleaning fluid and brushes, staples, staplers, paper, and number two pencils. Every two weeks, paper and other depleted supplies were replenished. When a unit was on the move, all newspaper equipment could be packed into the crate in which it first arrived and transported on a truck to the next destination. They would not be the most elegant of newspapers, but they would serve their purpose.

To provide guidance on what and how to print, the Special Service Division manufactured a variety of guides. For technical information on production techniques, mechanical questions, circulation tips, and basic organizational recommendations, the Special Service Division printed the *Army Newspaper Editors' Manual* to assist up-and-coming papers. To nurture budding journalists and provide an example of what a soldier periodical might offer, the War Department published a monthly trade magazine, *GI Galley*. It was an overnight success.

What made the *GI Galley* so popular was that each issue catered to its niche audience by authentically capturing the perspective of "lowly" privates who were battling to print newspapers despite a litany of challenges. Sage advice was interlaced with griping, teasing, swearing, and commiserating. This mixture of information and shared troubles produced a sense of fellowship among GI journalists that eventually spanned the world. The *Galley* celebrated the work of editors and reporters by telling their stories of circumventing army snafus and getting their papers out.

Rather than rely on its staff in Manhattan to guess which problems plagued editors in the field, the *Galley* asked GIs to submit their questions and complaints for publication. There was no shortage of them. "I'm fighting this war in one of the more tropical climates," wrote one soldier newsman. "I run into trouble all the time with mimeograph stencils which like to get all nice and mushy and soft because of the warm, humid climate." The *Galley*'s solution was to hang the stencils on a clothesline overnight so the cooler air would harden them, and work on the engravings first thing in the morning. The *Galley* also shared life hacks for supply shortages. When an artist for Fort Benning's *24th Hi-Lites* lacked a stylus, he discovered that a straightened paper clip could be used to carve illustrations into the mimeograph stencils. The *Voice of Shangri La* shared that "GI mucilage" helped bind stencils together in a pinch (to which the *Galley* countered, "Mimeograph manufacturers tell us mucilage won't work"). Next to technical difficulties, newsmen often solicited advice on how to improve the quality of their articles. "One of the unit contributors to our paper suffers from worditis," an editor complained. "He is a genius at making ten words do the work of two. How can I correct him?" The *Galley* advised, "Don't criticize his stuff directly but mention that most big papers and the better camp papers place the accent on terse composition."

The *Galley* lived up to its promise of being a clearinghouse of ideas. It showcased novel experiments, ingenious marketing ploys, and odd techniques to amuse and inspire editors. When Camp Roberts wanted to publicize a new movie with a female lead that was playing in the camp theater, a reporter discovered that dumping a bottle of perfume in the mimeograph machine's ink well resulted in scented copies of *The Cannoneers*. When there were no staples to bind the pages of the *Cobra Chronicle*, the staff used a sewing machine to stitch the paper together. Staffers on the *Post Review*, a newspaper for an air force basic training center in Utah, catered to their audience by liberally using GI slang—referring to "brass roosters" (bugles) and visiting the "gut hammer" (mess hall).

When it came to reporting headaches and work-arounds, there was no shortage of tales. When the Camp Edwards *News* ran out of newsprint, one journalist from the motor pool solved the problem by printing the newspaper on the back of old vehicle reports. "Better than no newspaper at all," he said. When a power outage darkened Stewart Field on press night, the editors of the *Prop Wash* worked by candlelight and manually cranked the printing machine to meet their deadline. As one journalist remarked, they could not let their readers miss a week's worth of "litterchure." The staff of *The Broadcaster* shared how a flood of biblical proportions swept Scott Field, Illinois, forcing them to spend five days in "fatigues working with spades and shovels rather than proofs and typewriters," but on the "sixth day they managed to return to editorial duty and turned out enough copy" to distribute a respectable newspaper on the seventh day. And editors in Alabama wrote the *Galley* for help when outspoken local ministers insisted they stop using the words *hell* and *damn* in their copy. (The *Galley* took the side of the editors; training could be hellish, and the editors would be damned if they did not say so.)

Although Marshall had envisioned troop newspapers as a domestic program, some units that embarked overseas in 1942 managed to bring their crated printing equipment with them. These early experiments in publishing in combat zones would ultimately embolden Marshall to sanction overseas newspapers in 1943. The first GI editors who attempted to publish abroad wrote the *Galley* to share an entirely different class of problems from what troops encountered while still in the United States.

"After 22 years of newspaper work I thought I knew what trouble was," one editor began his letter to the *Galley* from "somewhere in the Pacific."

"But I have a new slant on the word since becoming editor of *The Third Strike*." There was "one old, beat-up typewriter" and a mimeograph machine that his unit used for everything. Paper was scarce, their stencils were too hard, and their stylus "wasn't worth a tinker's dam." Adding to these troubles were "bombing raids on press night, bugs down the collar, assorted details and KP [Kitchen Police], building camps, running errands, swatting mosquitoes, and ruining your eyes under poor light." Still, with equal parts of sweat and profanity, they got the paper out on time, twice a week. Despite the parade of horribles he faced, the editor had not lost his spunk. "I remember reading or hearing that Japan has some good printing equipment," he remarked in closing. "If you hear that *The Third Strike* is a letterpress job in the future, you'll know what happened."

The *GI Galley* also shared stories of editors overcoming the obstacles presented by strings of bad luck, mix-ups, and combat. One such article chronicled the 1903rd Engineer Battalion's struggles as they attempted to publish their newspaper, the *Tough Sheet*. It read like a humorous cautionary tale. As boredom weighed heavily on the men during their weeks-long journey to the Pacific, the editors of the *Tough Sheet* thought they could entertain their captive audience by putting out a paper. Copy was written, the mimeograph machine was inked, stencils were carved and ready—but someone had packed the *Tough Sheet*'s paper supply in the hold of the ship. It took thirty-six hours to find it. A deliriously tired sergeant, dripping with sweat, marveled, "Here we are right in the middle of the biggest war in history and our biggest worry is getting the *Tough Sheet* printed. That's American Freedom of the Press for ya!"

But it was not just the high seas that vexed the *Tough Sheet*. Land somehow proved worse. "Because of typhoonic, hectic, and mechanicalic conditions (the latter meaning this G—Damned Typewriter) the Foxhole Press has been unable to supply you with the latest, up-to-the-minute news that it has spoiled you with up to a few days ago," the *Tough Sheet* explained from its new home, Ie Shima. The elements promised trouble for the duration of the war. Heat and humidity transformed mimeograph stencils into gummy sheets that were like magnets to sand

and coral particles; holes formed in the stencils, and they became un-usable. Sudden deluges sabotaged machinery. Plus, mortars and bombs threatened to annihilate everything with one well-aimed blow. Throw-ing in the towel was not an option, however. In the words of one officer, "The stateside press was giving Marine and Naval construction units full credit for transforming this mudhole island into one of the Pacific's most powerful bases." He needed to "give these Aviation Engineers full credit through the press for their accomplishments." With pressure from their superiors, enlisted men went through hell to get the news out.

Typhoon season not only wrecked equipment: it also brought supply problems. Staffers overcame a shortage of ink by making some—they mixed shoe polish with insect repellent. When the wrong-sized paper arrived, "4,000 bastard sheets were cut with a razor blade." And when headquarters ordered the unit to pack up and move out, just as one edi-tion of the paper was finally going to press, the staff wondered, "What ethics of that inky little god of journalism had they betrayed in their years of civilian and GI newspapering?" At the last moment, a merciful officer allowed the paper to be printed, even though the packing detail continued.

After listing the *Tough Sheet*'s many tribulations, the *Galley* could not help but remark that the paper was aptly named—it *was* a "tough sheet to get out."

While the *Galley* praised the hard work of GI newspaper staffs, it also created annual drama with a contest for the best troop newspapers in the army. Celebrity publishers sat as judges, handsome trophies hung in the balance, and certificates of honorable mention were hotly pursued. When each year's winners were announced, the *Galley* received an ava-lanche of letters that admired certain features and ribbed others. "After reading you and seeing pictures of some of the Army newspapers, I can see how outclassed this little mimeographed issue that we have here is," said the editor of *Sponge City Splash*, a paper for troops in Puerto Rico. Though the *Galley*'s judges awarded top honors to Fort Niagara's *Drum* in 1944, the editor of the US Army Air Force's *Trail Blazer* retorted that the *Drum* was "high schoolish and amateurish" in comparison to its offerings. So fierce was the competition that it seemed many units were fighting two wars—one with the Axis and the other to claim the top prize for their unit newspaper.

Yet alongside this cutthroat spirit was an undercurrent of friendship. After announcing its annual contest winners in 1943, the *Galley* suggested that editors write to each other and trade newspapers to share ideas and layout techniques. Pen-pal relationships flourished as swapping editors added personal letters with their latest issues. "Thought I would drop this note in to let you know I am still all OK and able to kick," an editor in England wrote to a newspaperman in the States on the eve of D-Day. "This may be the last paper for a while and it may not. You know why," he cryptically added.

———

While the *Galley* created an unparalleled support network for editors and journalists, many military newspapers lacked one necessary thing: sufficient content. Rigorous military censorship promised to eliminate nearly all newsworthy information. Army regulations empowered unit, base, and theater censors to scour articles for a long list of prohibited topics—including the location of US or Allied military installations; past or future movements of ships, aircraft, troops, supplies, or any equipment; information about the amount, condition, or character of troops, supplies, equipment, armaments, or training; any losses of "personnel or matériel"; transportation routes; the location of any high-ranking officials; and weather conditions. Some censors would not allow griping or criticism because they could fall under the catchall of "information determined by the area commander to be of aid or comfort to the enemy." Considering these newspapers were by and for those in uniform, it was difficult to figure out what was left to print. As one short-staffed editor wrote to the *GI Galley*, the only person he could ask for help was "the censor, who just cuts out rather than adds anything."

To assist GI papers in providing content, the Camp Newspaper Service ("CNS") *Clip Sheet* was created in late 1942. Printed weekly, it contained a mishmash of material, which included short snippets of small-town news to help troops feel a connection to home, amusing anecdotes about the army, and quizzes on technical knowledge. All of it was censor approved and could be cut and pasted into troop newspapers. Editors, however, were nonplussed by the early offerings. "That column 'News from Your Own Home Town' is of utterly no value to us," one editor complained. The new "G.I.Q." column "only wastes space on the Clip Sheet," said another. Instead, editors clamored for maps, photographs, and illustrations. And most of all, they wanted professional cartoons.

Luckily, a seasoned artist had already volunteered his services. Milton Caniff, one of the most popular American cartoonists of the era, believed that comic strips would be a useful tool in building comradery and pride among soldiers. His most popular strip for civilians had proven this point. Caniff had inducted into the Army Air Force the namesake of his legendary comic strip, *Terry and the Pirates*. Most Americans were following Terry's story—the strip ran in about 130 civilian newspapers with an estimated combined circulation of over twenty million. To make sure the strip was accurate, Caniff earnestly learned all he could about flight. He even underwent primary, basic, and advanced training at the West Point Flying School. Terry's adventures were so authentic that Caniff won the admiration and loyalty of Americans in uniform. "I, and I believe every Army pilot I have met, maintain an acute interest in the adventures of the characters in Terry and the Pirates," a member of a fighter squadron wrote Caniff. In fact, this airman insisted that many in his unit would not begin their day's flying without first consulting the strip. Caniff received thousands of letters from servicemen, thanking him for *Terry* and the strip's realistic portrayal of army life. These letters made an impression on Caniff, and he had no doubt that newspapers—and the cartoons inside of them—were wartime necessities. As Caniff said, cartoons and comic strips "played an important role in fostering people's sense of well-being," and they were good "for morale. . . . Particularly, the morale of soldiers."

Seeing the reaction that airmen had to *Terry*, Caniff reached out to his friend Marvin H. McIntyre, a member of the White House's secretariat and a personal confidant of President Roosevelt, and asked McIntyre to convey an idea to whoever was "in charge." Assuming that "newspapers similar to the old *Stars and Stripes* will spring up in every group to handle the news of interest to that local area," Caniff urged McIntyre to ensure that cartoons played a prominent role in these soldier papers. "The last war," Caniff said, "showed how much men in the ranks appreciated amusing drawings." If the army needed his help, Caniff was eager to contribute.

When Marshall learned that Caniff was willing to volunteer his artistic talents, he jumped at the chance. While a lucky handful of GI newspapers had their own staff artists (like Bill Mauldin, Don Freeman, George Baker, and Dave Berg), who dazzled with their comics and gag lines, other troop newssheets begged the *Clip Sheet* for help. "Our paper comes out weekly . . . very weakly . . . I do the cartoons . . . egad! What monstrosities!" wrote the editor of Fort Benning's *24th Hi-Lites*. Marshall offered Caniff, who was thoroughly dejected after being rated 4F and physically unfit for service, a job. Caniff was delighted to serve the army by creating an exclusive comic for troop newspapers. Initially, Caniff illustrated a GI version of his *Terry* strip for army newspapers, but this landed him in legal trouble when civilian publishers felt the army's special edition was a breach of contract. Caniff was thus forced to create an entirely new strip solely for the army called *Male Call*. It featured Lace, a dark-haired, femme fatale who, in Caniff's words, was "the kind of gal that guys can make cracks to and she snaps right back." She wore a "tight-fitting evening dress that became practically a uniform" and was always "in good taste." She was never far from a military base, hobnobbing with American GIs. Lace was such a hit that even navy and marine corps newspapers begged the army to place them on the CNS mailing list—just for the funnies. The army obliged, and soon all the services were receiving the CNS *Clip Sheet* and its extraordinary cartoons.

As he did with *Terry and the Pirates*, Caniff obsessively studied military equipage, lore, regalia, and airplane silhouettes and kept correspondence with many active-duty GIs. He wanted to know everything about military life to imbue *Male Call* with realism. It was a winning formula, and Lace's readers could not get enough. The navy's *Fore n' Aft* commented that it was "all the editors can do to contain themselves until the new clip sheets come out to get a 'look-see' at the doings of Lace and her cohorts." At Camp Butner, a field artillery battalion was asked to vote for "the girl whom we'd most like to see." Besting Hollywood actresses, radio personalities, and famous songstresses was Lace. Bergstrom Field's *Del Valle News* suggested that the *GI Galley* host a contest to find "the babe who looks the most like the favorite comic strip sweetie of us servicemen." Before the *Galley* could act, the *Marauder*, a Kansas air base publication, had already completed such a contest. Although chaplains occasionally voiced reservations about Lace's tendency to appeal to readers' more prurient interests, some men of the cloth overcame such qualms when they realized that Lace was "a sort of two-minute furlough for a lot of homesick GIs who looked forward to seeing her in their camp newspapers every week."

After *Male Call*, the second most popular feature of the *Clip Sheet* was *The Wolf*, a single-panel comic created by Sergeant Leonard Sansone. First appearing in *Duck Board*, Fort Belvoir's newspaper, *The Wolf* rose to international acclaim when it joined the *Clip Sheet* in late 1942. Clothed in an army uniform, Wolf, a furry-faced private, whistled and made passes at girls, was rebuffed, and came back the following week undeterred. The Casanovas in the military saw themselves in Wolf. As Caniff realized with Lace, "there would have been no particular point in providing girl-hungry GIs, isolated in remote de-feminized badlands, with a special strip of any other" type. Sansone also won points from his audience for never "writing down" to them; he assumed servicemen could decipher a joke without explanation and were "pixie enough to realize that the animal head was not evident to the other pen-and-ink people in the cartoon."

So popular were the CNS cartoons that nearly 95 percent of troop newspapers carried them. The only difficulty was the painstaking work of tracing the cartoons onto stencils so they could be included in mimeographed papers. This problem was solved in March 1943, when CNS began furnishing precut stencils to mimeographed papers—free of charge. They were a game changer. "We were about ready to start pulling the few remaining strands of hair from the top of our heads when you understanding fellows at CNS came through with the precut stencils," wrote the editor of *The Gremlin*. Before the stencils, "we made life unbearable for our staff artist," he added. These sentiments were universal. "The pre-cut stencil is like manna from heaven," said the editor of *The Voice of Shangri La*. Within five months of the stencils' debut, CNS received over six thousand requests from army, navy, and marine corps newspapers to be added to the mailing list for its stencils of *Male Call* and *The Wolf*. These numbers proved that Marshall's troop newspaper initiative had grown to proportions he had not imagined possible.

———

With the guidance of the *GI Galley* and the CNS *Clip Sheet*, thousands of unit newspapers were hatched in 1942. As Marshall had predicted, soldiers were eager to make sense of their unique positions and duties, see their names in print, and enjoy the civilian pastime of reading newspapers. No post was too small, no layover too short, to warrant a periodical. Newspapers sprouted up in induction centers, military hospitals, training facilities, overseas bases, troop transports, and even in German Oflags (prisoner-of-war camps). Laundry units, aviation cadets, military police, Women's Army Corps divisions, quartermasters, infantrymen, and every fathomable specialization had a newspaper unto itself. With 534 specialties that involved distinct training and one-of-a-kind hardships, it was a boon to see detailed coverage of a detachment's unique work. This singularity of purpose enabled newssheets to trumpet even the most idiosyncratic contributions—whether it be washing a record-breaking quantity of soiled garments or concocting new delicacies using the army's ubiquitous staple, Spam.

Many readers could decipher whether an army post had strict, humorless officers based on the tone of its newspaper. While some officers embraced Marshall's view and gave troops wide latitude, others cleaved to the notion that they were the officers *in charge* and stifled content that they deemed too unmilitary-like. Troops eager for some press freedom strategized and schemed. They found that puns, double entendres, inside jokes, euphemisms, and GI slang "comma-flaged" objectionable content so that it passed both censors and uptight officers. There was no better place to start pushing buttons than in a paper's name.

While the majority of papers adopted conventional titles—such as the *South Pacific Daily News*, *Camp Parks Log*, *Camp Barkeley News*, and *Iwo Jima Inquirer*—readers usually preferred a more colorful epithet. Some commanding officers obviously had a sense of humor when they approved the *Home-Wrecker* (induction station, Denver, Colorado), *The Ramp-Age* (Landing Craft School, California), *The Screamer* (502nd Parachute Infantry), *The X-Isle* (printed on "Island X" in the Pacific), and *SBAD News* (San Bernardino Air Depot). There were even a handful of mastheads that bore vulgarities—or at least, acronyms for them: *The FUBAR* ("'Fouled' Up Beyond All Recognition,"), *SNAFU* ("Situation Normal: All 'Fouled' Up"), and *TARFU* ("Things Are Really 'Fouled' Up"). There were trash-talking titles that paid homage to unit nicknames or reputations, like *Hell on Wheels*, *The Vigilante*, *The Barbarian*, *Gooney Tales*, *Devil's Digest*, and *Hellcat News*. And others nodded to the distinct jobs or interests of the men they served—such as the *Hospital Gauzette*, *615th Bakery Weekly*, *The Extractor* (for a laundry unit), *MP Blotter* (for the 716th Military Police Battalion), and *L'Chaim* (for Jewish servicemen).

While GI newspapers printed in the States usually adopted mild names, many overseas newspapers embraced monikers that reflected the jaded, homesick, war-weary men who read them. There were *Scars and Gripes* (Belgium), *Bi-Monthly Bitch* (somewhere in the Pacific), *Home Crier* (for a replacement depot in Italy), *59th Latrineogram* (New Guinea), *Gangplank Gazette* (at sea), *Bull Sheet* (Belgium), *Sorryburg Gazette* (location restricted), *Sunday Mud & Mildew* (Assam), and *Snarkyville Gazette* (somewhere in France). So unconventional and imaginative were World War II troop newspaper names that the scholar H. L. Mencken devoted a portion of his *American Language* treatise to them.

When it came to publishing stories that would appeal to troops, some newspapers had more difficulty than others. Posts that had frequent turnover suffered the most because staffers lacked the time to gain a foothold with censors and supervising officers. A typical example of this phenomenon occurred at the San Antonio Aviation Cadet Center, where some men cycled through training within weeks. Rather than give each new influx of cadets the discretion to print their own news, officers tended to use the base's newspaper, the *Tale Spinner*, to lecture the men. Its weekly editorials carried patronizing titles and harped on the importance of studying: "You Supply the Brains," "It's Time to Think," and "There's a Reason, Mister" (the latter described how a pilot who had forgotten one detail was found dead, "plastered 4,000 feet up on the side of a 6,000 foot ridge"). One editorial, "Hate Your Enemies," shamelessly tried to inspire rancor. "An eye for an eye . . . a tooth for a tooth. The hell with that! Two eyes for one. A whole jaw for a tooth," it said. "Hate the bastards, as they deserve to be hated." Despite this imperious content, the layout man obviously had a sense of humor. Wreathed around the "Hate Your Enemies" editorial were that week's schedule for religious services, a biography of the new chaplain, and an invitation to discuss one's moral qualms with the clergy.

Because the *Tale Spinner* could be mailed home (papers with more sensitive content were labeled "restricted" and could not be mailed), some men dismantled the paper's proselytizing for their family in the margins. "Cadets Can Now Enjoy Meals Under Changed Plan of Mess," one headline said. "Seeing is believing," a cadet wrote next to it. Underneath a cartoon captioned "How Long Did You Say You've Been a Cadet" were the scribbled words "Long enuff!!!!!!" And when an article captured what training was *really* like, it was circled and festooned with arrows and stars. "Just three short weeks ago, a timid, trembling horde crossed the magic road that separates Classification Center from Preflight. Struggling vainly to control wildly shifting eyes, they marched along to the tune of raucous shouts from demoniacal blue-tagged figures on every side. . . . At the end of that first horrible day, they were a scared, bewildered lot." Scrawled alongside this article, a cadet wrote: "*This* tells the story."

Though papers like the *Tale Spinner* had their rough edges, many included features or contributions that tempered their "get tough" tone.

For example, because the *Tale Spinner* was often mailed home, some parents could not help but write their own submissions for publication. These tender words softened the paper's feel considerably, like this mother's prayer that was printed for all to read:

> White clouds fold him softly,
> Evening star, shed your light,
> Moonbeams fall gently
> Where my boy flies tonight.
>
> Dear God, it is lovely
> Up in the sky at night;
> Send just one bright angel
> To guide him in his flight;
> To ever be proud of him,
> His loving watch to keep
> Over the little boy
> I used to rock to sleep.

———

Though there were plenty of newspapers like the *Tale Spinner*, whose supervising officers could not resist the temptation to "orient" troops through heavy-handed exhortations, the most-beloved gazettes gave readers space to explore how *dis*oriented they felt in the military. As enlisted men searched for a place to unpack their innermost thoughts and feelings, many found refuge in poetry. Censors tended to keep their scissors and blue pencils away from verse, causing poetry columns to become sanctuaries for soldiers' worries and complaints.

Men who had never attempted crafting a poem suddenly found catharsis in patching together rhyming couplets and lyrical odes that explored their unhappiness, sense of isolation, and frustrations. And there was no sense of embarrassment or weakness in doing so, as even top brass could not resist writing their own verses. Even the "two-fisted, gun-toting, commander," George "Old Blood and Guts" Patton, dashed off "God of Battles," a poem asking for divine guidance as he led his men into combat in 1943. (His wife, Beatrice, was so fond of it that she submitted it to a woman's magazine for publication, and troop newspapers reprinted it, relishing in the fact that they did so by permission of *Woman's Home Companion*.) "From pride and foolish confidence / From every waking creed / From the dread fear of fearing / Protect us, Lord, and lead," Patton's ode began. If commanding generals were doing it, surely it was acceptable for enlisted men to cobble together a few lines. Though Patton waxed poetic over battle, the topics troops tackled in their own verses tended to center on their daily indignities.

One of the most irksome issues that plagued nearly every soldier was the censorship of their letters home. The only way troops could communicate with their loved ones was by writing, yet censorship rules reduced their notes to empty ramblings. Any military-related information was barred, and it was hard to write a gushy love letter knowing a fellow soldier would be reading it in the censor's office. Meanwhile, troops felt obligated to reassure their folks that all was well (especially when it was not), the food was always delicious, and their health never better. As unsatisfying as it was to write reassuring falsehoods, recipients grew frustrated with opaque wording and nondescript updates. "Why don't you ever answer any of my questions?" one woman snapped at her husband in a letter. Because the truth would likely annoy the censor, her husband remained consistent and did not answer this question either.

But troop newspapers came to the rescue when such misunderstandings arose. "Approved by Censor," a popular poem that was reprinted in many papers, could be clipped and sent home. Offering some explanation for why their letters were always so vague, the poem absolved many troops of their letter-writing sins:

> Can't write a thing. . . . the Censor's to blame.
> Just say I'm well and sign my name.
> Can't tell where we sail from, can't mention the date.
> And can't even remember the meal that I ate.

Can't say where we're going, don't know when we'll land.
Couldn't inform you if met by a band. . . .
Can't keep a diary, for such is a sin.
Can't keep our envelopes your letters come in.
Can't say for sure folks, just what I can write.
So I'll call this my letter and close with "Good Night."

The army's censorship policy would not change, but by acknowledging it in newsprint, troop newspapers validated the universal frustration soldiers faced in trying to please both the censors *and* their loved ones.

Even the strongest relationships suffered under the trio of censorship restrictions, slow mail delivery, and misunderstandings nurtured by the vast time and distance that separated lovers. The pen could keep feelings alive or end a courtship. "My Girl and Me" cloaked this reality with humor.

"Dear John," begins her letter, but
The way she used to start
Was—"Dearest, Darling, Johnny boy,
My very own sweetheart."

"I would have written sooner but
I'm busy, that is why . . ."
(I know she must be busy, and
I wonder who's the guy.)
"The Weather's very pleasant, and
I hope you're feeling well . . ."
(What a difference from the things
She always used to tell.)

Her letter ends: "Sincerely," Boy!
Now isn't she a pal?
The Income Tax Collector writes
As friendly as my gal.

How fickle is the female sex!
An untrue dame is she!
My sweetheart, can I e'er forget
How much you mean to me?

What ho! It's after nine, and I
Don't want to make her wait.
(I mean the pretty PX girl,
With whom I have a date.)

Another popular theme was the rocky civilian-to-soldier transition. Group living was a particular source of irritation. The military did not care whether troops craved alone time because they were on a team now, and with their team they would always be. Outward appearances of harmony masked inner feelings of resentment and hostility. Odes to the loss of one's individualism and privacy appeared in many army newspapers. Suffocated by the lack of solitude he had, one man directed his anger at the army for the rank he was assigned in his "Lament of a Private":

In the Army they call me a private.
It is a misnomer . . .
I am the only living thing that has less privacy than a
     goldfish.
I sleep in a room with countless other men and eat with
     about nine hundred.
I take my baths with the entire detachment.
I wear a suit of the same material and cut as five million
     other men.
I have to tell a physician when I kiss a pretty girl.
I never have a single moment to myself.
And yet they call me a private!
Private!
What the -----!

Homesickness ran rampant as many civilians had left home for the first time and were plunged into the unfamiliar routines and culture of the military. Training manuals hewed to a policy of tough love. "Do what you are told to do, do it quickly and cheerfully, and you will be surprised how easy this military training becomes," one military manual advised. This attitude did little to lessen the sorrow that afflicted many men, especially as months and years slipped by and their hopes of returning home diminished. Although nothing (except discharge) could fully allay their heartache, poems at least provided the relief of knowing that others felt the same way. One bittersweet ballad, "Strictly GI," enjoyed wide circulation:

> Here I sit on my GI bed
> With my GI hat upon my head
> My GI pants, my GI shoes
> All is free, nothing to lose
> GI razor, GI comb, . . .
> GI wish that I was home.
>
> They've issued me everything I need
> Paper to write on, books to read
> My belt, my socks, my GI tie . . .
> All are free, nothing to buy.
> They issue me food that makes me grow,
> GI wish I were on furlough.
>
> I eat my food from a GI plate,
> And buy my needs at a GI rate,
> It's GI this and GI that
> GI haircut and GI hat,
> Everything is GI issue . . .
> Oh my darling! GI miss you.

By 1943, army morale had improved to such an extent that *Time* magazine christened George Marshall its "Man of the Year." "The American people do not . . . like or trust the military. But they like and trust George Marshall," *Time* said. The man who had been unfairly blamed for the low state of army morale in 1940 had now earned the public's confidence. In the words of *Time*, "American democracy is the stuff Marshall is made of."

And nothing was more democratic than giving American fighters the chance to express themselves in their own camp newspapers. By 1943, these homespun newssheets had become a cherished part of military service for a generation of Americans. It did not matter that they were largely produced by a group of novices who bungled formatting and graced the pages with amateur illustrations. They infused troops with pride because these newspapers were *theirs*. As one man described his unit newspaper, "although it did not take our breath away . . . it certainly was a source of amusement and information all the time. . . . I will keep every single number to bring home." Just as President Roosevelt had saved his shipboard newspapers from his presidential cruises, troops preserved their army newssheets—they were the only source documenting their experience. "Save these for me when I send them, will you mother?" one man wrote about his issues of *Sandfly*. "I want you all to read about my division and feel as proud as I am," an infantryman said when he sent his division paper home.

As the army continued to swell in size, GI gazettes continued to blossom. Whenever he visited an army post, Marshall made sure to read the newspapers troops were publishing. He was gratified to see more gripes and wisecracks finding their way into print, as well as signs of growing contentment in the army. One paper's "Cursified Advertising" column illustrated this phenomenon perfectly:

LOST: Two baseball teams in the vicinity of Philadelphia. Finder please return. Beebe.

WANTED: Set of ear plugs. Am being kept awake all night by Goffen. R. Stickler.

LOST: One basketball game. G. Stangel.

WANTED: Hammer to destroy all cowboy records in Rec Hall. Bob Irving.

FOUND: A home. Frank Kennedy.

# CHAPTER FOUR
## TEAR-STAINED PILLOWS

War has no use for free speech.

—Julius Caesar

Morale is to matériel as three is to one.

—Napoleon

While unit-based newspapers were remarkably popular for their ability to tell the unique stories of small detachments of troops, there was still a need to provide comprehensive war coverage. Thus, just as Marshall launched the army's troop newspaper program so that individual units could print their own homespun papers, he also made plans to create professional-grade, army-wide news publications.

What spurred Marshall into action were early reports from overseas that American troops had little understanding of the scope of the war and the purpose of their service. One report that reached Marshall's desk came from Major Ensley Llewellyn, a US Army censor in England. As Llewellyn read soldiers' letters to ensure no secret information was included, he was alarmed by how many troops wondered why they were in England when it was Japan that had attacked Pearl Harbor. Llewellyn stressed that US soldiers needed a firm understanding of the principles at stake in the war and why troops were stationed around the world. Llewellyn's missive only confirmed what Marshall was already thinking.

In early 1942, only the first trickle of American troops had been deployed, but Marshall would soon be sending millions of soldiers around the globe. And all of them would be desperate for war updates. If troops in an English-speaking country were having difficulty informing themselves of the war's progress, soldiers headed to areas where periodicals were printed in other languages (or not at all) could not possibly fare better. Taking a page from Pershing's playbook, Marshall seized the opportunity to resume publication of the Great War's famous army-wide paper, the *Stars and Stripes*, in England.

With Llewellyn at the helm, the army selected a small group of newsmen to join him in jump-starting an eight-page weekly from the printshop of Hazell, Watson and Viney in southeast England. In April 1942, the first copy of the *Stars and Stripes* rolled off the press. It was heartily read by US troops across England, and Marshall was eager to see the paper expand to all parts of the world where American troops fought. In November 1942, the *Stars and Stripes* became a daily newspaper, with satellite offices sprouting across the globe. By the war's end, there were thirty regional editions, from Algiers to Tokyo, and the paper boasted nearly one million subscribers.

Each daily edition ranged from four to eight pages long, and as the paper expanded from an audience in England to troops stationed in locales around the world, it became increasingly difficult to provide substantial war updates concerning its readers in all theaters. Plus, troops wanted more than just war updates. They craved news and features from newspapers back home. So the *Stars and Stripes* also delivered domestic sports news, cartoons, poetry, and letters to the editor. It was a perpetual challenge to cram as much war news into an issue while delivering all the other content troops expected.

What made the paper a success was its ability to capture the war from the perspective of the troops doing the fighting. The paper was permitted to send its staffers around the world to provide boots-on-the-ground reporting. The only way to win the confidence of readers was for the paper's journalists to live and fight alongside them. Only enlisted soldiers would be permitted to write, illustrate, and submit content for the paper.

To recruit journalists who had an intimate understanding of the war and the men fighting it, the Special Service Division requested that all troops with newspaper experience be identified for possible reassignment to the *Stars and Stripes*. Some soldiers volunteered, while others were chosen based on their army records. There were a few hiccups. While the journalists included men like Bob Moora (former *New York Herald Tribune* deskman), Bud Hutton (a Scripps-Howard city editor), and Andy Rooney (a copyboy for the *Knickerbocker News*), there was also Bill Estoff, who had identified himself as a "bookmaker" in his army paperwork. Either the army did not understand that Estoff was in the business of sports betting or, in the words of Andy Rooney, the army "decided there wasn't much difference between making a book and making a newspaper." Whatever the reasoning, Estoff was assigned to the circulation staff.

Like its predecessor, the revived *Stars and Stripes* fulfilled its duty to inform, but what made it enormously popular with troops was its style of reporting. *Stars and Stripes* journalists chronicled the war with vigor and verve. They cheered (but not too loudly) for the American fighters they covered, and injected humor into circumstances that could otherwise be tragically heartbreaking. Though its journalists typically eschewed the first-person singular "I-was-there attitude," they occasionally broke this rule to show readers that they also suffered their fair share of the war's frustrations and absurdities. For example, when the circulation staff needed to deliver the newspaper to troops on a beachhead that was barely under American control, the only transportation they could find was a donkey "'liberated' from a Wehrmacht service corps." When a photographer observed a "spraddle-legged" *Stars and Stripes* staffer riding a donkey with saddlebags stuffed with newspapers, he took a photograph of the spectacle and mailed it to the *Stars and Stripes*. Unable to resist an opportunity for laughs, the *Stars and Stripes* printed the photo with the caption: "Circulation Man Gets His Ass Up to the Front." It proved to be one of the most popular photographs the paper ever printed.

Most *Stars and Stripes* staffers felt they owed their loyalty to the paper first and the army second. They wanted to operate with the freedom they had had as civilians and tended to welcome the opportunity to exchange their guns for the mighty pen. As one staffer described his colleagues, they were "a collection of possibly the least martial souls on earth trying to put out a civilian newspaper in an army." Quirkiness and eccentricities were the norm. In the words of Hutton and Rooney, "The editorial staff might look like something from an Abbott and Costello movie and the business office staff as bad."

Although the *Stars and Stripes* correspondents had some freedom of movement and could leave an engagement in order to type copy and transmit it to an editor, this did not mean that they fled from the front as soon as danger lurked. Nearly all *Stars and Stripes* journalists spent time in the thick of combat. Though they wore correspondent badges on their arms, these reporters dug in next to the infantry as mortars sent the freezing mud soaring. They jumped with paratroopers. They flew in bombers through flak storms that tore planes to shreds (and learned on long flights back to base what the expression "a wing and a prayer" actually meant). They boarded navy vessels and became well versed in torpedoes and shore guns. And "some of them learned to fight and some learned to die." For the troops doing the shooting and the bombing, they were glad to have a photographer and reporter along—especially the infantrymen, who wanted Stripers "to stay around and get shot at and endure the misery of their lives." "It was a natural feeling on the doughboys' part," Andy Rooney said. "Only those who have been with them not only under fire but through the miserable and filthy days and nights of a ground soldier's existence can understand well enough the bleak futurelessness of their lives to write about them," he added.

With the majority of the staff bearing the low ranks of privates or corporals, tension inevitably arose between those who wrote for the paper and the officers and brass who did not like what they were reading. Frank Keppel, who was an officer in the army's Information and Education Branch and would later serve as dean of the Harvard Graduate School of Education and as the United States Commissioner of Education, advocated for independent troop newspapers. Keppel said that these papers thrived by "treating the soldier as an intelligent person whose tradition and cast of mind required that he be told as fully as possible what was going on." Keppel believed that educating troops about the war was essential because knowledge had the power to shift attitudes and "direct motivation into desirable channels." But to do this, troops needed to be given facts and allowed to draw their own conclusions. Likening orientation work to a weapon, Keppel warned that "the weapon rusts and even backfires when improperly handled." Many did not see things as Keppel did. Some commanding officers felt threatened by the prospect of an army that handed out explanations. To these officers, troops were supposed to do what they were told without question.

Marshall recognized this tension, but he also innately understood that an army newspaper like the *Stars and Stripes* would lose all credibility if officers manipulated it into a military mouthpiece. In an effort to keep the editorial decisions in the hands of GIs, Marshall submitted a letter to the editor that expressed what he hoped the paper would be. The letter was published for all to see, and the staff treated Marshall's words as the paper's constitution. "Like any other veteran of the AEF in France, I am delighted to welcome the new version of *The Stars and Stripes*," Marshall's letter began. He noted that, during the Great War, General Pershing had embraced a policy that "no official control was ever exercised over the matter which went into *The Stars and Stripes*"— it was to be "entirely by and for the soldier." Because this had been a winning formula for the paper in the 1910s, Marshall saw no reason to interfere with it in the 1940s. The policy of exerting "no official control" was "to govern the conduct of the new publication," Marshall said. With these words, staffers believed they had the power to print what they wanted, high-ranking officers notwithstanding. However, time and again, high-ranking officers could not resist the chance to tame the paper's content and its freewheeling journalists.

One of the most outrageous offenders happened to be the Special Service Division. This was deeply ironic considering it was the division's job to build morale. Yet as soon as the *Stars and Stripes* had developed a large and loyal readership built on the reputation of being faithful to the average GI, a high-ranking official at the Special Service Division insisted that it should use the paper to "'orient' the soldiers' thinking."

Although this seemed entirely antagonistic to Marshall's aims for the paper, the low-ranking staff members did not have the authority to ignore orders from a superior officer. The *Stars and Stripes* staff warned that "the combat man in a bomber or on the firing line feels that there is no particularly good reason why he should be told how to think by someone two or three or five hundred miles from the conditions under which he is doing his thinking." The Special Service officer disagreed. Pulling rank, he ordered the *Stars and Stripes* to print a particularly tone-deaf opinion piece and the paper was forced into submission.

The publication of the unsigned editorial entitled "So You Wanna go Home, Eh?" instantly drew the fury of all who read it. Chiding troops who missed their families and dreamed of their futures back in the States, the editorial opened by claiming that the growing chorus of "I-want-to-go-home" talk made it seem like "this was one panty-waist army" with "our great big American supermen . . . ready to pack up and leave this legalized murder to the nurses, WACs and clubmobile girls." This was not a war that could be won by "snapping girdles" or "stuffing [troops] with donuts," the editorial said. "It's man's work. Whether it's lifting stuff out of the holds of ships or highballing it to the front . . . it takes a hairy chest and a strong back." The editorial concluded by ordering troops who yearned for home to "lift their heads from their tear-stained pillows and take a look at the wreckage and misery of war around them and thank God their own homes don't look like that."

The blowback was mighty and swift. From foxholes, hospitals, rest areas, and the rear, GIs sent heated letters to the editor of the *Stars and Stripes*. Because the editorial had been unsigned, most readers assumed that it was the *Stars and Stripes* editorial staff that had written the piece. Thus, the newspaper—and not the Special Service Division—was assigned all blame. To make amends and try to repair its tarnished reputation, the *Stars and Stripes* printed an entire page's worth of letters lambasting the editor's ignorance and the staff's bad judgment. The paper's journalists could only hope that the Special Service Division would read, take note, and never submit another piece for publication.

"You're dam[n] right we wanna go home," responded Master

Sergeant Herman Surdan, an infantryman in Germany. "I'm sure that, man for man, there isn't 3 percent of all the GIs in foreign service who would take a discharge to return home and leave this legalized murder to the nurses, WACs, and Club-mobile girls, and of course, the staff of *The Stars and Stripes*, who, I am sure, have seen a great deal of front-line duty and could take over our positions very admirably," he said. "If any of your high-powered staff would venture to within Corps artillery range of the front lines I'm sure that you wouldn't find tear-stained pillows (if you even found such a thing as a pillow) . . . but rather stained with the mud and blood of combat. If they hadn't become too hard yet there might possibly be a tear or two for buddies who had been blown to bits next to him after being a happy, smiling GI a few moments before, but you wouldn't know about that," Surdan wrote.

Private Wesley G. Wilson, of the infantry, wrote on behalf of his unit to address the paper's "lousy editorial." He asked, "Have you ever stood by helplessly while your buddies around you fell? Have you ever heard the haunting sound of shrapnel and bullets whiz so close to your ears your heart stopped? Have you ever slept in mud and rain, or gone days without rations or water? Or would you like to trade (and I quote) your hairy chest and strong back for the place of one of us who'll never go back? . . . You won't meet a GI anywhere . . . who won't say, 'I still wanna go home.'"

Others took offense to the character of the editorial—they wanted news from the *Stars and Stripes*, not indoctrination. One unit asked whether "German propaganda [was] taking control of our paper" and offered "congratulations on your weak-kneed and hare-brained sassy remark." Technical Sergeant H. W. Mattick begrudged the editor's "patronizing air" and suggested that "the editor's 'hairy chest and strong back' . . . should qualify him for immediate front-line duty, because he doesn't seem to have the brains to write an acceptable editorial."

The "So You Wanna Go Home, Eh?" piece delivered such a blow to morale that General Dwight Eisenhower called the *Stars and Stripes* and asked to speak with the editor. Eisenhower "pointed out that almost never had he tried to influence in any way what went into the soldiers' newspaper," but "he didn't want anyone else doing it" either. The editorial reeked of propaganda and "brought a most unfavorable reaction from the fighting men and their commanders," Eisenhower said. If the *Stars and Stripes* wanted to remind readers "from time to time . . . [of] the basic cause for which we were fighting," Eisenhower suggested it be done "in a straight, factual manner," and not in such an arrogant and condescending way. The *Stars and Stripes* staff entirely agreed, and their appreciation and admiration for Eisenhower only grew. But when it came to "the polished Information and Education brass . . . we held another view."

Even after the paper published dozens of letters of complaint about the editorial and acknowledged what a mistake it was to print it, soldiers did not forgive the paper immediately. According to Rooney and Hutton, because of that editorial, "some of the ordinary staffers for months lived almost without surcease in the midst of the fighting, trying their best to restore . . . the paper's prestige with the guys who were winning the war, the guys who wanted to go home."

After weathering the fallout from this misstep, the *Stars and Stripes* eventually regained the confidence of its readers by never again allowing the voice of the paper to stray from that of low-ranking combat soldiers. By allowing troops to speak their minds, the *Stars and Stripes* reinforced that it *was* a soldiers' paper. The silver lining to this unfortunate episode was that the paper discovered it had at least one powerful ally in General Eisenhower.

––––––––

To Marshall, having one army-wide news source was not enough. Stateside, there was a growing trend among young people to read glossy periodicals rather than their parents' newspapers. As of 1939, there were 3,500 unique magazines in the United States, and most Americans bought about two per month. To ensure that the broadest possible audience would keep informed in the format they favored as civilians, Marshall approved the first army-wide magazine in 1942. It was called *Yank, the Army Weekly.*

The magazine was the brainchild of some of the most talented publishers and journalists of its day. Committees were formed to identify which characteristics would make the magazine a success among its khaki-clad readers. Among those consulted were former writers for the Great War's *Stars and Stripes* who had developed flourishing media careers after their discharge from the army: Harold Ross, who cofounded the *New Yorker* in 1925; Grantland Rice, a celebrated sportswriter and founder of the Football Hall of Fame; Mark Watson, an acclaimed journalist for the *Baltimore Sun*; Alexander Woollcott, an author and radio personality; and Franklin P. Adams, the creator of an enormously popular feature in the *New York Herald Tribune*. The guidance from these legends helped make *Yank* the most popular periodical of the war.

The group's recommendation was to stay true to the low-ranking troops who would be reading it. These veteran writers advised *Yank* to avoid government control so that it could maintain its independence. Based on this suggestion, *Yank* was offered by paid subscription only. If the War Department was not bankrolling the magazine, and soldiers were funding and producing it, there could be little leeway for army officers to force content into the magazine. Autonomy would ensure that *Yank* could avoid its own version of the "So You Wanna Go Home, Eh?" debacle.

After assembling a flock of journalists, photographers, and artists, the magazine granted its staff members complete liberty to search for stories, allowing them to roam American positions around the world and send their dispatches and corresponding visuals back to *Yank*'s headquarters in the Bartholomew Building in New York City. From "Fort Bartholomew," as staffers called it, *Yank* journalists pieced together twenty-four pages of content, which usually included two to three detailed feature articles that ran several pages, along with sports updates from home, letters to the editor, and a full-page pinup. *Yank* also expertly captured the experiences of low-ranking soldiers through cartoons like Sergeant George Baker's *Sad Sack*, which featured a down-on-his-luck private who was never promoted, given the worst assignments, and always getting into trouble. And to show that heroics were not only performed on the battlefield, *Yank* dared to tell the stories of support troops, soldiers stationed on neutralized islands where the fighting had long ceased, and others who served valiantly—though not in combat.

*Yank* also printed a robust poetry column that displayed the full panoply of emotions soldiers felt. While *Yank* published plenty of humorous odes and stirring rhymes about the army, it also printed heartbreaking poems that acknowledged soldiers' feelings about the anonymity of loss—a topic too many soldiers experienced but rarely wanted to discuss. One such poem, "The Death of Private Jones," eloquently honored a friend who died in the chaos of an amphibious landing:

> Let's say that Private Jones died quietly.
> Let's say that when the first wave stormed the shore
> a single shot went through his heart, and he
> slipped lifeless to the sand. Not one man saw
> him die, so busied they with lying hid
> and crawling on, yet all men felt the breath
> of leaden wings come close, and when they did,
> it made his passing seem a public death.
> So much for Jones. He died as one of scores,
> and on a distant beach. But when they bring
> the news to those who count the cost of wars,
> a private's death becomes a private thing.
> How strange that war's arithmetic discounts
> the spread of sorrow as the sorrow mounts!

Of all the features that gave GIs a voice, the most popular was "Mail Call," where troops were able to gripe to *Yank* about any topic they found aggravating. Complaints ran the gamut. "What I and many of my comrades want to know is who designed the present Army raincoat? . . . It rains every day here, and we have proved that a GI gets wetter with the present raincoat on than he does without one," Technical Sergeant E. J. Lambiotte wrote from Guadalcanal. "I am one of the many GIs who have, sad to state, achieved only 19 years of age. We are allowed to die for the glory and the safety of our country and its ideals, but we are too young to vote. It would seem one is old enough to vote when one is old enough to kill people," Private William Whitman commented while convalescing at the Cushing General Hospital in Massachusetts. And from New Hebrides, Private H. Moldauer captured the feelings of many support troops who were waiting for the war to end while stationed on isolated Pacific islands: "Monotony, monotony, all is monotony. The heat, the insects, the work, the complete absence of towns, women, liquor. . . . The irregular mail, which has become regular in its irregularity. . . . On a more personal basis, the monotony of prefixing the name with those three little—awfully little—letters: pfc."

In the words of *Yank* journalist Barrett McGurn, the "Mail Call" column "offered every serviceman the opportunity to speak across continents in his own voice" and "wedded necessary military discipline with the American democratic soul." No letter was too critical, caustic, or bitter to publish. Even the chastened Special Service Division, which had infringed on the *Stars and Stripes'* autonomy, understood that it was imperative to refrain "from interference, particularly in regard to the Letters to the Editor, [even though they] were thought to tend toward the seditious."

The likely reason *Yank* was able to print such inflammatory material without repercussions was that President Roosevelt had personally dedicated the magazine to printing whatever troops wanted. While Marshall had christened the *Stars and Stripes'* inaugural 1942 issue with a letter for publication, Roosevelt volunteered to write a piece for the first issue of *Yank*. Just as he had dedicated the American war effort to "Four Freedoms," Roosevelt urged *Yank* to serve as a model of press freedom everywhere in the world:

> In YANK you have established a publication which cannot be understood by your enemies. It is inconceivable to them that a soldier should be allowed to express his own thoughts, his ideas and his opinions. It is inconceivable to them that any

soldiers—or any citizens, for that matter—should have any thoughts other than those dictated by their leaders.

But here is the evidence that you have your own ideas, and the intelligence and humor and the freedom to express them. Every one of you has an individual mission in this war—this greatest and most decisive of all wars. You are not only fighting for your country and your people—you are, in the larger sense, delegates of freedom.

With the wave of his pen, Roosevelt empowered *Yank* to publish GI perspectives with impunity. And perhaps as a vote of confidence or as a threat to commanders wishing to interfere, Roosevelt let readers know that he would be among those subscribing. "I look forward myself to reading YANK—every issue of it—from cover to cover," he said.

*Yank* allowed its readers to fulfill their role as "delegates of freedom" by giving all troops the opportunity to be heard. Eventually, every issue dedicated two pages to letters to the editor, as well as responses to prior letters. In this way, a single letter could spark conversations among troops stationed around the world, and an ongoing dialogue (through follow-up letters and responses) could span weeks and months. And because *Yank*'s readership ranged from privates to the president, when a GI's letter was published, it had the capacity to console fighters in foxholes, while also attracting the attention of top brass and the army's commander in chief. In this way, *Yank* fulfilled the original meaning of "arsenal of democracy" better than perhaps any other periodical of its day. At its height, *Yank* had two million paying subscribers and, because troops abided by the unspoken rule of always sharing their reading material, a probable readership of ten million. As one soldier described *Yank*, it was "the best damn weekly publication ever to receive ink from a printing press."

———

There was one final army-wide periodical that Marshall personally mobilized during the war. As Americans went overseas to fight, some inevitably would receive an early ride back to the States because of injury. In a split second, a man could go from healthy to hurt with no chance to say goodbye or exchange addresses with friends with whom he had fought. Back in the States, military hospitals were filled with troops who required months of convalescence, physical therapy, and counseling. Rather than feel relief for having survived the war and making it home, many felt guilt because they had left their buddies shortchanged at the front. George Marshall was sensitive to this dilemma. "A basic point carried through all military training teaches the individual to think of himself as a member of a team—that if he fails in his job he lets the entire outfit down," Marshall said. This training had the unfortunate by-product of causing wounded troops to feel shame and disappointment upon leaving their unit and friends because of injury. The sudden rift in communication and connection made hospitalization more of a punishment than a therapeutic course. More than anything, the wounded wanted information about their friends who were still at war.

Censorship made this practically impossible. Even if a soldier had the Army Post Office addresses for his friends, troops who were in combat could not write about what they were doing or where they were. And those who were hospitalized could face similar restrictions. Thus, to restore the sense of kinship that injury often severed, Marshall proposed *Outfit*, a monthly magazine for convalescing troops that was distributed for free in US military hospitals around the world.

*Outfit*'s mission was to squeeze as many names, divisions, and war updates as it could in each issue's sixteen pages. It proved impossible to give troops the specific information they wanted about their own unit in so little space. In November 1944, when the first issue of *Outfit* was published, the magazine provided vague coverage for happenings in Alaska, Europe, the Mediterranean, the Middle East, the Pacific, China-Burma-India (CBI), and the Caribbean. Aggravating matters, the magazine was bound by the military's continued insistence on secrecy—especially when it came to information about the location of Americans in combat zones. Since the vast majority of injured troops had come from the front lines, it was an exercise in futility for troops to exhaustively search each issue of *Outfit* for news about the friends they had left—and find nothing.

Rather than ignore this problem, *Outfit* printed letters from hospitalized troops that both begged for information and bragged about their old unit. One issue even devoted a column to letters from "Guys Who Miss Their Buddies." "I have been reading your magazine since I returned to the States from the ETO and I've not yet seen the 334th Regt, 84th Div. mentioned. I sure would like to hear something about my old buddies from B Co., 1st Bn.," wrote Private Alex Chavez from Mason General Hospital in New York. "I would like to see just a couple more words about the best infantry division in the whole damn world, the 'Red Arrow' 32d. We've had so many firsts to our credit, it's taken for granted, and where it's toughest is where you'll find the 32d," wrote Technician Howard Givens from the Ashford General Hospital in West Virginia. "Perhaps you have heard about the 428th Sig. Construction Bn., the 426th and the 445th," Corporal Henry C. Basinger wrote *Outfit*. "All are colored. . . . I think they and others are doing a wonderful job over there. . . . To let America know would make us very happy," he said. "Bear with us, boys," *Outfit* replied. "We can't go around breaking WD secrets." But *Outfit* added that it would continue to cover "the bang-up job being done by Negro outfits."

Since up-to-date war coverage posed a constant censorship challenge, *Outfit* worked around this roadblock by paying homage to individual divisions through full-page cartoon strips that detailed their history and heroics. Having subsisted on a steady diet of military cartoons, it was refreshing not only to see a comic strip but to see one's division at the heart of it. *Outfit* also worked to stoke pride and restore spirits by turning an eye on those who were reading the magazine. A weekly "Fighting Faces" column featured photographs and stories about individual soldiers; it celebrated the wounded and created the feeling that these men had sacrificed their own limbs and well-being for the sake of their friends.

Despite its flaws, *Outfit* was one of the most popular magazines in every US military hospital. Because it was published by and for the army and had limited circulation to *only* those rehabilitating in an army hospital, it created a much-needed sense of belonging—sometimes reinforcing a bond with an old unit, but also coalescing convalescing men. In the words of Charles G. Bolte, an American who endured a lengthy hospitalization after his leg was amputated in Africa, "What happens during convalescence from a serious wound can sour or sweeten a man for life. The pattern of the way he handles himself and the way he looks at himself and the world can be determined for good or for bad in that period of time. Boredom can corrode him, brooding can embitter him," but the written word could restore him. *Outfit* went a long way in easing the emotional wounds of recuperating soldiers by creating a connection with their friends and demonstrating that they were still valued members of the team.

———

Between Marshall's army-wide troop publications and the small-scale newspapers troops were printing themselves, the US Army was generating a deluge of reading material by the end of 1942. However, as millions of US troops began to embark on journeys to locations around the world, the struggle to maintain morale and inform troops would be tested to the extreme. Combat shattered confidence and hopes of survival, and enemy propaganda attempted to destroy any remaining will to fight. Newspapers had their work cut out for them.

# CHAPTER FIVE
## HELLO, SUCKERS!

We shall not land troops like William the Conqueror. . . .
Our weapons are not "visible ones."

—Adolf Hitler

New York. Newport News. San Francisco. Troops knew they were going overseas when they arrived at these ports of embarkation. Shouldering their bulging barracks bags, soldiers left staging areas and found massive gray hulls awaiting them. As they approached their ships, Red Cross volunteers doled out donuts, brass bands belted out patriotic ditties, and final roll calls were taken amid the commotion. They climbed rickety gangplanks, descended into the bellies of boats, and were led to towers of bunks. It looked impossible to stow their gear and still have room to sleep in such cramped quarters, yet they made do. Anxiously, they waited for anchors-up, when they would finally be told where they were going. Their destination could be almost anywhere.

Some of the ships leaving the United States in 1942 were headed to North Africa, where troops would meet the German Army for the first time. It took several torturous weeks to get there, fueled by seasickness and boredom, uncertainty and curiosity. Some ships buoyed passenger spirits by printing shipboard newspapers filled with gossip, humor, and cartoons. But these were the last newspapers troops would see for a while. It was one thing to publish newspapers on friendly territory, and quite another while under fire. Many unit commanders questioned the wisdom of sending troops into war zones—where their focus should be on fighting—and distracting them with newspaper publishing. Adding to this reluctance was the fact that supply lines were already stretched thin and preference was given to shipment of the absolute essentials—weaponry, food, clothing, medical supplies, and the like. Crates of recreational equipment from the Special Service Division were ranked low priority. With no unit newspapers, and because there were no army-wide periodicals in North Africa yet, all information provided to troops came from Washington. Troops quickly discovered that the "chairborne," thousands of miles from the frontlines, had little useful information to impart.

One common orientation tool from the War Department was "country guides," which provided troops an overview of the customs, religions, history, language, weather, and geography of the discrete region where they were headed. In 1942, many troops figured out where they were going when they received *A Pocket Guide to North Africa* along with complementary War Department language guides for North African Arabic and French. These guidebooks had their issues. According to their country guide, troops could expect dry weather in North Africa. "If the stuff that came down day after day along the Algerian coast in a piercing, chill, Englandlike downpour wasn't rain, then I must have been shell-shocked," one man said in exasperation. The language guides were no better. As one soldier remarked, "Even with the [French] language guide, it took [us] half an hour to find out what time the train left next morning, and another fifteen minutes to learn that the train carried freight only." The North African Arabic guide seemed to begin with a sense of pessimism, stating, "Some Arabic sounds [a]re almost impossible for Americans to learn." Tossing the guides aside, many troops communicated with locals by drawing pictures, pantomiming, and just plain hollering. Americans made a terrible first impression, much to Germany's gratification.

Before the Allies landed, Germany had done an expert job of unleashing a torrent of propaganda on civilians. By flaunting Germany's success in Europe, emphasizing the superiority of the German military, and pegging Americans as "soft," Germany made a strong case for why North African nations should side with the dominant and victorious Nazis. When the first American troops were observed, Germany's claims only seemed more plausible. As the celebrated war correspondent Ernie Pyle conceded, "Our troops made a poor impression, in contrast to the few Germans [the locals] had seen. . . . Our boys sang in the streets, unbuttoned their shirt collars, laughed and shouted, and forgot to salute. A lot of Algerians misinterpreted this as inefficiency" and "thought such a carefree Army couldn't possibly whip the grim Germans." The army paid for its failure to acclimate and prepare its troops when North African forces initially hesitated to join sides with the seemingly undisciplined Americans.

Local civilians were not Germany's only target for its propaganda campaign. The war in Europe established the efficacy of Germany's strategy of spreading disinformation and fear to soften military targets. Green American troops were susceptible. They were far from home, getting their first acrid taste of battle, and realizing the only way back to their families was through injury, death, or an end to the war. In between strafing runs and bombings, the terrible whine of enemy aircraft brought a weapon that was potentially more damaging: doubt—thousands of sheets of it, fluttering onto soldiers like giant snowflakes. "Hello, suckers!" began one leaflet. "I'm sure you'll pardon the salutation, seeing as how it comes from a 'Sucker' of 1918! Yes, I was one of those mugs who fought to Make the World Safe for the British Empire in the reign of President Wilson," it said. This flyer attempted to exacerbate the jealousies and fears of American troops, whether it was low soldier pay ("While we were in uniform and earning the magnificent sum of *one Dollar* per day, the fellows back home were living off the fat of the land and making their five to ten dollars per day"), being two-timed ("The 'stay-at-homes' got our jobs and dated our best girls"), or fighting another nation's war at the cost of American lives and prosperity ("While his nephews were fighting and dying to Save King George's Empire, Uncle Sam was going into debt to the tune of some 20 odd billion dollars"). It painted President Roosevelt as a liar, quoting his promise in 1940 "that no American boys will be sacrificed on foreign battlefields." Finally, it vowed to send more leaflets. "Watch for next issue," it said. Most troops saw these leaflets for the Nazi propaganda that they were.

Many crumpled them up or used them for toilet paper. However, some tucked Germany's propaganda into their pockets or mailed it home.

The army, used to issuing equipment to deal with war conditions—a wool coat for the cold, a gas mask for a poison vapor attack—had no apparatus in its arsenal to protect American minds from psychological warfare. In time, top commanders would realize that finding ways to boost morale was the best antidote for the hazy distortions contained in the enemy's blizzards of paper. They also recognized that the best way to fight a war of words was with their own.

But the army always seemed to be behind the eight ball. Just as it struggled to procure supplies and build camps at home in 1940 and 1941, the army was unprepared to meet the dual demands of arming men for battlefield fighting and shielding their minds from persistent enemy propaganda. Readying soldiers for combat was prioritized—and with good reason. As difficult as training had been back home, now that troops faced actual fighting, they felt unprepared and unsure of themselves. Many had been shuttled through basic training using only fake weapons. The troops who fought the Germans first felt like guinea pigs. When combat veterans were later polled, two-thirds stated that they had "too little training in the United States" and should have learned about "enemy weapons and [the] best defense against them," as well as "how to find and handle land mines and booby traps" and "how to operate against different types of enemy defense."

As confidence in their training lagged, combat conditions further wore down troops' mental and emotional defenses. There were days when they fought and advanced without sleep, and others spent pinned down in foxholes as German snipers eyed the landscape for targets. They dug foxholes with abandon and flung themselves into these ditches, clinging to the earth for dear life as German planes swung low for strafing. Their diet was limited to joyless packages of C rations, which one man described as "dehydrated eggs, dehydrated potatoes, and that detestable canned meat called Spam." There was also synthetic lemonade, which earned the moniker "battery acid" because it could "clean and bleach" just about anything. Under a blanket of stars, troops took turns standing guard and attempting to doze off despite the "inhuman" cold and nightmarish symphony of artillery fire. Many compared their foray into warfare to a baptism by fire. It was an apt comparison. Like religion, the army required each man to have faith—in one's commander, in one's unit, in one's training—to sustain them through each day's tribulations.

But blind faith only got them so far. Knowledge and information were essential. Soldiers had many questions in need of answers. Why were they in Algeria, Tunisia, and Morocco instead of taking the fight to the German mainland? How was a firefight in the desert contributing to victory? Where else were Americans fighting? Spotty information came in dribs and drabs. Rumors were whispered down the line. Radios were the main source of news, but they were in short supply. The few pithy news reports that were intercepted were often beamed from thousands of miles away—from the BBC in London, or, if the men had a short-wave radio, from the States. "It seemed ironic that what was happening two hundred miles from us had to be flashed to America and then back again before we could hear it," Ernie Pyle observed. These broadcasts might mention the action in North Africa in a couple of sentences, if at all. Most of the time, troops had no idea what was happening around them or anywhere else in the world.

Facing commanding officers who were still wary of distracting combat troops with newspaper publishing, the army initially turned to civilian-run periodicals to fill the void. In World War I, Marshall had observed how General Pershing endorsed the distribution of thousands of American magazines and attempted to get hometown newspapers across the pond. Marshall hoped that the Special Service Division could make arrangements with American publishers to get an even larger quantity of newspapers and magazines into the hands of his men.

The Special Service Division began with newspapers. When home-front publishers learned of the War Department's desire to get local newspapers into the hands of troops, they were eager to do their part. Between late 1942 and early 1943, domestic newspapers secured corporate sponsors to cover layout and printing costs and created truncated editions just for troops. In Boston, shoppers at the Jordan Marsh department store were encouraged to take a free "overseas edition" of the *Boston Herald* to send to a loved one abroad. The overseas issues were reduced to nine by six-and-a-half inches so they were a convenient size for mailing. They contained world news, music, and movie reviews, excerpts from Boston-area sermons, sports coverage, cartoons, and a crossword puzzle. Many other large city papers did the same. For example, New York's Spear and Company furniture store partnered with the *Daily Mirror* to create a free servicemen's edition that offered a taste of the big city to troops afar.

Other novel arrangements were made by domestic newspapers to create troop-sized editions. The *Providence Sunday Journal* delivered its service edition within the pages of its Sunday issue—along the centerfold, a dotted line demarcated a six-by-eight newspaper that could be clipped, folded, and mailed to a soldier. Portland's *Oregonian* ran a daily servicemen's edition that was available by subscription. To ensure the swiftest overseas delivery, Dayton, Ohio's *Journal Herald* printed a weekly troop edition directly on a V-mail form so it could be delivered within days to troops across the globe. Never mind that troops had to squint in order to read these rags or that the exceptionally small text made their eyes burn; in their hands were newspapers printed back home just for them. To receive a letter with one of these newspapers inside was a boon. They were passed from one man to the next until the newsprint disintegrated.

These hometown gazettes were treasured, but not because they imparted up-to-date war news. Months could pass between the mailing of a newspaper and its delivery overseas. Rather, these newspapers were cherished because they represented "home." The longer a man spent overseas, the fuzzier his memories became of what home was like, which only intensified the desire to return. As Ernest Norquist, a GI in the Philippines lamented, "Oh, I long for the familiar things of home. The curtains and rugs and pictures and vases with cared-for flowers in them. There is even the SMELL of home that I want to experience again. . . . I want to hear the sounds of home—the water running in the kitchen sink, the treading of familiar footsteps, the sound of beloved voices, all these and more I want to hear." And yet, Norquist added, "We CAN'T get away. We CAN'T go home, we CAN'T: no matter how much we WANT to. It has required a revolution in our thinking for us to recognize our utter helplessness." Although a hometown newspaper might seem a minor comfort, it was capable of delivering a swell of nostalgia to very homesick men. Few things were more coveted.

Yet newsprint rationing stymied the production of these tiny servicemen's editions. Beginning in 1943, the War Production Board (WPB) required newspapers to reduce their consumption of newsprint because huge quantities of paper were needed to package war supplies. This announcement angered publishers who were mistrustful of the government's motives in regulating free presses. The twin menaces of the US Office of Censorship's regulations and military censorship rules had already curbed newspapers from printing all they wanted to. Now, the government's rationing limits on newsprint promised to physically shrink the amount of news that could be reported. One of the most vocal critics of the WPB's paper restriction was the *Chicago Tribune*, which charged that rationing newsprint was a blatant attack upon the freedom of the press. "It is designed to put the bureaucracy in a position to coerce newspapers, and to punish or destroy those that expose its blunders or resist its tyrannies by denying them the paper necessary for their publication." The *Tribune* urged all newspapers to band together and "react vigorously against this attempt to destroy them." But the WPB insisted that newsprint rationing was a necessity because there was a shortage of pulpwood and manpower in Canada, and military demand drained supplies.

As domestic newspapers struggled to stretch their limited newsprint quota, some decided to discontinue their overseas editions for troops. After all, they were hard to justify. Why waste newsprint on news that had gone stale before delivery? Many publishers did not realize the sentimental value of troop editions until it was too late. When Louisville's *Courier-Journal* announced that it was discontinuing its servicemen's edition in 1944, it was inundated with letters begging it not to. As one heartbreaking letter from a soldier said, "Your overseas edition was almost as welcome to me as a letter from home. I think I am speaking for

Kentuckiana service men when I say that the bad news about stopping the overseas edition is like a sweetheart writing about meeting another fellow and informing you that she will never write again."

Recognizing that hometown newspapers played an important role in maintaining morale, the War Department considered subscribing to major regional newspapers. The idea was quickly scrapped because it would be too labor-intensive and impractical to subscribe to domestic newspapers, collect them at a stateside distribution center, and then ship them to bases overseas. The process would take weeks at best. Rather than focus on daily newspapers, the Special Service Division shifted its focus to monthly magazines. Most young Americans had a habit of reading magazines as civilians. Why not give troops their favorite periodicals while at war? The man placed in charge of this literary operation was a thirty-three-year-old officer, Ray Trautman. Thanks to his boundless imagination and creativity, it is estimated that nearly one billion magazines were purchased and distributed to American troops around the world. It was an incredible feat, far surpassing Marshall's wildest expectations for what was possible.

Like Marshall, Trautman innately understood the power and importance of supplying the written word to troops. After graduating from the University of Kentucky in 1932, Trautman opened his own bookstore in Lexington, Kentucky, and later took a job as manager of the H. A. Moos Bookstore in San Antonio. Mingling with customers, Trautman kept his finger on the pulse of reading habits and what genres were most popular. He never imposed titles on readers. Instead, he operated like a matchmaker by learning a customer's preferences and then connecting them to a title that they would enjoy. From highbrow literature to the silliest comic book, Trautman made sure to have a wide variety of reading materials, so he had something for everyone.

As the Great Depression swept the nation, Trautman, like so many young men, joined the Civilian Conservation Corps. His college degrees earned him the position of educational adviser of the CCC camps in Kentucky. In this position, Trautman ordered truckloads of books and magazines, providing countless Americans free access to books and periodicals for the first time in their lives. CCC recruits savored the chance to entertain themselves and find escape by turning to Trautman's reading materials. It was gratifying for Trautman to watch as thousands of men took advantage of the opportunity to read and better themselves. Even the US Department of Education took notice of the correlation between Trautman's inspired work and the soaring morale being reported by the CCC camps in Kentucky. Reading was changing lives. It was an invaluable education for a man who would soon be choosing books and periodicals for over twelve million Americans in uniform.

The CCC sealed Trautman's interest in becoming a professional librarian. In 1939, he moved to New York City and attended Columbia University's School of Library Service. One year later, he graduated with a degree in library science. When he entered the army in 1940, Trautman's unusual background in books, army know-how from his years in the CCC, and librarianship earned him the position of chief librarian of the US Army.

When Trautman began his quest to procure popular magazines for troops, he faced more obstacles than a steeplechaser, but he had the agility to clear every hurdle. His foremost problem was budgetary. In 1941 and 1942, the Army Library Service placed thousands of magazine subscriptions with the Washington News Company, which offered the most competitive rates for popular magazines. However, Trautman's limited budget meant he could send no more than one magazine for every twelve to thirteen soldiers. Clearly, this was not enough. As one soldier described the situation, "We are crying for reading material." Trautman wanted to fill the void, but problems kept mounting that threatened the entire enterprise.

Just as he was trying to build momentum, the War Production Board announced that all magazines would be subject to paper rationing and therefore limited to using whatever tonnage of paper they had used in 1941. This quota strangled growth. Nothing sold magazines like war, and the rate of readership spiked after the attack on Pearl Harbor. For example, *Reader's Digest* sold nearly 3.7 million magazines in 1941 and 5.1 million in 1942. To keep the number of magazines being printed as high as possible, publishers reduced the size of each issue, eliminated underperforming features, reduced advertising space, and used thinner paper to stretch every ounce they were allotted. Clearly, it was an inopportune time for Trautman to seek tens of thousands of magazine subscriptions at reduced rates. Magazine publishers could hardly meet the raging civilian demand while charging full price.

Trautman felt he had no choice but to approach WPB officials and ask that they grant an extra paper allotment to magazines that contracted with the army to supply periodicals for soldiers. In an uncharacteristically swift decision, the WPB agreed. Suddenly, Trautman became one of the most influential figures in the magazine industry; his signature on an army contract enabled a publisher to print exponentially more magazines—and gain more readers. To put this in perspective, Trautman's contracts with *Time*, *Newsweek*, the *Saturday Evening Post*, and the *New Yorker* alone led to an additional allotment of 1,300 tons of paper. And these were just four of the dozens of titles Trautman ultimately purchased for troops.

Trautman exercised his power with tremendous restraint. He believed his job was to make sure that each ton of paper produced the maximum number of magazines for soldiers. Thus, each army contract with a magazine publisher included paper- and money-saving conditions. No advertisements could be included, they had to conform to the army's standards of reduced size and format, and they would be sold to the army at cost (or less). To ensure that all these requirements were satisfied, Trautman personally negotiated prices and fiddled with production techniques to create some of the smallest magazines in history.

Trautman initially turned to *Newsweek* to experiment with creating miniature magazines for the army. First, Trautman turned to V-mail technology. In January 1943, Trautman took a pair of scissors to several copies of a *Newsweek* issue, extracted every article of significance, removed every advertisement in the magazine (he had to abide by his own rules), and then pasted all usable content onto paper that could be fed through a V-mail machine. When the thirty-seven-page magazine was reconstituted at a quarter of its original size, the four-by-five-inch

magazine could fit inside a uniform pocket. But the font was so minuscule that it was hardly readable. Trautman had to go back to the
drawing board.

Next, finding inspiration in magazines like *Omnibook* and *Reader's
Digest*, which were more like booklets than their sprawling glossy-paged
cousins, Trautman combined forces with *Newsweek*'s production staff
to design ad-free magazines on newsprint. Their prototype weighed a
few ounces, measured five-and-a-half by eight inches, and had a small,
but legible, font. It became the model for all other American magazines
that wished to print servicemen's editions for the army. Alongside *Newsweek*'s miniaturized "Battle Baby," soon came *Time*'s "Pony Edition"
and the *New Yorker*'s overseas edition. Besting them all, however, was
the *Saturday Evening Post*—which measured only three by four-and-
a-half inches. Dozens of other magazines omitted advertisements and
used low-weight paper, but kept their large size. As long as they met
the army's specifications, a magazine would become a mainstay of the
Army Library Service. Each week, the army shipped a fresh batch of
popular magazines from home. Titles were chosen based on their mass
appeal. Beginning in mid-1943, a unit could expect to receive a monthly
shipment of periodicals that included at least one copy of each of the
following: *American, Baseball, Collier's, Detective Story, Flying, Esquire,
Infantry Journal, Life, Look, Modern Screen, New Yorker, Newsweek, Omnibook, Popular Mechanics, Popular Photography, Radio News, Reader's
Digest, Saturday Evening Post, Superman, Time*, and *Western Trails*. As
more publishers agreed to abide by the army's specifications for overseas
magazines, additional titles were added. Trautman's monthly packages of
magazines were an immediate hit with troops. Domestic magazines were
so beloved that when their arrival was postponed by shipping delays,
some units attempted to placate readers' disappointment by producing
hand-drawn replicas of *Time, Collier's*, and other popular titles.

For publishers, creating servicemen's editions of their magazines
caused headaches. Though eager for new readers, some cringed at the
contortions their magazines had to go through to appease the army.
When the *New Yorker*'s Harold Ross learned that Trautman could grant

a paper allotment for an overseas edition, he was eager to strike a "deal with the Army to get us, outside of our ration quota, the paper for the issue." However, once Ross's wife, Jane Grant, successfully brokered a deal with Trautman, Ross was the source of never-ending complaints. The army's persnickety restrictions on page count and size tortured him. The "halftones took an awful licking in the miniature edition," Ross grumbled, and he could hardly bear how the cover art was "mutilated" by the change in page size (the "peewee" edition, as Ross called it, was six by eight-and-a-half inches). Though he was unhappy with the appearance of his magazine, he could not help but feel gratified when 20,650 miniature issues of the September 1943 *New Yorker* were shipped to military installations around the world. Circulation numbers for overseas editions only increased as the army's appetite for magazines proved insatiable, and the navy piggybacked on the army's magazine contracts.

From an initial 120 *Newsweek* subscriptions in early 1942, Trautman's army periodical program ballooned to over 156 million magazine issues per year. Americans in far-flung locations were grateful for every periodical that reached them. Shipped to places where no other English-language reading was available, each box of magazines was greeted by a captive audience that "gobbled them up quickly." All abided by an unspoken rule: as soon as one man was finished, he passed his periodical to the next man until the print was smeared and the pages were falling out.

Testimonials from overseas proved how valuable magazines were in the battle for information and the maintenance of morale. As the communications officer for the USS *Alcyone* explained in a letter to *Time*, after a long engagement at sea, a pile of magazines reached the ship, and one issue of *Time* happened to cover the *Alcyone*'s recent mission. "So help me," one of his fellow sailors said upon reading it, "this is the first time I've known what the hell went on out there." As the communications director explained, when in the thick of fighting, "The welter of detail sometimes gets so confusing on this end that it's a pleasure to sit down and read the story after someone has taken the time to whittle down the detail and reduce everything to its proper proportion."

Gil Sandler, a US Navy navigator who spent nearly three years stationed in the Pacific, never forgot the day a small boat pulled along-side his ship to deliver boxes of periodicals. "I found myself reading a magazine I had never read before, it was called *The New Yorker*. . . . And the writing in it, and the writers (E. B. White, James Thurber, Brendan Gill, Dorothy Parker, John O'Hara, A. J. Liebling) were to influence my life profoundly." He explained that his ship experienced "great stretches of time between battles" with little to do but "stand routine watches." The advent of miniature magazines that informed them of the world they had left behind and the one they were fighting to save was a godsend.

———

While Trautman's magazine program would revolutionize American troops' access to reading materials, it took time to become fully operational. For those serving in North Africa in 1942, their fighting would be over by the time civilian magazines were shipped overseas in sufficient numbers. Something else was needed to fill the information void. The army could not afford to keep its troops in the dark while Germany routinely peppered Allied forces with myriad propaganda leaflets casting doubt at every turn. Though supply lines were overburdened and the US Army was reluctant to ship anything that did not clothe, feed, or arm troops, Germany's psychological warfare forced the War Department to treat information as essential armor. As Marshall said, "It is true that war is fought with physical weapons of flame and steel but it is not the mere possession of these weapons, or the use of them, that wins the struggle." Dispirited and unsure of the importance of their fighting, overseas troops needed the War Department to supply them with a shield of information. The Special Service Division's field kit for newspaper publishing was relatively small and could be shipped anywhere, if only it was given prioritized status. In January 1943, Marshall did exactly that. The Special Service Division's newspaper kit was designated "specialized equipment" and given equal standing with conventional weaponry. Thus, alongside cartons of ammunition were crates of paper and ink.

Though Marshall could solve the issue of supplies, the rest was out of his hands. Combat proved to be one of the most inhospitable environments in which to publish, yet troops showed that war was no match for their ingenuity. According to one overseas editor, printing a paper was feasible so long as the staff included "good newspapermen, full of life, a little skeptical of officers' ideas of what is news, and as resourceful as frontiersmen."

By the time the field kit for newspaper publishing made its way across the sea, the fighting in North Africa was coming to an end. However, these troops knew more battlefields were in their future—possibly in Italy or the Pacific. To work out any kinks before they were put to the test of publishing in combat, they fitfully began to assemble newssheets from "somewhere in Africa." Some, like the 903rd Engineer Air Force Headquarters Company's *Engineerful*, were printed to entertain and amuse. The *Engineerful* printed humorous pieces, such as the unit's "favorite recipe," which instructed, "Take one draftee slightly green. Stir from bed at early hour. Soak in shower . . . Dress in olive drab. Mix with others of his kind . . . Grate on sergeant's nerves . . . Season with rain, sun or snow . . . Bake in 110 degrees in summer and let cool in below zero weather. Serves 140,000,000 people." It also experimented with printing some of the most risqué pinups of any troop publication, including nude illustrations.

On the other end of the spectrum was the army's *Bonjour*, printed in West Africa beginning in the spring of 1943. It printed the occasional message from top command but otherwise masterfully conveyed the spirit, attitudes, and brio of the enlisted men. Submissions acknowledged the nearly universal dream of "getting the hell out of here," boasted about how *Bonjour* was so good that "the *New Yorker* will be over here begging for copy," and marveled how only the army could take perfectly good food and make it unappetizing. Even soldiers' gripes made headlines. When enlisted men were unfairly treated because of their low rank, *Bonjour* took their side. "What certain dog faces want to know is why a certain MP officer made them leave the festival in the next town Sunday night, after they had paid $2.00 to enter plus a huge amount for each drink . . . and at the same time permitting the officers to remain and enjoy themselves," the paper reported. "Rank is a fine thing and something we all respect, but such treatment can be only described as 'RANK.'" Perhaps this article brought results, as a few weeks later an enormous headline read, "OFFICERS DO K.P.!" The very thought of officers peeling piles of potatoes must have cheered many an enlisted man's heart. "Will wonders never cease?" the article asked.

*Bonjour* also addressed the pesky wisps of paper that kept falling from the sky from German planes, and how this was a two-front war being fought with traditional and psychological warfare. The mental fight featured novel weapons—there would be "Axis Sally" and other propaganda-laden German radio programs, pro-Nazi posters in occupied towns, and more German leaflets urging surrender. While many US troops would laugh at Sally's lies, see through the Nazis' bombastic slogans, and perceive Germany's desperation, they also wanted to retaliate with their own psychological blows. "On [Hitler's] own soil it is not only possible to smash his . . . backbone," *Bonjour* said, "but it is possible to break his heart, as well as the hearts of all of his people." To achieve victory in this war, Americans would have to crack Germany's army *and* assail the ideology that fueled it.

# CHAPTER SIX
## 45TH GIORNALE MILITARE

Here we go again!

Heigh-Ho and here we go on another year of war!

Another year of toil and sweat and tears and blood. One more year of struggle and strife, of loneliness and disappointment—far from Mother and Sweetheart, Wife and Child.

And with the coming of each day will come the dread spectre of death. Thousands of lives will be thrown away.

Who knows what the new year holds in store for you? What new weapons will be introduced and what new difficulties lie ahead?

Look around you at this moment, take notice of the friends and associates whom you have learned to respect:

How many will still be there at the end of 1945?

—German propaganda leaflet

When it came to keeping troops informed while deriding Nazi Germany, perhaps no overseas newspaper could compare to the brazen and impudent offerings of the *45th Division News*. It developed a penchant for making trouble at home before heading overseas. The paper began under the inspired command of Lieutenant Colonel Walter M. Harrison, the former editor of the *Daily Oklahoman* and an army intelligence officer at Fort Sill, Oklahoma. After gathering a handful of experienced writers and artists, Harrison invited these newsmen to create a paper that captured the humor, frustrations, and achievements of the division. The staff came out swinging and spared no barbs. In less than a year, the *45th Division News* had gained a reputation for its hell-raising content and un-army-like independence.

The staff member who created perhaps the most incendiary material was the *45th Division News*'s artist, Bill Mauldin. His boyish appearance and petulance made him seem like a wayward teenager, but Mauldin had an innate understanding of humanity, and he used his artistic skill to distill complex problems and emotions into a single-panel drawing and punchy tagline. His cartoons proved so popular that the *Stars and Stripes* soon carried them, and by the war's end, Mauldin was a world-renowned, Pulitzer Prize winning artist. Yet perhaps his greatest achievement was making millions of soldiers feel understood.

What enabled Mauldin to tap into the veins of discontent coursing through the army were his own unpleasant experiences. Though Harrison would sometimes excuse newspaper staff from certain details so that they could work on the paper, he refused to give Mauldin a break. In order for Mauldin's cartoons to offer catharsis, Mauldin needed to take turns scrubbing pots on KP, cleaning toilets, shoveling coal, and carrying (in Mauldin's words) a twenty-gallon "honey bucket . . . full and foaming" for disposal (the bucket was provided to dissuade men from urinating on the ground outside of their tents). As Harrison said, "How can you find material for cartoons if you're not soldiering most of the time?" The disgust Mauldin felt for these jobs made its way into his cartoons. And these cartoons made their way into the hearts of soldiers who took turns doing the same thankless jobs.

But they had the opposite effect on the higher-ups. "[Mauldin's] cartoons have an irreverent quality about them which has not escaped notice," Harrison explained. Even so, as the officer in charge, he did not buckle under criticism. "This happens to be exactly the kind of paper I had hoped for," Harrison retorted. There was no point in publishing unless the *News* remained independent and true to its readers. Harrison understood that soldiers needed a place to gripe, and they felt better after getting their troubles off their chests. If a cartoon griped for them, that was even better because it demonstrated that a man was not alone in feeling unhappy. For as long as he could, Harrison guarded his staff against easily offended outsiders. And the staff knew they could continue publishing the content their readers wanted because anytime the paper came under attack, Harrison, "our little colonel, would snarl back . . . and circle about us protectively, throwing up smoke screens like a destroyer escort."

The ultimate test of the paper's freedom was its ability to keep its GI flavor in combat.

————

In June 1943, the Forty-Fifth Infantry Division—known as the Thunderbirds—was given orders to embark on a multiweek voyage through U-boat-infested waters to Oran, Algeria. Even though the Allies held North Africa, the Thunderbirds made their amphibious landing on the shore at Arzew in full combat gear; it was their final practice before a more contested landing as part of Operation Husky, the invasion of Sicily. They spent two weeks in Algeria writing letters home and getting their "land legs" before shipping out. When the day came, they boarded transports outfitted in steel helmets, wool shirts and pants, cotton jackets, service shoes and leggings, ammunition belts packed with eighty rounds, and inflatable life belts. Each man stuffed his haversack with rations, a mess kit, a blanket, a poncho, a shelter half and other tent supplies, socks and underwear, and miscellaneous personal items. A bayonet, entrenching tool, and gas mask topped off the load. Seasickness quickly overshadowed the fifty pounds of gear they carried. Churning seas tossed ships around like toys in bathwater. Holds were "an inch deep in vomit." One man recalled, "You wouldn't believe a land-locked body of tepid water could behave so violently." The sight of enemy territory had never been so welcome. The Thunderbirds made the precarious climb down nets and into landing craft. Zigzagging through the choppy surf to the melody of US Navy destroyers bombarding the coast, many Thunderbirds disregarded orders to keep their heads down and stole peeks of the shore they were about to take.

The invasion was riddled with miscalculations. Landing craft deposited men on the wrong beaches, some became stranded on sandbars and outcrops of rocks, and still others lowered their ramps into water so deep that the equipment-laden men plunged in and drowned. The Thunderbirds who made it to the shore scrambled to form makeshift units and start moving inward toward the two airfields they were supposed to pry from the Axis. Tens of thousands of German and Italian soldiers were waiting for them. It was not long before the men of the Forty-Fifth got their first glimpse of the savageries of war. Bodies dotted the landscape, and cries from the wounded punctuated the stagnant air. Rather than asking for medics, these young men cried for their mothers. There was no chance to process it all; war did not stop for casualties. Dazed by the horror of combat and the prospect of death, troops silently trudged forward.

"It was D plus one and time to think about getting out the *45th Division News,*" recounted its longtime editor, Sergeant Don Robinson. A somber mood had settled over the division, and the appearance of something familiar, the newspaper that had accompanied them for over a year of training at home, would be a comfort. Like the rest of the division, the *News* had not endured the landings unscathed; half of the newspaper's staff was missing and presumed dead. "We decided the best memorial to the boys would be to put out the first Allied newspaper on Axis soil in World War II," Bill Mauldin said. If they were going to be the first, they would have to hustle as competition was on their heels. British troops managed to land with a truck outfitted with a tiny high-speed press mounted to its bed, an invaluable advantage.

With sand pouring through the figurative hourglass, the *45th Division News* got a crash course in the quagmires of overseas publishing while fitfully trying to print before the British did. Because the crate containing their mimeograph machine and typewriters was nowhere to be found, Robinson and Mauldin attempted to find presses they could use. They found a printer in the nearby town of Vittoria, who agreed to take their business. However, the Italian typesetters struggled to transcribe the Americans' stories, which were handwritten in English. Given the slow progress, Robinson settled for a short, two-page paper instead of the usual eight pages. Next, however, he learned that the Italian alphabet lacked the letters *w*, *k*, and *y*, and the typesetters were running out of their limited supply usually used to spell foreign names. Copy was rewritten to avoid these letters.

Meanwhile, Robinson needed the latest war news. As Mauldin would not be contributing a cartoon to the inaugural Sicilian issue because illustrations would have introduced an additional round of complications, Mauldin volunteered his reportorial skills. The last place he had heard English-language news was back on the ship that brought him to Sicily. So Mauldin managed to "borrow" a bicycle, ride it to shore, and bribe a sailor for a ride to a navy vessel. After getting the news, Mauldin returned to shore and pedaled back to Vittoria. On the way, his burnished bike caught the eye of an enemy dive-bomber, who, in Mauldin's words, "couldn't resist a bit of sport." After a few unsuccessful strafing runs, the pilot lost interest, and Mauldin ditched the bike, hitched a ride, and returned to the printer by nightfall. Inside were two *News* staffers who had been rumored dead. One was cursing about running out of *m*'s after turning them upside down to pose as *w*'s, while the other was painstakingly rewriting copy using his neatest penmanship to avoid typos by the Italian typesetters.

It took all night because the factory lost electricity, forcing the men to switch to a hand-operated press, but volume IV, number I of the *45th Division News* was cranked out during the early morning hours of July 13, 1943. Three thousand copies told of the Eighty-Second Airborne Division's "paratroopers who had preceded us into Sicily by several hours and met us as proudly as a little boy who has slipped through the pantry window and opened the front door for his mother." The issue also included combat stories and general interest pieces. Was it the first Allied or American paper on Axis soil? "Despite the fact that [Britain's] Eighth Army *News* had mobile printing equipment, we beat them by a day in getting out," Robinson bragged.

After navigating this host of printing problems to put out its Vittoria edition, the division's mimeograph machine miraculously arrived and was used for the next two issues. The division's constant movement, however, prevented the newspaper from remaining self-sufficient. Carrying a pencil and notepad was one thing, but a truck was needed to cart around the mimeograph machine, typewriters, and the mishmash of accouterments to produce the paper. The newspaper's crate of supplies usually wound up in the rear of a convoy, arriving just in time to move out again. Thus, the *45th Division News*—if it was going to exist at all—was forced to find newspaper presses and amenable printers in cities no longer under siege. Because the Thunderbirds continued their relentless drive forward, the newspaper was continually on the search for proximate print shops. All the while, difficulties stalked the paper like a shadow.

The paper was set up next in the Sicilian town of Caltanissetta, where the Italian typesetters solved the dilemma of *w*'s, *k*'s, and *y*'s by switching font sizes and styles whenever their supply was exhausted. The newspaper they produced looked like a ransom letter. Staffers were embarrassed by the amateur appearance of the paper's mismatched type, but it was received by soldiers with appreciation and trust. Untrue rumors spread rapidly at the front, and troops looked to the *45th Division News* to set them straight. One story making the rounds was that General George Patton had to be evacuated from Italy in a straitjacket after worrying himself sick. Because the Thunderbirds assumed that "if anything newsworthy had happened [the *News*] would have printed it," unconfirmed rumors such as this quickly lost momentum.

With a little overseas practice under their belts, Robinson decided it was time to treat readers to a cartoon. Bill Mauldin was sent to nearby Palermo to search for an engraving facility. All that remained was a bombed-out shop. The owner agreed to relocate his damaged equipment to a nearby chicken coop and attempt to refurbish it to make a printing plate of one of Mauldin's illustrations. But he lacked acid and a zinc plate for the engraving. Mauldin acquired the acid from a local chemical plant and then visited a casket maker who removed a sheet of zinc from the lining of a coffin. Back at the chicken coop, the engraver heated the metal plates over a wood-fed fire, and slowly, an impression of the cartoon was transferred. It showed Mauldin's famous characters, Willie and Joe, in a mountain of debris. One was rattling off his gun at an enemy airplane that was swooping toward them, while the other was wearing a roof tile on his head for camouflage and yelling, "Stop shootin' at him, ya idiot! Wanna give away our position?" It took a day's worth of work, but the Caltanissetta issue of the *News* finally carried a Mauldin cartoon.

Soon, the paper's entire staff moved to Palermo, where they discovered a mildly damaged printing plant with a professional Linotype machine. "Our paper became again the size it was in the States, with pictures, cartoons by Mauldin, and all the regular features," Robinson remembered. "We rode high." Five issues of the *45th Giornale Militare*, as the staff affectionately referred to the Italian edition of their paper, were printed in quick succession. The next issue carried the colossal headline "Finito." The battle for Sicily was over.

———

The swift, six-week battle for Sicily gave false hope for a quick end to the campaign for the Italian mainland—an objective that ultimately took nineteen months. From the beaches of Salerno to Anzio, Axis forces took advantage of Italy's terrain. Its flat shoreline became crowded with Allied troops and equipment during amphibious landings and was an easy target for German flyers. Italy's mountains offered high perches to levy attacks on invaders approaching from the lowlands. The mountainous region around Cassino offered such perfect protection to a defender that war colleges worldwide studied its topography and seeming impregnability. When geographic challenges were combined with one of the most frigid and wet winters in Italian history, infantrymen faced casualties, not only from enemy fire, but also from pneumonia and trench foot. Although the army had plans for the rotation of units, soldiers scattered across the impassable hills and valleys of the Italian countryside suffered for weeks without being relieved. As one soldier said, "Just about the only way the combat man could get out was to be carried out." Under the circumstances, mere survival was a gift. Fresh socks would have been a miracle. And newspapers seemed a distant, civilian luxury.

Yet they were printed, albeit intermittently. Not only did they build morale, but GI journalists found great meaning in printing the first independent newspapers in Italy. For years, Italian publishers had been censored and forced to paint the Fascist regime in glowing colors, giving the appearance of unanimous support for Prime Minister Benito Mussolini. Soldiers felt the power of liberating printing facilities as they crept northward, closer to Germany. When they came across one publishing house that had belonged to Mussolini's son-in-law, they learned that "the last job they had done was a 2-tone picture of Hitler in 1938." Upon getting the factory's machinery in working order, the Americans ensured that the next job consisted of free words written by the soldiers of a democratic army.

In keeping with tradition, the *News* strove to be the first American newspaper to be published on the Italian mainland, and it was. But the newsmen faced worse conditions in Salerno than they had in Sicily. Each week seemed to offer a new threat to the paper's existence. Robinson bemoaned the paper's streak of bad luck: "Week No. One, German bombers got a near miss on the engraving shop and put it out of business temporarily. Week No. Two, the CID [the Criminal Investigation Division] picked up all our printers and put them in the clink on suspicion of counterfeiting bread ration tickets. Week No. Three, the bombers were back, and this time, got a direct hit on our print shop, filling the presses with plaster and scrambling the type." Despite the adversity they faced, the staff of the *45th Division News* never considered quitting. Their readers were already enduring deprivations of all sorts; their newspaper would not be one of them.

In Italy, the *News*, like the infantrymen who read it, became more grizzled. Mauldin's Willie and Joe grew beards (as did most men in the Forty-Fifth), and their repartee was less lighthearted and more sardonic. Armed with his drawing board, Mauldin waged attacks on the army's utter neglect of infantrymen in the mountains, who languished under terrible conditions while receiving only a trickle of replenishments, and he chastised overzealous military police who jailed men for ludicrous infractions, like not being clean-shaven. For those fighting the Germans and the conditions, Mauldin's cartoons showed that someone was standing up for them. High command, however, was less enthusiastic. At one point, there was even a concerted effort by top brass "to purge the Italian campaign of the cancer of insubordination" by wiping Mauldin's cartoons from the pages of any troop newssheet that dared to print them. According to a stenographer at a secret Fifth Army conference of field generals, General Theodore Roosevelt Jr. quashed this anti-cartoon crusade. Opposing the view that Mauldin's sketches were encouraging dereliction, Roosevelt insisted that they nurtured resolve and morale because troops felt vindicated in knowing that others felt as they did. Cartoons would not cause a mutiny; rather, they were helping to prevent one. Roosevelt's impassioned plea seemed to quell the dissenters of the Fifth Army.

Mauldin gained other supporters in high places. General Dwight Eisenhower was a regular follower of the misadventures of Willie and Joe, and General Mark Clark even arranged for Mauldin to have a "specially equipped Jeep in Italy so that he could go where he wanted and draw what he wished." For every friend Mauldin made, however, he seemed to have at least one outspoken enemy.

As Mauldin was publishing sketches of scraggly infantrymen, General George Patton was keeping busy by erecting signs throughout Third Army territory that threatened to fine soldiers who failed to maintain their appearance and hygiene. The general demanded that his men shave, polish their shoes, and wear proper attire. Patton, a West Point graduate, was known for his tough love and strict adherence to order—he encouraged and bawled out his men in equal measure. Throughout his military career, he cleaved to the notions that "iron discipline was . . . essential to success in battle" and that strict adherence to cleanliness, grooming, and proper saluting fostered a spirit of obedience and efficiency. When the *Stars and Stripes* published a Mauldin cartoon of Willie and Joe sporting mangy beards while beholding one of Patton's very own signs, "Old Blood and Guts" was not amused. Patton demanded a meeting with Mauldin.

On Mauldin's day of reckoning, Patton immediately launched into a profanity-laced diatribe.

"Now then," Patton began, "about those pictures you draw of those god-awful things you call soldiers. Where did you ever see soldiers like that? You know goddamn well you're not drawing an accurate representation of the American soldier. You make them look like goddamn bums. No respect for the army, their officers, or themselves."

After accusing Mauldin of encouraging such impudence, the general produced "some prime goddamn examples of what I mean by creating disrespect." Patton displayed one of Mauldin's cartoons depicting an opera house with a marquee announcing a USO show featuring women from the States and demanded an explanation.

"Queued up in the snow at the front door was a long line of weary-looking soldiers . . . with their coat collars turned up against the raw weather and their sad faces filled with anticipation of the charms within," while there was a line "at the stage door [of] officers . . . all spruced up and waiting to take the girls out," Mauldin described. Patton could see this much.

"You've got a bunch of messy goddamn soldiers in one line and a bunch of officers in another. What does it mean?"

"General . . . suppose a soldier's been overseas for a couple of years and in the line for a couple of months without a break, then he gets a few days in a rest area and goes to a USO show. He knows there's not much chance of getting next to one of the girls, but it would mean a lot to him if she'd circulate among the boys for a while. . . . Usually, there's not a chance. She arrives in a colonel's jeep two seconds before showtime and leaves in a gen— . . . some other colonel's staff car before the curtain's down." Mauldin then explained that when the soldier returns to his foxhole, he starts "stewing about officers and thinking he's got the short end of the stick in everything, even women. . . . The fact is he feels there's been an injustice, and if he stews long enough about this, or about any of the other hundreds of things soldiers stew about, he's not going to be thinking about his job.

[But if] he picks up his paper and reads a letter or sees a cartoon by some other soldier who feels the same way, . . . he says, 'Hell, somebody else said it for me,' and he goes back to his job." Patton did not see things this way.

"I don't know where you got those stripes on your arm, but you'd put 'em to a lot better use getting out and teaching respect to soldiers instead of encouraging them to bitch and beef and gripe and run around with beards on their faces and holes in their elbows."

The meeting ended at an impasse, yet Mauldin was undeterred. He continued to draw bearded soldiers in shabby uniforms who railed against slights and injustices. But he also made sure to stay outside of the territory of the Third Army and Patton's reach. It was a wise move. In the words of General Patton, "If that little son of a bitch sets foot in Third Army I'll throw his ass in jail."

Patton's distaste for newspapers and cartoons that undermined strict adherence to his rules on military comportment never lessened. Even as victory in Europe loomed, Patton continued to attack Mauldin and the newspapers that printed his cartoons. He did not care that some of these newspapers, like the *Stars and Stripes*, were read and beloved by millions of soldiers. Patton would rather deprive his men of information and amusement than be the butt of any joke or punch line. As he noted in his diary in early 1945, "Wrote the Editor of the *Stars and Stripes* protesting against his paper as subversive of discipline. . . . I stated that unless there is an improvement, I will not permit the paper to be issued in this Army, nor permit . . . reporters or photographers in the Army area. It is a scurrilous sheet."

Though he may have felt this way, Patton's threat was an empty one. The *Stars and Stripes*, replete with Mauldin's cartoons, continued to circulate right beneath his nose. Even a four-star general was powerless to do anything about it.

———

As the Americans inched toward Germany, the Axis lobbed, dropped, and scattered paper bullets on the Allies with growing intensity. In Italy, propaganda was dumped on American troops in such abundance that historian Rick Atkinson claimed that leaflets covered the ground as thick as Vesuvian ash. Graphic images accompanied inflammatory taglines. One leaflet showed the streets leading to the Colosseum macadamized in bones with the caption "The roads to Rome are paved with skulls. There is plenty of room for more of them!" Another strung together pithy statements: "Why are you still fighting in Italy?"; "Fighting on is senseless"; "Retreat yesterday! Retreat today! Retreat tomorrow!" Others told elaborate stories. "I fought in Italy too," said an apparition of a soldier on yet another leaflet. This "dead pal" described how he had advanced on the Germans and received a mortal head wound. He remembered blood trickling down his face as his family flashed across his mind's eye. "Our sacrifices are of no avail!" the specter hopelessly concluded.

As the propaganda fluttered down, American soldier newspapers took stabs at their antagonizing messages. One of Germany's favorite themes was the superiority of its weaponry. "Thousands of German machine-guns, mortars, 'Whining Winnies,' panzers and guns of all calibers are waiting to take their toll of life on the road to Rome," one leaflet promised. The *45th Division News* set the record straight on its front page under the headline "Sssssssss! But no boom," which ridiculed the impressive quantity of defective German shells. It claimed that troops did not need to count sheep to cure insomnia. They counted duds instead. One sergeant's tally in a single evening was forty-eight whistling shells and only four explosions. The *News* observed that with those odds, slumber was not so hard to come by. Meanwhile, the *45th Division News* reported that Americans had fired so many shells at the Germans that "all slit trenches in the area have been lined with cardboard shell casings for comfort," and still there was a surplus of packaging to be carted away.

The *News* seemed to enjoy printing stories that would taunt any German who found a copy at the front. In this way, this soldier newspaper doubled as a tool to demoralize and rankle the enemy. It even printed one piece entitled "A Little Story for the Nazis." Under this headline, the *News* told of a wounded German who had been taken to a battalion aid station where three Americans carefully treated his injuries. "The Aryan spoke to them in German, the aidmen answered him in Yiddish."

While the *45th Division News* was the first American newspaper to publish on Italian soil, it was eventually joined by others in late 1944 and throughout 1945. *The Spectator* by the Twenty-First Engineers documented the reconstruction of Foggia and the Twenty-First's establishment of a military air base there. In a display of Allied cooperation, American and British forces jointly churned out the *Palace Guard* and *The Cocktail*, both of which were replaced by a single effort called *The Chronicle*. In its heyday, *The Chronicle* served as many as fifty thousand Allied troops, sharing stories of individual units as they journeyed from Africa to Italy and providing the all-important *Wolf* cartoon from the CNS *Clip Sheet*. In *Sortie*, the Fifteenth Air Force celebrated its skilled flyers with sensational stories of bravery and courage. And other papers delivered much-needed levity. To "orient" troops to their surroundings, one American gazette even satirized the army's language guides by providing Italian language lessons for "commonly used phrases." Among these were "Sergeant, please wake me at ten," "I am an honest millionaire of good family," and "I forgot I have a wife and twins but we will always be friends."

––––––

While trench newspapers approached Germany's psychological assaults with lighthearted counterattacks, the US Army fought paper attacks with paper by scattering pro-Allies propaganda across Europe. With cooperation from the Office of War Information (OWI), leaflets were divided into categories: news, photographs, morale boosters for Allies, bomb warnings for civilians, and rescue appeals pertaining to Allied airmen who bailed from aircraft over occupied lands. According to the OWI, American "news" propaganda leaflets aimed to "tell the truth" about enemy losses (German and Japanese radio programs often minimized Axis casualties and Allied advances), expose Axis war-supply shortages, and recognize the indignities enemy troops suffered under the hands of their own officers. On the back of many American leaflets were surrender passes that promised Axis troops good treatment if they waved the white flag.

To ensure that US leaflets struck the right tone, the Military Intelligence Branch of the US Army conducted polls of captured German prisoners of war. These polls aimed to gauge "trends in enemy thinking" to maximize the power behind every propaganda punch. According to James Erdmann, an authority on World War II propaganda warfare, "The overall conclusions drawn from a large number of POW interrogation reports [suggested] that tactical and strategic propaganda were beginning to work a basic malaise in Axis morale." However, it was difficult to isolate the impact of propaganda leaflets from other conditions that weakened resolve, such as "general attrition and fatigue" and the toll of severe casualties. Nevertheless, as an ever-increasing number of German troops surrendered and redeemed "safe conduct passes" (or *Passierscheine*) as they gave themselves up, it was clear that the leaflets had been read and saved. Meanwhile, aware of their capitulating troops, German and Japanese authorities threatened that those caught reading or listening to American propaganda would be punished. On the whole, the leaflets seemed to make a difference.

However, if American paper bullets were eroding the enemy's will to fight, the War Department could not ignore the possibility that Germany's frequent gusts of propaganda could have the same effect on American troops. There was no sugarcoating that the US Army needed a defensive strategy to ward off Germany's psychological warfare. Commanding officers turned to the Information and Education Division to strengthen morale to such a degree that Americans would be impervious to the Axis's war of words. It was not an easy task as morale was not like typical armor. It could not be purchased, distributed, and worn like an article of clothing. Morale was a feeling that had to develop naturally. To nurture esprit de corps, the army aimed to provide materials that would inform, entertain, and build pride. Few took this need as seriously as General Eisenhower, who believed his men would need every ounce of courage and faith that the army could bestow upon them as they invaded France and aimed for the heart of Nazi Germany.

# CHAPTER SEVEN
## A MONUMENT TO INTOLERANCE

For we had just learned a most traumatic lesson. We
found out why we were fighting this war. True, we . . .
were fighting for our country, our freedom, our way
of life—for justice and even to save the world. We
believed it as an accepted truth. But we believed it in
our heads. Now, suddenly, as if we had been struck
by a bolt of lightning, it became a revealed truth. It
had burned its way into our being. Yes, Dachau was a
lesson, a most expensive lesson. We had to pay for it
with our innocence.
—Sam Dann, H Company, 222nd Infantry Regiment,
Forty-Second Infantry Rainbow Division

In the spring of 1944, General Dwight Eisenhower was preparing for
the long-awaited Allied invasion of France. Like a maestro guiding an
orchestra through an elaborate masterpiece, Eisenhower had choreo-
graphed a multifaceted invasion with each element timed to the minute.
There would be paratroopers dropped behind enemy lines to secure
bridges and other logistic landmarks, assault engineers to remove and
disable underwater mines that lined the shores, naval gunfire to pummel
German fortifications, and a never-ending stream of landing craft to
carry men and supplies. Undoubtedly, the invasion would claim thousands of lives. In fact, a rather optimistic estimate of first-wave casualties
was 30 percent.

Like Marshall, Eisenhower was devoted to the well-being of the men under his command. "Morale," Eisenhower said, "given rough equality in other things, is supreme on the battlefield." As troops gathered in England for the crossing, Eisenhower cooperated with the Special Service Division to ensure that all soldiers were equipped with supplies to keep their spirits up. This included athletic equipment, books, movies, and radios. He also endorsed troop newspapers because he believed morale would be higher, and soldiers happier, if they were given the leeway to publish informational newssheets of their own so long as war conditions would allow. Leading by example, Eisenhower printed his own newsletter, the *S.H.A.E.F.*, the "daily organ of Supreme Headquarters." It consisted of a single sheet, folded in half to create four panels. Each section was printed in a different language—German, Polish, French, and English. From airplanes, the "parachute edition" was dropped daily, supplying objective war news to American soldiers, as well as civilians the Nazis had kept in the dark for years. Knowing that the invasion of Normandy would likely be a bewildering and chaotic experience for ground troops, Eisenhower also arranged for Special Service officers to print a newspaper on the beaches to impart the latest war updates. On June 6, 1944, thousands of copies of the mimeographed *Invasion Bulletin* informed troops that their landing had been successful.

Once the beaches were taken, the drive inland was slow and deadly. This was not going to be another Sicily that took only weeks. Troops battling for Europe were in it for the long haul. The grind of war—the shrieking shells, mud-encrusted uniforms, tin-can meals, and mounting casualties—took its incalculable toll. As the months and years crept by, troops felt robbed of their youth and time with their loved ones. There was no way for the military to compensate for these sufferings and losses, but the Marshalls and Eisenhowers of the army understood that some of the bitterness and anguish could be ameliorated by praising jobs well done, building pride in what was being achieved, and letting troops know the meaning and purpose of their sacrifices.

Troop-written newspapers delivered all these benefits, but the war in Europe often made publishing impossible. Logistics foiled ambition. When a division was on the front lines, all manpower and resources were committed to battlefield victory; the men had no time to tinker with mimeographs and newspaper copy. Many units were constantly on the move, and even if they wanted to print a newspaper, the Special Service Division's crate of supplies never caught up with them. Still, some enterprising GI journalists hatched novel schemes to disseminate the news anyway. When one division lacked newsprint, journalists added a few layers of carbon paper as they typed copy and tacked these contrived newssheets onto trees. One unit cobbled together a hodgepodge of clippings from other newspapers and posted them on a bulletin board for all to read. When another division could not locate typewriters, paper, or a mimeograph machine, their newsmen delivered the news via loudspeakers mounted to a truck that rolled through the area where their readers were stationed.

Still, a handful of divisions bucked the odds and managed to publish during the war, including two of the most storied divisions to fight in Europe, the Eighty-Fourth "Railsplitter" Division and the Forty-Second "Rainbow" Division. They printed for different reasons. For the Eighty-Fourth, their newspaper resumed publication on the heels of the Battle of the Bulge because censorship had barred civilian correspondents from reporting the true story of the ambush. If home-front newspapers could not publish how this was a surprise attack that caused significant American losses, then soldiers would honor both their dead and their truth by committing to print what they saw. For the Forty-Second Division, printing an overseas newspaper was their custom. The division had done so during the Great War, and they rolled through Europe with a professional press in World War II. Yet this tradition was infused with deeper significance when the division entered the Dachau concentration camp and liberated it. Having witnessed Nazi ideology taken to the extreme, the Forty-Second felt a moral obligation to carefully chronicle what they saw and publish it for the widest audience they could command. As these divisions made history, they demanded to write it.

---

Months after Eisenhower sent the first wave of troops into Europe, the Eighty-Fourth "Railsplitter" Division landed on Omaha Beach. It was November 1944, D plus 146, and this was the division's first rendezvous with war. Although the Railsplitters had enjoyed a number of troop newspapers over the years, including the *Camp Howze Howitzer* in Texas, the *Camp Claiborne News* in Louisiana, and finally their own *Railsplitter*, when the Eighty-Fourth shipped out for France, publication ceased. Once on French soil, their nomadic existence slashed any immediate hopes of resuming their journalistic endeavors. First, there was the fifteen-hour, fifty-mile march inland. Exhausted, the men flung themselves onto their tardy convoys. They motored through Versailles and Paris and continued to Belgium. Rattling past roadside graves, soldiers bowed their heads and mouthed silent prayers for those who lay beneath crosses fashioned from wood scraps and twine and crowned with a helmet. Instead of picturesque scenes of quaint towns and bucolic landscapes, troops saw whole villages that were reduced to rubble, fields pockmarked with craters, and charred remains of tanks and jeeps dotting the landscape. The earth was branded by the terror of battle. A mixture of emotions swept the advancing forces. Some felt vindictive and wanted to avenge the deaths of the Americans whose graves they passed. Others felt nausea and dread for the battles they would soon face. They journeyed on to Holland and were given a short rest before receiving their marching orders for the front.

In the first twenty-four hours of combat, green infantrymen were schooled in war's rhythms and brutalities. One of these men was nineteen-year-old Private Roscoe Blunt, a scrawny college freshman who was drafted into the army. A drummer, he was supposed to be transferred to a music unit but never was. Next, he was tabbed for officer school, only to be told there had been a "clerical mix-up" and he would never be an officer. Instead, Blunt became a "foot soldier," an infantryman who learned how "to shoot a nine-pound M-1 rifle and slosh on his belly through the mud." When he found himself somewhere in the Netherlands, ordered to the front to fight, Blunt was terrified. His first hours of combat were unlike anything he had ever experienced. He became an expert in contorting his body to fit into the smallest of foxholes and adjusting to the deafening silence that hung in the air after a shelling. He saw the appalling variety of ways a man could die—from sniper fire, land mines, artillery attacks, strafing, and hand-to-hand combat, to the blade of a bayonet. He learned to distinguish incoming from outgoing "mail," and how soldiers' bodies and minds reacted to the "incoherent rage of battle." Blunt recalled, "I learned afterwards from grizzly old regular Army non-coms that an infantryman is considered a veteran if he survives his first day of combat." Blunt became a veteran that day.

In mid-December, after the Railsplitters had been in Europe for only a few weeks, the German Army launched a surprise attack on the Allied forces in the Ardennes. Caught in the midst of it was the Eighty-Fourth Division. When the Germans attempted to surround and decimate the American forces, severe losses mounted as the Allies strove to push the German Army back. The fighting would continue for over a month, and the Bulge would earn the unenviable distinction of being the largest and most deadly battle of World War II.

For the Railsplitters, the Battle of the Bulge consisted of weeks of complete chaos. As Private Blunt described, "There were no front lines, no rear echelons, there were no company or battalion boundaries, no safe or unsafe sectors. The Germans were everywhere, and so were we." When "replacements" arrived to take over the positions of the dead and wounded, distrust and confusion proliferated as German paratroopers, who spoke perfect English and wore American uniforms and dog tags taken from prisoners or the battlefield dead, began infiltrating American positions. Everyone was on edge, not knowing whether a new face was a friend or foe.

Exacerbating matters even further, Germany made sure to take advantage of the Allies' bewilderment by seasoning them with propaganda. "THE P.O.W. WILL SAFELY RETURN," one leaflet screamed in red ink. "THE DEAD WILL NEVER RETURN!" said the back side of the same leaflet, with lists of names of those killed in action printed faintly in the background. Germany also demonstrated an uncanny ability to pinpoint the exact location of the Railsplitters so that personalized propaganda flyers could be dropped on their precise position. During the Battle of the Bulge, Railsplitters were awestruck when the leaflets that fluttered into their foxholes were addressed to the "Men of the 84th." One such leaflet read, "After two days of back-pedaling and hill-chasing, you've gotten an idea of how this maneuver is going. Your front is caving in on you. You've been flanked time and again." The leaflet predicted death within two days and offered the alternative of surrendering.

It was hard for the Railsplitters to evaluate whether there was any truth to Germany's claims. Were they surrounded? Outnumbered? Outmaneuvered? It was impossible to know. So little information had reached them. They were not even sure where they were. Heerlen, Marienburg, Geilenkirchen, Haversin, Grandménil—each town they saw was "another in a long list of names that meant nothing to me," Blunt recalled. Of all Germany's claims, however, there was one that soldiers knew to be false. The obscure villages they passed shared the same horrific scene: lined against a wall or building, groups of civilians—even children— lay frozen on the ground, their hands tied behind their backs and their bodies riddled with bullets. If SS troops were capable of such atrocities against innocent noncombatants, why would enemy soldiers be treated with greater mercy?

Perhaps the only thing that gave the Railsplitters a brief reprieve from the stress of fighting was the arrival of mail. To receive a letter from home "was a very special event for a GI," Blunt explained. "It allowed him a few minutes to withdraw into his private shell [to savor] our only precious link to the sanity of our earlier lives." The familiar penmanship of a parent was balm for the soul. Sometimes newspaper clippings were added when the division made headlines back home. At first, these reports were devoured—any news that reached the front was. But the Railsplitters quickly discovered that the home front was not being given the facts about the severity of the Battle of the Bulge. Unbeknownst to troops, the US government had initially imposed a thirty-six-hour press blackout on all coverage about the battle, which meant that war correspondents could not report any information about the German Army's gains, American losses, or how the Allies were caught off guard.

The danger of silencing the American press was understood by US war correspondents who witnessed Germany's prolific propaganda about the Bulge. CBS war correspondent William Downs refused to stand down. He protested the news blackout and censorship by broadcasting from Holland on a radio frequency that would reach listeners in the United States. He demanded that the Allied command release information. "There is little necessity for censorship regulations that have made the story of this great battle a confused and uncorrelated group of facts," he scolded American commanders. And to his listeners, Downs insisted, "You should be told the exact number of our casualties. Army authorities who know should tell you the truth—bluntly and now. As a democracy we can stand the shock of a setback as well as we can rejoice in a victory."

Despite Downs's plea, news was not forthcoming. Even after the press blackout was lifted, censors made sure that new reports about the Bulge were sanitized to the military's satisfaction. The tidbits of information approved for publication emphasized "intermittent Allied successes" despite the far more significant German gains. During the last two weeks of December, as American forces were pushed back and tested to the extreme, newspaper headlines at home inexplicably announced victories:

Dec. 20: "Nazis Stopped at Monschau"
Dec. 23: "Bomber Fleet Pounds Nazis"
Dec. 24: "Nazi Drive is Stopped"
Dec. 29: "German Drive Stopped"

Soldiers knew the battle continued to rage. While rosy headlines and the cherry-picking of slight gains might fool the home front, the soldiers fighting the Battle of the Bulge immediately recognized these half-truths and whitewashed reports for what they were.

As misleading press coverage about the Battle of the Bulge reached the front lines, troops grew incensed. When Blunt's family sent him an article from their hometown paper that described casualties in the Battle of the Bulge as "light," Blunt demanded that his parents stop sending him newspaper clippings. "I couldn't figure out what war these clippings were referring to, surely not the one in which I was engaged," he remarked. He added that he had personally "observed the numbers of American dead . . . and could offer eyewitness testimony" that countered the lies the government was peddling to the home front.

Having lost faith in the optimistic accounts in domestic newspapers, American troops turned to other sources for facts. Because Germany was churning out stories about the Bulge in a variety of formats, troops were especially susceptible to enemy propaganda. Having "liberated" small battery-operated radios from captured or dead German troops, Americans tuned into Reich Radio's news programs for information. In addition, some troops were fooled into reading Nazi propaganda when German leaflets took the guise of US troop newspapers. One faux newssheet that Germany disseminated was the *Home Telegram*. It looked legitimate. Emblazoned across the masthead was a hand-drawn image of the Manhattan skyline and the Statue of Liberty. It contained a comic strip, and its articles had datelines from Madrid, London, and New York. Although it appeared to be a genuine American-made troop newspaper, its substance was unquestionably propaganda: "It's time to fold up! The US war aims have been reached," one article said. "What remains are ideological reasons and they shouldn't count when the lives of fighting Yankees are at stake. Why then are Americans still in this war? . . . For the celebrated Four Freedoms? Nobody believes in them anymore." The paper emphasized how well the Germans treated American POWs, claiming that detainees gorged on coffee, chocolate, and cigarettes. Plus, they enjoyed athletic fields, medical care, educational opportunities, and regular mail. "One thing is sure," the article concluded, "his relatives prefer a living POW to a dead hero."

Between German radio programs, enemy-created troop newspapers, and showers of surrender leaflets, Germany created a potent elixir of distortions and doubt. In the words of one correspondent, Allied foxholes "seeth[ed] with damaging rumors and completely fantastic stories" of events that "never happened." Forced into action, the army started distributing factual booklets, only to be outwitted by Germany. To counter

Germany's claims of treating POWs well, the War Department distributed a pocket-sized tract entitled, "If you should be CAPTURED these are your rights." It opened by stating, "Being a prisoner of war is a grim business. You live behind barbed wire, under constant guard . . . The monotony is deadly." Not missing a beat, Germany rapidly produced a propaganda leaflet that was the spitting image of the War Department's booklet, even matching the font style and navy-blue cover. The title was slightly modified to read, "If you should be CAPTURED *you will be safe.*" The back of the leaflet emphasized Germany's excellent treatment of American prisoners. It even reproduced an article from the *Boston Herald*, with the headline "Nazis Found Fair to Yank Wounded." The War Department could not print and distribute booklets fast enough to deal with Germany's ever-escalating war of words.

But troops on the ground could print the truth contemporaneously—if a commanding officer would give his blessing to do so. Thanks to Germany's relentless campaign to sway Allied soldiers' thoughts, Major General Alexander R. Bolling, commander of the Eighty-Fourth Infantry Division, was provoked into retaliatory action. He restored the division's newspaper and insisted its journalists publish the news before, during, and after combat no matter how difficult. He explained, "As an ideal, we have always believed that every man should know—before every battle—what he is going into and why. We have also believed that every man should know—after every battle—what he, his organization and his army have accomplished and why." During the Battle of the Bulge, troops were forced to operate on hope. As the fighting subsided in January 1945, Bolling knew there would be plenty of battles ahead, and he wanted his troops to have the facts. They saw the carnage of combat and knew the steep price in human lives that had been paid for a French forest. To honor those who were lost, and to acknowledge the relentless fighting that others survived, the truth needed to be told. As Bolling said, each soldier "will fight better if he knows from past experience that his share was indispensable in the battle, the campaign, and the war as a whole." Back in Camp Claiborne, the *Railsplitter* had crystallized the division into a cohesive fighting unit. Now, Bolling hoped it would strengthen resolve as troops recorded their battlefield accomplishments.

Oversubscribed supply routes could not be relied upon to transport paper, ink, and a mimeograph machine, so like their brethren in the Forty-Fifth, the Eighty-Fourth Infantry Division was forced to scout for printing facilities in the small villages they passed and ask locals for help. Belgians were gratified to assist the American Army in publishing free and independent words. For years, Belgian publishers had lived under German occupation and had lost control of their presses. Quietly, they had resisted. When a May 1940 German decree stipulated that no Belgian newspaper could be published without Nazi consent, many large papers closed their doors rather than print what the Nazis ordered. Unsatisfied, Nazi leaders seized and reopened Belgian newspaper offices. Editors resigned, journalists were replaced with Fascist contributors, and uncooperative proprietors and newsmen faced arrest, imprisonment, and exile. Around this time, an Antwerp paper, *La Métropole*, boldly asked journalists to risk it all to preserve the freedom of the press. "It has always been our belief that the journalist's role . . . is that of a soldier armed with the pen, who volunteers to serve all good and just causes. . . . For it must be known and made known, that silence is often worse than betrayal." *La Métropole* issued an ultimatum: publish the truth "secretly or in exile," or do nothing and provide tacit approval to the Nazis. The fourth estate answered by resurrecting the newssheet *La Libre Belgique*, a well-known vestige of Belgian defiance in the Great War. Over thirty additional underground newspapers followed, many bearing the mark of skilled journalists. These papers not only unified Belgians, but they also publicized ways to sabotage the Germans, from arson and severing railway lines to neutralizing munitions. Anyone caught producing, contributing to, or distributing these illicit papers would be murdered by the Nazis. Hundreds of journalists accepted the risk.

As the smoke cleared over the Ardennes, enterprising American soldiers worked with a local printshop that had been recently liberated. Together, they produced weekly issues of the *Railsplitter* from "somewhere in Belgium." It immediately gained an avid readership. The paper proved its GI mettle by reporting the extraordinary exploits of the division's men. This included an eight-man reconnaissance patrol that took the town of Deiffelt, four Railsplitters who stopped a German advance into Belgium from their third-floor window in an abandoned hotel (and earned Bronze Stars), and three unarmed medics who sneaked past enemy positions to rescue injured troops. For the latter story, the paper reported, "For once the weather was kind and sent a heavy fog to dim the moonlight and make it possible for the medics to carry the three wounded men back to friendly lines without mishap."

The paper also gave voice to those grieving for soldiers who had given their lives. Countering the false reports printed back home of "light" casualties, the *Railsplitter* honored those whose time had been cut short. On the front page of an issue of the European *Railsplitter* was a tribute to the "Men We Won't Forget":

This is a note to the guys in the 84th Division who only bought a one-way trip to Europe:

It's a funny thing how they handed them out. Nobody paid any money at all. We got a ticket good for the trip over and the trip back. And then somewhere along the line, They decided to take yours away from you . . .

One minute you were clutching on to that return ticket stub which said: "Good for one trip back home to live in the Greatest Damn country in the World."

Then the next minute the wind of a mortar, the breeze of a machinegun bullet had whisked it out of your hands.

Some of us saw you lose those tickets.

Where was it?

That foxhole at Lindern, the snow drift under the clean-smelling pines of the Ardennes? Or maybe it was in the mud before Golkrath and Baal.

So now we—who still have our tickets—are going home. And you're going to stay here—forever.

Time is going to pass, and years go by, and maybe it'll look like we've kinda forgotten you. Oh, they'll put up some memorials to you fellows, and every now and then some pompous old man will get up on Memorial Day or the Fourth of July and tell us what a swell job you did.

Imagine anybody telling US what you did. You were the guy who slept in the same room with us at Heerlen during that rest before we jumped the Roer.

We used to march behind you when we snaked our way across Germany.

And they don't want US to forget YOU. . . .

[O]ne of these mornings, gang, we'll be trudging up that gangplank and pulling out of here.

And our sincerest wish will be that we could have picked up those return tickets you dropped, and given them back to you again.

Throughout February and March, the Eighty-Fourth made advances despite bad weather, pockets of fierce resistance, and relentless streams of leaflets imploring them to surrender. Their progress was so impressive that Major General Bolling took to the *Railsplitter* to express his unbridled pride for the job his men were doing. After the Eighty-Fourth covered forty-two miles to the Rhine in just five days, Bolling could not help but gush, "You men can accomplish anything you set out to do!" After detailing how his men had driven through the Siegfried Line, pushed the Germans back in the Ardennes, and smashed through enemy strongholds, Bolling bragged that the Railsplitters had "covered a greater distance than any other division on the line—and through heavier fighting." What's more, when the Railsplitters had reached the shore of the Rhine River, "after long, hard grueling days and cold, sleepless nights, you still wanted to push on, and asked for authority to cross the river." Bolling was humbled by the resolve and bravery exhibited by his men. "You have accomplished what many thought was impossible. Without your drive and determination, without your spirit and courage, the drive would not have been accomplished as expeditiously—the credit is yours," Bolling said. "I am, as you are, very proud to be a 'Railsplit-ter,'" he concluded. After reading this, troops mailed their newspaper home. If censors were not letting civilian correspondents tell the real story, the *Railsplitter* would.

With the support of Major General Bolling, the *Railsplitter* became the most frequently published GI newspaper in Europe, with three issues rolling off the presses each week. It also changed formats, from a tradi-tional newspaper to a tabloid-style orientation that would make it "easier to read, easier to send home, [and] easier to find out what-in-'ell is going on in the division." The paper cheered the progress of the Railsplitters as the division delved deeper into Germany by the day. Headlines encour-aged troops as it became clearer with each issue that their fight against Germany was coming to an end. First came the banner, "Nazis Giving Up to 84th As Resistance Collapses," then "84th Takes 4 Nazi Gener-als," and finally the one they had all been waiting for— "VICTORY!"

———

While the Eighty-Fourth's newsmen had to scavenge for newspaper supplies as they trekked across Germany, the Forty-Second Division carried the torch of tradition by traveling across Europe with its own professional newspaper press. The last time the division was in France in the 1910s, it recorded its historic feats in a no-nonsense single-page newssheet under the banner *Ohio Rainbow Reveille*. When the division was reactivated at Camp Gruber, Oklahoma, in July 1943, their trusty newspaper was reborn as simply the *Rainbow Reveille*. With a bright three-tone rainbow sweeping across the masthead, the paper's new it-eration delivered a robust smorgasbord of photographs, comic strips, individual battalion news, sports updates, and a wallet-sized pinup— the "billfold girl of the week."

From the beginning, the *Rainbow Reveille* kept a jocular tone while also recounting the division's illustrious past. One of the paper's mainstay journalists was Scott Corbett, whose wit and low rank offered plenty of GI perspective combined with a recalcitrant streak. Corbett complained about the things every soldier disliked. Back in Oklahoma, when forced to eat outside in the rain to "get a taste of combat conditions," Corbett reported that "combat conditions taste like . . . wet chicken." When Corbett was put on a KP detail, he shared that it was a "nerve-wracking" experience, with officers stopping by so often that he "leaped to attention from so many different positions that a scout for Ballet Russe would probably have become interested in me." When Corbett's unit underwent a nighttime bivouac exercise, he spent the entire evening trying to pitch his tent—never getting it right—much to the chagrin of a barking officer. Corbett also frequently touched on the theme of his "tendency away from wholesome exercise." When a "speed march" was announced, Corbett cringed at the thought of huffing it in double time while carrying a full field pack. "It was a rough night, hot as hell out, and I was sweating so much the guy behind me was running ankle deep in mud, but we still kept getting that old double-time," Corbett related in his column. Troops loved it.

In November 1944, the division received orders that it was time to ship out. Staffers crated their newspaper equipment, loaded it onto Pullmans, and hoped to put it to future use. After weeks of trains and transports, France greeted the men with bitter cold, blackout restrictions, German aircraft grumbling overhead, and rumors that the Allies were being pushed backward by German forces in the Battle of the Bulge. The Rainbow infantrymen were sent to the western shore of the Rhine, where the Germans waited for them on the other side. Similar to the Railsplitters' experience, their first month provided a terrifying initiation to combat. The Rainbowmen proceeded through forests riddled with mines, bore freezing temperatures and relentless snowfall, and met fierce German resistance that destroyed their equipment and killed 50 percent of the division's riflemen in less than one month. After regrouping in Nancy, the Forty-Second returned to the Strasbourg area, where they spent much of their time focused on reconnaissance. Troops, confident they could smash the German Army if allowed to dabble beyond mere patrols, grew tired of waiting. "This is a silly damn way to fight a war," one Rainbowman complained in February 1945. "We just go out and chase the [Germans] off that hill and then come back. We could have them half way to Berlin if we kept on going," he added.

Finally, in March 1945, the Forty-Second stopped surveying. The division was tasked with taking the Hardt Mountains and pushing through the Siegfried Line. The terrain was so rugged that motorized equipment couldn't navigate the land. Only mules could accompany foot soldiers. Top command recognized that the assignment "would require the utmost in courage and physical stamina." Infantrymen unleashed their pent-up eagerness to fight and sliced through the thick woods like a hot knife on butter. While battling the Germans, the craggy landscape, and their obstinate mules, the men of the Rainbow also published their trusty newspaper. Each story was told with zest and an eye to antagonize any Germans who happened to find a copy. "They Cried Uncle—Uncle Sam," the March 8, 1945, *Rainbow Reveille* proudly declared on its front page. "Here's the kind of German advance we like to see," read the caption beneath a picture of German troops surrendering to Americans. Living in foxholes, eating out of cans, and swashbuckling through the French wilderness, the men were delighted to see their feats published in their own house organ. All the features they expected were surprisingly intact—the billfold gal, *Male Call*, *The Wolf*, miscellaneous articles about the accomplishments of individual men and batteries, and Scott Corbett's regular feature. "There was a time . . . when T-5 Bill Newmark and I were known as the worst tent-pitching team this side of the Girl Scouts. Right now we're pitching a billet together and my troubles are starting all over again," he reassured his readers.

The *Reveille* was back, but irregularly. The next issue took a month to produce. But the headlines trumpeted their progress. "Rainbow Smashes Siegfried Line," the front page of the April 5, 1945, edition declared. Sharing the same front page was a story of how the Forty-Second had happened upon the "castle" belonging to the mastermind of Germany's concentration camps and mass-genocide program. "Heinrich Himmler would have been more than a little upset if he had known that he was the unwitting host to Rainbowmen . . . during the 42d's drive into Germany," the article said. The division stumbled upon his summer château and used it as a rest spot, heating their K rations in the castle's spacious kitchen. "It was a nice spot to run into," said Technical Sergeant Raymond Edwards in the *Reveille*, "but what we really want to see is Himmler's place in Berlin."

As the division gained momentum in their quest for Himmler's other home, their newssheet blossomed and evolved. Between February and April 1945, it went from a monthly to a weekly and then to a semiweekly sheet. It doubled in size from a four-page French edition to a spacious eight-page German imprint with a two-page spread of illustrations. With this additional space, the Forty-Second added a little gossip and humor, like how one man spotted a book he wanted to read in a Red Cross mobile library only to find his mother's inscription inside the front cover, or how another man was getting by on limited clothing because a shelling occurred as he was getting dressed and it blasted his entire wardrobe.

In mid-April, however, the paper went quiet. The United States Seventh Army (of which the Forty-Second was a part) continued its drive to Munich, advancing 105 miles from Fürth in under three days. When they were less than ten miles from Munich, they "ran into an installation many of us had never heard of, Dachau."

Two newspaper reporters, Marguerite Higgins of the *New York Herald Tribune* and Sergeant Peter Furst of the *Stars and Stripes*, intercepted the assistant commander of the Forty-Second Infantry Division, Brigadier General Henning Linden, and asked the general where Dachau's infamous concentration camp was located. General Linden ordered his aide, Lieutenant William K. Cowling III, to find the camp and "take a reading of the situation."

Just off the main road, Cowling, Higgins, and Furst found Dachau. The camp was bordered by a railroad siding jammed with boxcars. Cowling looked inside one of the carriages and was horrified to discover stacks of dead bodies "in an emaciated condition from starving." Some showed "signs of beating and had been shot in the head." A German SS officer appeared and relinquished the camp. Cowling ordered all German guards to surrender to the Americans. Some resisted and were killed. Once the Americans infiltrated the camp's gates, they entered a deserted courtyard that was eerily silent. "About a minute and a half later," Cowling said, "people began pouring from the low, barracks-type black buildings. They were thin, dirty, half-starved." The prisoners surrounded Cowling, Higgins, and Furst, reaching out to touch the Americans to confirm that these symbols of freedom weren't hallucinations.

That morning, the Forty-Second's newspapermen—journalists Scott Corbett and James Creasman, artist Ted MacKechnie, and photographer William "Hap" Hazard—were given the assignment to record their observations of the camp. Words failed the journalists. As Corbett said, "Nothing can adequately describe the horrors we saw there." The railway siding, the stacks of clothing and dead bodies, the skeletons who still lived—even battle-hardened soldiers struggled to keep from sobbing and retching over the inhuman treatment they encountered. On battlefields, they had become accustomed to death and suffering, but not like this.

Once the camp was secured, Corbett and Creasman, along with other journalists who streamed into the area, were sent to the Corps Public Relations Office, where typewriters and liquor awaited them. Corbett explained that the alcohol was necessary: "We had to relax to get some of it off our chests for a while." Officers from the Signal Photo Company who had taken pictures for the War Crimes Commission were also there, and the group tried to collectively process and describe the scenes of that day. "We would write, and then someone would exclaim about something, and we would all stop and talk about it," Corbett remembered. For hours, they filled page after page with the macabre details, not finishing their work until five thirty the next morning. "We never wanted to see Dachau again," Corbett remarked. But for many, the grotesque scene they walked into on April 29, 1945, was branded into their memories forever.

Major General Harry J. Collins authorized James Creasman to publish an immediate account of Dachau in the headquarters' mouthpiece, the *42d Rainbow Infantry Division World News*. Circulated to officers and enlisted men, the May 1, 1945, mimeographed edition carried one story under the handwritten headline "Dachau." Attempting some balance between objectivity and abject emotion, Creasman's raw account is perhaps the most important contemporaneous description of what the Rainbow Division witnessed:

DACHAU is no longer a name of terror for hunted men. 32,000 of them have been freed by the 42d Rainbow Division. The crimes done behind the walls of this worst of Nazi concentration camps now live only to haunt the memories of the Rainbowmen who tore open its gates and first saw its misery, and to accuse its SS keepers of one of the worst crimes in all history.

When Infantrymen of the 42d Division fought their way into Dachau against fanatical SS troops who met deserved violent deaths along the moats, behind the high fences, and in the railyards littered with the bodies of fifty carloads of their starved victims, these hardened soldiers expected to see horrible sights.

But no human imagination fed with the most fantastic of the tales that have leaked out from the earliest and most notorious of all Nazi concentration camps, could have been prepared for what they did see there . . .

Riflemen accustomed to witnessing death had no stomach for rooms stacked almost ceiling-high with tangled human bodies adjoining the cremation furnaces, looking like some maniac's woodpile.

And when an officer pressed thru mobs of the forgotten men of all nations inside the electric barbed wire enclosure and entered a room where lay the dying survivors of the horror train, he wept unashamedly as limp ghosts under filthy blankets, lying in human excreta, tried to salute him with broom-stick arms, falling back in deathly stupor from which most would never rouse.

Ten days before the arrival of the Rainbow Division fifty carloads of prisoners arrived at Dachau from Buchenwald concentration camp in a starving condition after 27 days without food. . . .

In those stinking cars were seen the bodies of those prisoners too weak even to get out. A few tried, and they made a bloody heap in the door of one of the cars. They had been machine gunned by the SS. A little girl was in that car. . . .

Some of the cars had been emptied and the bodies carted to the crematory. In one room adjoining the furnace-room on the left they were neatly stacked. The stripped corpses were very straight. But in the room on the right they were piled in complete disorder, still clothed.

With the help of a husky Yugoslav inmate who worked at the furnaces and who told that all four of them had been going "tag und nacht" . . . "day and night" with a capacity of 7 bodies each, the explanation was partially unfolded. The straight neat ones had probably been brought in alive, showered in the "Brausobad" or shower-room, then gassed or hanged from hooks on the rafters in front of the furnaces. Those on the right were just as they were dumped out of the freight cars where they had died of starvation.

It was incredible that such things could happen today, but there was the visible proof.

It was unbelievable that human beings were capable of perpetrating such unspeakable atrocities, but there were the men who did it. The SS . . .

Now the SS Guards were dead. But their deaths could not avenge the thousands dead and dying there in Dachau.

Those tortured dead can only be avenged when our world is aroused so much by what the 42d uncovered at Dachau and by what others have found at all the other Dachaus scattered throughout Germany, that never again will any party, any government, any people be allowed to mar the face of the earth with such inhumanity.

———

The next time the *Rainbow Reveille* was printed, the usual swagger and humor in its articles were conspicuously absent. Although V-E Day had come and gone, there was little in the way of celebratory prose. To be sure, the May 11 edition recounted the division's five-month advance, its conquest of six thousand square miles of Nazi territory, and its arrest of more than forty-five thousand German prisoners of war as it "captured the most important cities of Southern Germany." Yet it was not the division's battlefield victories that claimed the bulk of the paper. It was Dachau.

"Enough copies of this issue have been printed to provide one copy for every three men," the paper noted, so "don't mail a copy home till at least two other men have had a chance to read it." This was a paper not just for the soldiers, but one that needed to go home, to those who had never set foot in a theater of war but who needed to understand what this war was all about. It could not be left to civilian journalists or army communiqués, or to people who might have seen Dachau days or weeks after it was liberated and not what it was *really* like when the Americans first arrived. It had to be a story told by the soldiers who had seen it firsthand. Nine photographs taken by "Hap" Hazard accompanied the text penned by Corbett. It was all there: the stacks of naked bodies outside the crematory, the ovens, the boxcars filled with "victims in the agonized attitudes of death by slow starvation," the prisoners who had attempted an escape only to have "machine guns mercilessly cut them down," and the rescue of a single Polish survivor from the railcars carrying an estimated 1,800 people.

After detailing the heinous barbarities that had been committed within Dachau's gates, Corbett tried to make sense of how it happened. He was forced to the conclusion that it was "the natural outcome of the Germans' belief in themselves as a master race, a natural outcome of their contempt for the political and religious beliefs of all who differed from them." The ideology that fueled Hitler's rise to power was the same that attempted to destroy the "spirit of democracy, of decency and tolerance . . . in the flames of its hideous crematories." Corbett concluded that Dachau was "a monument to intolerance carried to its ultimate."

After Germany's surrender, the War Department made plans to ship most troops out of Europe. Some would get an honorable discharge and a ticket home while most faced redeployment to the Pacific. Though millions of troops would leave Europe, what had happened in Europe would never leave them.

The thousands who had liberated concentration camps finally understood why they were wearing a uniform and what they were fighting for. And they believed in their cause. Though going home was their ultimate goal, now many felt compelled to finish the job and ensure such horror was the last of its kind. It was difficult to explain to loved ones. But these soldiers had made up their minds. As one of the Rainbow Division's lieutenants wrote his parents after they complained that they did not want him going to the Pacific:

> I have only been in the Army a couple of years. Some of these people were in the hell hole of Dachau for years. If I spend ten years in the Army during war I will never go through what those people go through. Even if I were killed, I would be lucky compared to those people. So if you still feel the jitters remember the people of Dachau and think how lucky I am no matter what happens.

Preventing another Dachau was worth whatever price it commanded. The Rainbowmen would see the war to its end, and if that meant going home via a detour through the Pacific, many were willing to take that route.

The Rainbow Division would never forget Dachau. By documenting the painful details of what they had encountered, committing them to newsprint, publishing thousands of copies, and sending them home with careful instructions to keep the paper forever, troops hoped that others would never forget either.

# CHAPTER EIGHT
## DON'T SEND ME IN

"FUBAR"

Have you ever sat through a picture show
While the rain seeped through your trousers, Joe?
Have you ever labored in mildewed clothes
Or stepped on a lizard with your naked toes?
Have you ever stood, till you thought you'd choke,
In line for beer or a glass of coke,
Only to hear that familiar shout,
"Sorry, guys, we just ran out?"
To be just a little more specific,

Have you ever been in the South Pacific?
Have you ever wakened in chilling fright
To the awesome sounds of the jungle night?
Has your skin ever turned a yellow-green
From your daily doses of atabrine?
Has sweat ever dripped on your writing pad
As you penned a letter to Mom and Dad?
Have you ever been tempted to moan and sob
At the fate of a lonely land-based gob?
Have you ever wished you could strip down bare
And roll around in the snow "Back There?"
If you don't think that would be terrific
Then you've never been in the South Pacific.

—author unknown

Four years after the Pacific war began with the attack on Pearl Harbor, American troops had fought across almost three thousand miles of ocean in deadly battles for flecks of land that seemed insignificantly small. Some held invaluable traits, such as a strategic airfield, a treasure trove of natural resources, or a perfect launching point for the Allies' island-hopping campaign. Japan knew the importance of its holdings; it had spent years fortifying them. For the Allies, each stepping stone to Japan seemed deadlier than the last.

Amphibious landings were the norm. If all went according to plan, barrages by the navy and air force would knock out enemy strongholds before the marines and infantrymen waded ashore. Under the worst-case scenario, the navy and air force missed their targets, and ground forces had to essentially advance before a firing squad. If they survived the landing, troops faced relentless combat, withering temperatures, tropical diseases, and constant stress. Those who lived long enough to see an island neutralized were given a brief respite before shipping out to the next amphibious landing. It was a crushing cycle. In the words of E. B. Sledge, a marine:

> I found it more difficult to go back each time we squared away our gear to move forward into the zone of terror. My buddies' joking ceased as we trudged grim-faced back into that chasm where time had no meaning and one's chances of emerging unhurt dwindled with each encounter. With each step toward the distant rattle and rumble of that hellish region where fear and horror tortured us like a cat tormenting a mouse, I experienced the greater and greater dread. And it wasn't just dread of death or pain, because most men felt somehow they wouldn't be killed. But each time we went up, I felt the sickening dread of fear itself and the revulsion at the ghastly scenes of pain and suffering among comrades that a survivor must witness.

War overloaded the mind and senses. Whistling shells, chattering machine guns, and booming artillery enveloped the men in deafening sound. Piercing this maddening crescendo were the cries of the wounded. As quickly as this pandemonium erupted, it would cease. The search for cover began. Foxholes were dug. Cigarettes were smoked. In the eerie, postbattle silence, men reflected on what they had experienced. One inch, one hilltop at a time—this was how Pacific islands were taken. Dead bodies were tallied and buried. The emotional toll evaded measure.

There was no way of sugarcoating that these were fatal missions. As Sledge described it, living "seemed more unlikely by the day." The mental arithmetic required to prepare for a foray into combat, knowing it could be the end, was exhausting. "I concluded that it was impossible for me to be killed, because God loved me. Then I told myself that God loved us all and that many would die or be ruined physically or mentally or both by the next morning and in the days following," Sledge said. He struggled to quiet his heart's philosophizing. Some nights, he soothed himself to sleep by repeating the Lord's Prayer.

Many in the Special Service Division believed that if ever there were a place to cater to the psychological, emotional, and mental needs of American troops, it was the Pacific. And yet, this was where Frederick Osborn, the leader of the Special Service Division, seemed to fail most at his job. Osborn was not Marshall's pick to lead the army's morale efforts, but Osborn's friendship with President Roosevelt and Secretary of War Henry Stimson had helped seal his nomination. Retired from business at the age of forty, Osborn devoted his time in the 1930s to the study of eugenics and the idea that people either had "good" or "bad" genes. He believed eugenics was "racial preventative medicine" that could be used to identify "defectives" and prevent them from procreating. Beginning in the 1930s, the research by American eugenicists was used and twisted by Hitler, first to justify a program of forced sexual sterilization of those deemed genetically inferior, and then for concentration camps and the Holocaust. Osborn openly admired Hitler's eugenics program, describing it in 1937 as "excellent" and "perhaps the most important social experiment which has ever been tried." His views did not seem to change even after witnessing the horrors of Hitler's ideology carried to its most extreme. Osborn toured the Dachau concentration camp weeks after its liberation in 1945, and his diary reveals a rosy description of the camp, stating the crematorium was located "in a nice little park," noting the "nice concrete floor" of the "gassing" room, and remarking that the few remaining prisoners, though "so thin they looked like skeletons," were "out enjoying the fine warm sun." Whereas battle-hardened soldiers cried and grieved over the inhuman conditions they witnessed, the leader of the army's morale efforts found compliments for the death camps and was undeterred in the continuation of his study of eugenics after the war. And it is not that Osborn eschewed criticism or unkind words. Days after his tour of Dachau, he documented in his diary his displeasure with his room in a luxury hotel: "Badly quartered at the Ritz, a disgusting caravansary." To say the very least, Osborn was a strange choice to lead the army's morale efforts during World War II.

One of Osborn's main objectives as head of the Special Service Division was to cater to the recreational needs of troops, but much to Marshall's chagrin, Osborn seemed indifferent to the value of recreation. Osborn told the *United States News* that "entertainment and diversion [might] remove some local irritants," but they did little to improve troops' overall well-being. He did not seem to appreciate how the monotony of off-duty hours with no recreation caused discontent to fester. Nightly boredom was far worse than a mere "irritant" like a buzzing insect. Movies, magazines, and music provided troops with an escape from the military and the war. To Marshall, recreation was essential to building the best fighting force in the world. Osborn's nonchalance toward recreation, and Marshall's passion for it, soon came to a head.

When George Marshall toured the Pacific in late 1943, he was outraged by what he observed. "I was much disturbed in the Southwest Pacific to see how little had been accomplished by your activities," Marshall wrote to Osborn. "General MacArthur himself seemed almost entirely unaware of what your activities were," he added. Rather than ensure that troops received information and recreation, Osborn had primarily conducted research polls to gauge the emotional and mental impact of combat on troops. While these questionnaires might have satisfied his interest in social science and eugenics, they achieved nothing in actually improving morale. Marshall knew that many troops in the Pacific wanted to know where they were, why their missions were essential, and how their work directly contributed to ending the war. They needed newspapers, not research surveys. Since it seemed Osborn did not understand the magnitude of the morale problem in the Pacific, Marshall ordered Osborn to go see the conditions for himself. "I want you to go direct to Australia and see General MacArthur personally and explain to him what your activities are and what can be done, and endeavor to find out for yourself why it has not been done," Marshall said.

It was a formidable task. Not only was Osborn dubious about the recreational offerings he needed to market to MacArthur, but the Supreme Allied Commander of the Southwest Pacific was not known for taking an interest in the well-being of his men or having warm feelings toward the press. Convincing MacArthur to encourage troop newspapers would be like trying to make it snow in one-hundred-degree heat.

MacArthur, the son of a decorated Civil War general, was literally born into the military at Little Rock Barracks in 1880. He graduated first in his class at West Point Military Academy and spent the next six decades serving his country. Steeped in military tradition, MacArthur failed to relate to those who were not. When he was sent to France in 1918, MacArthur chased glory. As chief of staff to the commander of the Forty-Second Division, MacArthur was not supposed to lead reconnaissance missions or participate in frontline fighting, but he believed that the "real promotions" would go to the men in the thick of the fighting. And so he led men into battle often without regard to the human cost of victory (a concern that reemerged during his "island-hopping" campaign during World War II). In one well-publicized episode during the Great War, MacArthur dramatically announced that his brigade would capture Châtillon or "take 100 percent casualties," to which one soldier under his command retorted, "Generous son of a bitch, ain't he." MacArthur ordered a frontal, daylight attack, and losses mounted quickly. As promised, Châtillon was captured. As he had predicted, decorations flowed. MacArthur received Silver Stars, the Distinguished Service Cross, and the Croix de Guerre. He had no qualms when the press sang his praises. In fact, he relished the admiring articles about him.

But when it came to criticism, MacArthur had thin skin. "Nothing affected MacArthur like being attacked in print," biographer Geoffrey Perret observed. As the army's most senior commander in the South Pacific, MacArthur could control the access correspondents had to his theater, and his censors could monitor their coverage. As historian and special correspondent Phillip Knightley said, "If the policy of shielding the nation from reality, maintaining morale by avoiding the truth, and convincing the public that the war was being conducted by a command of geniuses could have been typified in one area and by one commander, that area was the South-West Pacific and that commander was General Douglas MacArthur." MacArthur banned correspondents from visiting advanced bases and court-martialed any soldier who conspired with the press to circumvent this dictate. He rigidly enforced censorship rules and required correspondents to obtain many levels of clearance before an article could be published. By denying access to the fronts and supplying communiqués that cast each battle in the warmest glow, he thwarted correspondents from reporting the full truth. Hog-tied, one journalist penned a sarcastic poem that perfectly captured the spirit of "Doug" MacArthur's distorted press releases:

> Here, too, is told the saga bold
> Of virile, deathless youth,
> In stories seldom tarnished with
> The plain unvarnished truth.
> It's quite a rag, it waves the flag,
> Its motif is the fray.
> And modesty is plain to see
> In Doug's Communiqué. . . .
>
> And while possibly a rumor now,
> Someday 'twill be a fact,
> That the Lord will hear a deep voice say,

"Move over, God—it's Mac."
So bet your shoes that all the news
That last great Judgment Day
Will go to press in nothing less
Than Doug's Communiqué!

MacArthur's efforts at controlling the press only led to the demoralization of his troops. Even Ernie Pyle, the most beloved and famous correspondent of the war, faced the ire of soldiers who felt that he was not being honest in his reporting. While he was accompanying the infantry (which, Pyle admitted, "is not the way to live to a ripe old age"), one soldier snapped at Pyle, "Why don't you tell the folks back home what this is like? All they hear about is victories and a lot of glory stuff. They don't know that for every hundred yards we advance somebody gets killed. Why don't you tell them how tough this life is?" "That was what I tried to do all the time," Pyle responded. Try as he might, Pyle had to operate within the bounds of military censorship and tiptoe around a general with an easily bruised ego.

Thus, just as the Eighty-Fourth Railsplitter Division felt compelled to write the truth about the Battle of the Bulge, and the Forty-Second Division insisted upon recording what Dachau was really like, troops across the Pacific turned to their own newspapers to honestly chronicle their stories and, most of all, their unhappiness. For troops, there was a great deal more to say about the Pacific than what could be found in MacArthur's communiqués, and little of it was complimentary. Whether they would be able to get the publishing kit from the Special Service Division depended on Osborn.

———

When Osborn went to Australia under Marshall's orders, it is unclear whether he fully comprehended the fog of despondency that had enveloped the theater, but the situation was dire. As one historian described it, the "morale situation in [the Pacific] was increasingly bleak as it became obvious to MacArthur's men that the only ticket home was a coffin, blindness, or loss of a limb."

Though charged with the task of ensuring the Southwest Pacific would be saturated with morale-boosting equipment, Osborn instead had a fruitless two-hour meeting with General MacArthur. According to Osborn's diary, MacArthur "took me very fully into his confidence" and revealed his "disinterestedness of my position." MacArthur wanted his troops focused on fighting to the finish. He felt the publication of newspapers, as well as nearly every other entertainment offering from the Special Service Division, was a distraction from that focus. Besides, data collected by MacArthur's counterintelligence staff revealed that soldiers thought MacArthur was "a brass-hatted old bastard," a "flannel-mouth fool," and an "egotistical ass," among other derogatory things. There was no way MacArthur was going to give his men newspapers so they could print these opinions. As biographer Geoffrey Perret commented, MacArthur was "too sensitive to slights ever to allow his troops to run a newspaper that had anything resembling freedom of expression." Osborn left the meeting with nothing to show for it.

However, already in hot water with Marshall, Osborn decided that rather than acknowledge his defeat, he would tell the chief of staff that his meeting with MacArthur had been a success. Osborn told Marshall that MacArthur "became first convinced of the integrity of our purpose, and then enthusiastic about the value of our work." In actuality, if anyone had embraced the work of the Special Service Division, it was the commanding officers who were many ranks below MacArthur. These officers fought alongside their men for every expensive inch of little-known islands that could become their final resting place. Those who experienced the terror of amphibious landings and island fighting believed that if troops wanted to admit how terrible it was, why shouldn't they?

Perhaps Osborn believed that his cheery report to Marshall would be the end of the matter. But Marshall's commitment to the well-being of troops required more than mere assurances. Believing that Osborn had paved the way for the Special Service Division to permeate the Pacific theater, Marshall wrote to MacArthur directly, reporting that "[Osborn] gave me a most favorable report of your interest in this field and the tremendous assistance you afforded him during his stay in the Southwest Pacific. This was very encouraging to me, for I feel that Osborn and his organization have filled a very definite need of our troops overseas."

Osborn's lie to Marshall may have forced MacArthur's hand. After all, Marshall, as chief of staff, had leverage over MacArthur. Shortly after Osborn's visit, the Special Service Division began to supply the Pacific theater with its recreational field kits so troops could watch movies, read books, make music, and play sports in their downtime. And in 1944, MacArthur begrudgingly approved a theater newspaper, but there was one caveat: MacArthur would exercise complete control over it. The resulting *SWPA Maptalk* provided a dry, textbook-style description of the latest war news. There were no editorials, photographs, sports scores, or cartoons. A pinup was out of the question. It was as popular with servicemen as MacArthur was.

Fortunately for troops, even though MacArthur had control over his *theater* periodical, army regulations provided that each localized detachment could have a *unit* newspaper as long as a commissioned officer approved one. Some officers allowed their death-defying men to publish anything. Others struck a much more frightened tone, perhaps intimidated by the iron grip of MacArthur. "If we printed the truth we'd be buried so deep in the dungeon that air and sunshine would have to be piped to us," said the editor of New Guinea's *Latrineogram*. Whether troops printed caustic opinions or inoffensive content tended to depend on their proximity to MacArthur.

On the whole, what passed for a newspaper in the Pacific felt and looked nothing like the newspapers printed under Eisenhower's command in Europe. In the ETO, Americans wrote about their engagements and heralded their battlefield accomplishments; they used professional printing presses liberated from the Nazis and churned out papers on actual newsprint. As they printed and read their own newspapers, many troops felt like they had a personal role in exercising freedom of expression everywhere in the world, as FDR had declared. And although they faced miserable conditions and high casualties, their newspapers rarely carried traces of bitterness. On newsprint, they made sense of their battles, honored their dead, and saved their sarcasm and ribbing to antagonize the Germans.

On the other hand, troop newspapers published in the Pacific exposed the rancor, depression, and resentment many troops felt. No other theater had newspapers that explored the depths of soldier discontent. Examples are legion. One Pacific newspaper interviewed a soldier who had attempted suicide. The private admitted "his morale was shot, his nerves were shot, his love life was shot, and his chance for a T/5 rating was shot so he . . . might as well be shot bodily." A demoted soldier penned a eulogy to his fleeting eminence in his paper's "Obitchuaries" column: "In fond memory of my constant friend and companion, two T/5 stripes. A true friend to the end." Striking a more jocular tone, the Ryukyus' *Tough Sheet* published a classified ad that read, "WANTED! Responsible Aviation Battalion wants ride to San Francisco. Will buy own meals and help drive." When the *Bamboo Bulletin* asked readers what they would like to get out of the army, one man answered, "What I want most out of this army is me." And from an unknown island, a group of marines reported their feelings by stringing together a list of book titles: *Days Without End, No More Gas, Return of the Native.*

Troops in the ETO undoubtedly felt despair and wanted to go home, but they never seemed to feel a need to air these feelings in print. Perhaps General Eisenhower's outspoken concern for the well-being of his men ameliorated some of their unhappiness. Troops knew that if conditions could be improved, Eisenhower would attempt to make them better. In contrast, MacArthur's blind drive to victory at any cost only stoked the flames of indignation. It was demoralizing to operate under the belief that their commander did not care how many men lived or died as long as the war was won.

Troops wanted the war won too. But they also wanted to live. And so they took to the pages of their defiant newspapers to record their stories and heartaches, prayers and poems, jokes and fears. They put their humanity on display, and it made them feel less like mere "cannon fodder" and more like men.

As MacArthur kept his laser-sharp focus on the Pacific battles he waged, newspapers printed outside of combat's spotlight escaped his attention. Many were printed with impunity. And although these newspapers could not extract the terror from battle or lessen the heartache for those lost, the printing of honest words about the Pacific war bestowed the gift of community. Troops felt less alone when they shared their burdens and fears. Some pieces so effectively captured the feelings of troops that they went viral and were reprinted in GI newspapers across the Pacific. One such composition was an anonymous soldier's version of Cole Porter's hit song "Don't Fence Me In." After changing the title to "Don't Send Me In," the lyrics were refashioned to express the troops' universal dread for MacArthur's amphibious landings. It went like this:

Let me float in a boat
'Til the enemy's remote
DON'T SEND ME IN

Let me land on the sand
With the General and the band
DON'T SEND ME IN

Send me back to my farm
Raising pigs and pullets
And big beefsteaks for civilian gullets
Don't mind the guns but I can't stand the bullets
DON'T SEND ME IN

Just turn me loose
Let me dally in the galley
While the beach is under fire.
On my caboose in my sack it seems a racket
But you know how fast I tire.

Oh, it's a lie I ain't shy
But I'm much too young to die
DON'T SEND ME IN

You can have my souvenirs
I don't have many
Keep your medals 'cause I don't want any
Just want to carry home a healthy fanny
DON'T SEND ME IN.

Undoubtedly, if MacArthur had caught wind that troop newspapers in *his theater* were publishing songs like this, a swift and complete moratorium on all newspapers in the Pacific would have been implemented. And because censorship regulations prohibited the printing of content that might "aid or comfort the enemy," MacArthur likely could have leaned on the army's own policies for justification. Wouldn't the Japanese be satisfied to know that Allied soldiers feared having to fight them? But MacArthur never learned about the song, the papers that had printed it, the spirited sing-alongs inspired by it, or the commissioned officers who approved its publication.

Across the Pacific, officers performed a delicate balancing act of trying to please opposing needs. Some fumbled and made miscalculations. When this happened, intrepid troops fought restrictions and pressured officers in charge to give them the freedom of expression they were supposedly fighting for. One of the greatest examples of Pacific troops fighting for free presses occurred on the heels of the Battle of Saipan.

———

In 1944, the marines engaged in one of the "bloodiest battles of the Pacific," as approximately fourteen thousand lives were taken to claim the mountainous, seventy-five-square-mile island of Saipan. Prized for its airstrip and proximity to Japan (America's long-range B-29 Superfortress bombers could fly the 1,465 miles to Tokyo and back), Americans slowly advanced and eventually cornered the island's defenders at the cliffs of Marpi Point. Japanese propaganda convinced locals that suicide was preferable to life under American captivity. Thus, when the US Marines closed in, Japanese soldiers alongside civilian adults and children leaped to their deaths. Local lore holds that, after this mass suicide, white birds began to inhabit the cliffs. They were believed to house the souls of those who had perished there.

After the marines moved out, the Ninety-First Air Service Group moved in to keep the runway operational. Before arriving, the Ninety-First was briefed. As one officer instructed, "Remember . . . the water about the island has coral formations with razor sharp edges, the water is also infested with sharks . . . On the land there are many poisonous snakes, bottomless swamps filled with tropical sword grass that will cut through the clothing like a razor, fever-producing mosquitoes, no wholesome water, and a hot and humid climate." When the officer asked if there were any questions, one man raised a hand and asked, "Why don't we just let the Jap[anese] have Saipan?"

Efforts were made to improve island life. An indefatigable Red Cross worker named Orville "Uncle Bob" Roberts performed miracles to give his "boys" a taste of home. While on a trip to Hawai'i, he purchased two donut machines and shipped them to Saipan. Once they were operational, Roberts assigned himself a "donut detail." He circled the airstrip in his truck from 1:00 to 4:30 a.m., delivering fresh donuts and sweetened coffee to the tune of 750 donuts and thirty gallons of coffee per day. This was just the beginning. He requested Red Cross canteens, instruments for a full orchestra, and printing supplies for a troop newspaper. Uncle Bob made good on it all.

*This Is It!*, appearing in October 1944, was a weekly mimeographed paper that aimed to be "constructive—not destructive" and promised to publish news that would be of the greatest interest to the men of the Ninety-First. It asked for contributions, suggestions, and complaints. In reality, it printed only meek or humorous gripes. "We wish to commend those who put out the electrical power—it no longer is so intermittent," said one of the snarkier letters to the editor.

Instead of low-ranking troops speaking their minds, patronizing articles by officers dominated the paper. For troops, it was a drag to read. Issue after issue praised censorship regulations (which the troops hated) and included stern warnings to strictly adhere to the censor's orders. Editorials schooled the men on the dangers of Japanese radio propaganda. Most men thought the haunting birds at Marpi Point were reminder enough. Editorials also chided troops for gossiping. Troops grew tired of being told what not to say, what not to listen to, and what topics were off-limits for discussion. These condescending articles prompted a near mutiny.

Troops did not feel that "their" newspaper was really *theirs*. So the men of the Ninety-First conspired to flood *This Is It!* with letters of complaint. Some questioned why the newspaper asked for gripes about credible problems if it was not going to acknowledge them. Others criticized the paper because it was so full of indoctrination that it failed to include actual news. Troops wanted to know how their work factored into the fight with Japan. What was happening beyond the outskirts of their airstrip? Why was all of this censored?

Incredibly, this tidal wave of discontent brought change. *This Is It!* published these letters, and the paper's editorial policies shifted. Suddenly, it began to feel like the paper was truly on the side of the personnel in the Ninety-First Service Group. For starters, Lieutenant Montana Reese, the officer in charge, allowed the paper to print a poem by a corporal lampooning the paper's penchant for whitewashed content:

> A paper for the group by the group
> Namely, the enlisted men;
> It very rarely has a scoop,
> It repeats again and again.
>
> Contributions they are seeking,
> Must be unassuming and nice,
> For should you know of something reeking;
> That would definitely not suffice.
>
> You can write of muck and mire,
> And it may be slightly fictitious;
> But should it contain witty satire,
> That would be termed malicious.

So if you're not an obsequious flatterer
Your penning may as well cease,
For you'll never pass the iron hand
Of Lt. Montana Reese.

Next, the paper announced that a weekly "Problem Hour" was scheduled to allow troops to voice complaints and get answers. And war updates became a regular feature of *This Is It!* With an especial focus on B-29 bombing raids, the paper showcased how the work of the Ninety-First Service Group impacted the trajectory of the war. During the battle for Iwo Jima, *This Is It!* reported the latest progress made by the marines and how they benefited from the Ninety-First's assistance. When Okinawa was invaded in April 1945, *This Is It!* published hand-drawn maps, descriptions of the island and its assets, and articles detailing the tactical and strategic support provided by the bombers assisted by the Ninety-First. Troops could no longer complain about a news short-age or fail to understand how their work factored into the war's bigger picture. By giving them the information they craved, members of the Ninety-First Service Group were able to appreciate how their role on a remote island was indispensable to the fighting hundreds of miles away. With its improved news coverage, many troops mailed copies of *This Is It!* to their loved ones back home. It was the only record of the experi-ences and achievements of their group.

Alongside this newly added war coverage were cartoons and pop-ular illustrations. Many in the Ninety-First believed they would be the last Americans sent home after V-J Day. This sentiment was captured in a cartoon showing a soldier crouched in his foxhole while small explo-sions riddle the landscape as he makes calculations on a scrap of wood. "According to my figures, I've been home six months," said the caption. When a new service club opened, troops doubted it would ease their boredom. A cartoon depicted the new hangout, which bore a large mar-quee reading: "The Club Atoll. No Women Atoll, No Food Atoll, No Nothin Atoll." And to make up for the absence of women on the island, the paper made sure to include pinups that troops hung in their bunks and painted onto the noses of airplanes. Not everyone was pleased with this addition. "The word is out that some of the Chaplains . . . , with little sin to wrestle, are currently concerned with the pin-ups—those paper dolls we call our own," *This Is It!* reported. "Some hard eyes have also been cast upon the luscious creatures adorning the planes—Our Baby, Heavenly Body, Million Dollar Baby, and Supine Sue, etc." However, neither the nose art nor the pinups were going anywhere. "Happily," the article said, "no one can locate any paint remover," and pinups were too popular to be discontinued.

In the spring of 1945, *This Is It!* ran a front-page story announcing that Uncle Bob was leaving. A "favorite friend," his "unique coffee-and-donut run has given a lift to hundreds of night workers, but it has raised the dickens with his own health," the paper reported. Although Uncle Bob was being sent home to recuperate, the silver lining was that he left knowing his men had gained a voice, and if they needed something, they had a newspaper where they could make demands and get results.

———

One theme in many Pacific newspapers was how misunderstood troops felt. It seemed *civilians* were eager to tell *troops* what war was like. Because of the offerings of the Special Service Division, like civilian magazines and Hollywood movies, troops could read and watch how the home front was depicting the military. Little of it was accurate. For amusement and catharsis, many GI newspapers in the Pacific razed the delusional perspectives being sold to the folks back home. The newssheets on Iwo Jima did an expert job.

The 1945 battle for Iwo Jima was one of the costliest in the Pacific. The marines "expected . . . a bloody and disagreeable time," and with good reason. The only possible landing point was Iwo Jima's southeast beach. "We would have surprise on our side like a burglar with whooping cough," one officer said. Japanese defenses were elaborate, with intricate caves, reinforced pillboxes, and antitank ditches ready for any invaders. Offensively, the Japanese were poised to launch attacks with artillery, antitank guns, rockets, and mortars. When the invasion began, it took days for the US Marines to gain control of the beach and begin moving inland.

While the opening days of the battle for Iwo Jima had gripped the United States—claiming headlines, prime-time coverage on the airways, and detailed profiles in many magazines—as the fighting dragged on from days to weeks, the home front's interest waned. For the marines who stuck with their mission, fighting for five weeks straight to take Iwo Jima, it was infuriating that the home front ceased to care. Alongside sketches by Sergeant Dave Berg (who made a career of cartooning for *Mad* magazine after the war), the VII Fighter Command took to their newspaper, *Fighter Post*, to lament the flippancy of the civilian media and its audience. Likening the taking of Iwo Jima to a three-act play, an editorial began with the opening days of the campaign when the island was front-page news back home and the public was at the edge of their seats in suspense. "Iwo Jima was the most heavily fortified island in the whole world, and during the first wild act of the drama, the audience sat spellbound." Then came the second act, after the beaches had been taken. Enemy planes "came over in the weird dark green of night, and sent sleep-filled soldiers scurrying to Bomb Shelters, planes, and gun emplacements. By this time, some of the audience had lost interest in the plot as other shows were just starting down the street, and a few left; but the actor was just as interested in his part as ever, and acting it just as well." During the mopping-up phase—the third act—"most of the audience failed to come in from their smoke in the lobby." Although the crowd had gone and the spotlight had dimmed, the men were still doing their jobs. "As this issue goes to press, the soldier is sitting in the darkened theatre at the end of the season. Is he going to get home soon? His job is done, and the audience doesn't think about him as much, but he shouldn't be left in the dark of a theatre that once changed the course of history."

———

Many places in the Pacific theater could relate to the *Fighter Post*'s darkened theater analogy. As the war was constantly moving closer to mainland Japan, occupation troops remained on secured islands and performed a variety of jobs to support those in combat hundreds of miles away. They often felt like military castaways who were neglected, unimportant, and entirely forgotten.

With most large periodicals covering the latest amphibious landings and aerial battles, it was rare to find one that honored the tedium that occupation troops tolerated as they performed backbreaking work to support those in the limelight. One of the exceptions was the Seventh Air Force's magazine, *Brief*. Its editorial policy was unusual for a military periodical. "Whether you want to sit down and bitch without being interrupted or whether you have a plan that will end the war next week, take ten and write a letter to BRIEF. If we have room, we will print it." This was a policy that MacArthur never would have approved, but because the magazine was produced in the distant land of Hawai'i, it escaped his editorial preferences.

When the magazine invited complaints, it was not an empty gesture. There was a "Bitching Post," where profanity-laden protests were printed. It also advertised the formation of a "Gripe Club," although it noted that the group's "real name . . . is somewhat stronger." Each week, a handful of letters to the editor were printed that detailed indignities the men hoped the magazine could correct. There was no shortage of impetuous submissions from low-ranking soldiers, many of which were published. The magazine's features and articles brazenly gave voice to the tens of thousands of support troops who felt hopelessly insignificant and unappreciated.

*Brief*'s unique editorial policy was fortified after it had the moxie to print an early submission entitled, "Heroes Don't Win Wars." The piece was the by-product of a beer-fueled, late-night bull session in the Marianas. These troops were stuck at the end of the "third act" of their wartime play. The press had moved on and no longer covered the island they were stranded on. As their indignation boiled over, Private Earl "Bud" Nelson jotted down the passionate words of one of the men, a cook, and sent it to *Brief*.

"Why [doesn't] anybody ever mention the poor bastard who got dragged into the Army, got stuck out here on one of these godforsaken holes, and is doing nothing but his job? . . . Ninety—or maybe ninety-nine percent of the guys in the Army never had anything happen to them," the cook had said.

Take, for example, a guy I know named Chuck who was on KP today. Nothing ever happened to him. He doesn't even get into trouble.

What does he do all day? He drives a truck. He goes back and forth over the island one hundred miles a day. He goes to a movie at night; probably a very bad and very old movie which he has already seen four or five times. He goes back to his tent and writes a gushy letter to some babe who has probably thrown him over a year ago. He lies in his slit trench at night during air raids. He goes on KP about every fifth day.

He sure as hell isn't going to get any medals or citations. He won't kill any [Japanese] or down any Zeros. He won't do a damn thing to get his name in the papers. He won't even get a rating.

But somebody's got to drive that truck. Somebody's got to pull KP, or be latrine orderly, or clean up the dayroom, or file letters, or type special orders, or drive some Major over to the hospital to see a nurse. . . .

Hell, . . . I personally think it's just as dangerous to light one of those damn field stoves as it is to go over a target. A lot of cooks have been blown to hell-and-gone by them. And a hell of a lot more burned to a crisp. But can you imagine a General pinning a medal on a guy and saying: "for heroism in lighting a stove . . . day after day for two years?"

Or a guy getting a citation which read: "for typing our correspondence eight hours a day, every day, for two years without making a mistake?"

Don't you think those guys would like to see their names

in print, saying how they're fighting the war, too? Don't you think they're just as fed up with this war, just as sick of all the chicken down here, just as disgusted with all the crap they have to put up with?

Don't you think a mechanic down on the line thinks what he's doing is just as important as what the gunner, or the pilot are doing? . . .

Heroes don't win wars—they just get their names in the paper. The guys who win wars are the guys who lug reams of paper around, or open cans of C-rations, or clean pots and pans, or grease jeeps or dig sump pits or do any of a thousand jobs that nobody ever heard of, except the poor bastard that has to do it. . . .

The guy who's just a serial number, the guy who says 'Yes Sir' like an automaton, the guys whose jobs have become so monotonous and regulated that they can do them while their minds are 10,000 miles away. . . . He's told down to the twitch of his shoulders just how he should do whatever he's doing, and he damn well better do it that way whether it's the best way or not.

He's the guy . . . that is winning this war—if it is being won. And he's the guy I think somebody ought to write about.

Inexplicably, Nelson's submission survived army and navy censorship and was printed. Any other paper would have been shut down if it published something this contemptuous, hot-headed, and divisive. Letters poured into *Brief*'s APO box. Gunners and airmen went on the offensive, emphasizing the importance of their jobs. A few pilots offered to swap places with file clerks any day of the week. The overwhelming response, however, came from "Chucks" who agreed with the cook. No newspaper dared write about them; there was nothing flashy about their work. It was dull, tedious, and disenchanting. They had no escape, save victory and an eventual discharge. But even then, because they had no medals, no citations, no rank to pull, they would be last in line to go home.

While the military typically did not tolerate the kind of talk in Nelson's article, there was little that could be done once it was published. Some wondered if some form of punishment was in the cards. But *Brief* and the commanding officers of the Seventh AAF did the opposite. Nelson was awarded a weekly column devoted to the "poor bastards" he wrote about. It was called "One Damned Island After Another." And the Supreme Commander of the Southwest Pacific remained blissfully unaware that such free expression was being written, distributed, read, and enjoyed right under his nose.

# CHAPTER NINE
## DEMOCRACY?

Let America be America again.
Let it be the dream it used to be.
Let it be the pioneer on the plain
Seeking a home where he himself is free.

(America never was America to me.)

Let America be the dream the dreamers dreamed—
Let it be that great strong land of love
Where never kings connive nor tyrants scheme
That any man be crushed by one above.

(It never was America to me.)
                                    —Langston Hughes, 1936

By mid-1944, Marshall's troop newspaper program had spread across the world, and over 4,600 distinct army newspapers were in print. On the whole, the project was a resounding success. Troops were informed of current events, and many were able to freely express their experiences and ideas.

But not all. Some groups in the army struggled to gain recognition for their contributions to the war. At a time when Japanese Americans were being sent to internment camps in the United States, approximately twenty thousand entered the US Army and were funneled into segregated units. Although they were assigned to some of the toughest fighting in the Mediterranean and European theaters, Japanese Americans seldom received any coverage in army periodicals. Native Americans also remained on the periphery of the press despite their willingness to volunteer and fight on behalf of the United States. Approximately forty-five thousand Native men aged eighteen to fifty years joined the US military during World War II, many of whom provided crucial assistance in transmitting communications in the Pacific. Yet GI newspapers rarely cast a spotlight on their unique contributions.

There were two groups, however, whose large sizes made them difficult to ignore entirely. Over eight hundred thousand Black Americans and approximately three hundred fifty thousand women served in the US military during World War II, yet the military accepted them with tepid enthusiasm. For Black troops and women volunteers, newspapers were one of the only ways to extend their reach outside of their segregated and separate worlds and show that their work was meaningful and worthy of praise. They hoped army-wide periodicals might assist them in gaining awareness of the important war work they performed. Results were mixed.

———

When the Selective Training and Service Act was passed in 1940, it provided that "any person, regardless of race or color . . . shall be afforded an opportunity to volunteer for induction into the land or naval forces of the United States." By the first anniversary of Pearl Harbor, nearly four hundred thousand Black Americans had joined the army. However, recruitment offices and brochures neglected to mention that the US military adopted strict regulations against "racial intermingling," believing that integrated units would destroy morale and inhibit the military's preparation for war. Judge William H. Hastie, who had been appointed civilian aide to the secretary of war, urged the army to rethink this policy, stating that the "inflexible separation of white and black soldiers was 'the most dramatic evidence of hypocrisy' in America's professed concern for preserving democracy." But Secretary of War Henry Stimson insisted racial segregation was necessary and was most consistent with the "prevailing public sentiment against mixing the races in the intimate association of military life." Already overwhelmed with trying to raise and equip a rapidly growing army, Marshall decided that the "settlement of vexing racial problems cannot be permitted to complicate the tremendous task of the War Department and thereby jeopardize discipline and morale." In time, Marshall's own newspaper program would reveal the backwardness of his position.

The army's inflexible policy meant that, beginning with induction, Black Americans were subjected to racially segregated barracks, training programs, replacement centers, post exchanges, service clubs, mess halls, and army transportation. As one man described his experience, Black troops were subjected to "separate and very unequal facilities." Not only were buildings and equipment subpar but so were the opportunities available. Black troops quickly learned that the army's panoply of specialties was not open to them no matter their education or experience. Instead, most were consigned to servile or menial jobs, like preparing food or unloading equipment. Making matters worse, the majority of military installations were located in the South, where Jim Crow was the norm, and the army opted to conform to local attitudes and customs. For the sake of consistency, all army establishments adopted compatible policies, and so the army "actually introduced Jim Crow in some places at home and abroad." It did not take long for Black troops to realize that this was not a war "of Americans against Germans, it was black Americans versus white Americans on . . . army post[s] that perpetuated segregation and prejudice."

In a war for freedom and the preservation of democracy, it seemed counterintuitive for the US military to adopt a racial segregation policy that seemed "consonant with the racial theories of Nazi Germany." In the words of the NAACP's monthly magazine, *The Crisis*, while its editors were "sorry for brutality, blood, and death among the peoples of Europe . . . the hysterical cries of the preachers of democracy for Europe leave us cold. We want democracy in Alabama, Arkansas, in Mississippi and Michigan, in the District of Columbia—in the

*Senate of the United States.*" The NAACP's point was not lost on the Axis. Well before the war, Germany recognized that America's history with race could be manipulated to nurture hate, misunderstanding, and dissension. As Germany's minister of propaganda, Joseph Goebbels, stated in September 1941, "America of today will never be a danger to us. Nothing will be easier than to produce a bloody revolution in the United States. No other country has so many racial and social tensions. We shall be able to play many strings there." An army splintered by prejudice and bias would be easy to topple.

Although the overwhelming majority of overseas commanders refused to accept Black combat units through much of 1943, attitudes and circumstances began to shift as Black troops proved themselves in the field. Back at home, GI gazettes published by and for Black troops—like the Tuskegee Army Air Base's *Hawk's Cry*—chronicled the accomplishments of Black combatants. The *Hawk's Cry* did such an expert job that it consistently won honorable mentions in the *GI Galley*'s annual army-wide newspaper contests, besting thousands of other contenders. The *GI Galley* cast a spotlight on the editor of the *Hawk's Cry*, Sergeant Leon E. Smith, when it asked him to contribute to the *Galley*'s regular feature "A 'Perfect' Paper." When given this international platform, Smith explained that his paper's success was the product of understanding what his readers wanted and ensuring each issue satisfied their interests. "This doesn't mean, however, that the wants of the GIs at this station are different from those at any other place where men wear khaki, make formations, go to sick call and wait in line on pay day," Smith noted. "Our news has a universal appeal, not only for Negro GIs but for the entire armed forces." As army-wide periodicals began to cover the feats of Black troops, Smith's conviction that inclusive news had mass appeal would be confirmed.

One of the most important publications to cover the deeds of Black troops was *Yank, the Army Weekly*. Not only did it have the largest circulation rate of any military periodical, but it also operated with an unusual degree of independence. Perhaps because it was not bankrolled by the government, *Yank* did not shy away from publishing articles that exposed the War Department's duplicity in telling troops to fight for democracy, while treating its own troops differently based on race.

*Yank* made its stance clear beginning with a summer 1943 multi-page article detailing the inaugural battle between an all-Black air force squadron and a fleet of German planes near Tunisia. "Over the Mediterranean, [Black Americans] for the first time in history fought for their country in an aerial battle against the enemy . . . beating off superior forces without loss to themselves and with probable loss to the enemy," *Yank* reported. Millions of soldiers read the article and saw the accompanying images of the pilot, ground crew, and post-mission debriefing with army intelligence staff. As usual, letters to the editor followed. One letter from a Black engineer thanked *Yank* for its excellent coverage. Another letter asked *Yank* for its "ideas on the race problem after the war. The Negroes will think they are equal to the whites because they have fought in this war." Usually, *Yank*'s editors kept their opinions out of the magazine. But this time, they were asked and so *Yank* answered: "*YANK* takes its views on the post-war 'race' problem from the founders of the United States, who believed that *all* men were created equal." To that end, *Yank* continued to publish combat stories involving Black troops.

By mid-1944, the initial hesitance of many commanders to accept Black units eroded, possibly because of *Yank*'s coverage. Black troops were being requested for combat duty in all theaters. Though the army insisted on keeping ground troops segregated, the battlefield proved to be a place where troops were not white or Black; they were either allies or enemies. Racially segregated units may have entered the battle, but the chaos of combat caused Black and white ground troops to fight side by side, living and dying together. Stereotypes and prejudice faded as all troops worked together to achieve a common goal.

Questionnaires administered by the army's Research Branch in May and June of 1945 confirmed what was already known on the field. A poll of white officers who observed integrated fighting forces in Europe showed that 84 percent believed that Black troops had performed "very well" and reported that combat seemed to forge unity and "good relationships" between Black and white troops. Some white enlisted men admitted that they initially disliked "the prospect of having black troops in their companies," yet "three-quarters of them changed their minds after serving with [Black troops] in combat, their distrust turning into respect and friendliness." Despite the overwhelming data that integrated forces were just as effective as segregated units, and had the added benefit of combating racial prejudice, the War Department kept its surveys secret. The army could bury its head in the sand, but the troops knew the truth. And *Yank* and the *Stars and Stripes* did not shy away from printing it.

––––––

Although *Yank* began its coverage of Black units in 1943, it took many letters of gentle goading to encourage the *Stars and Stripes* to include stories about the work of Black troops in the army. This began with published criticisms of its limited coverage. "It is an obvious fact that *The Stars and Stripes* deals chiefly with the white American GI in the ETO, thereby seemingly ignoring the part played by the Negro soldier," said an October 1944 letter signed by six Black troops in a quartermaster bakery company. "Would it be asking too much to request that MORE articles be printed reporting the deeds and accomplishments of our Negro soldiers? What could be a more appropriate time to reach a better understanding between our races than now, while we are fighting together for a common cause, mainly . . . DEMOCRACY!" The editor made no reply to this question, and weeks passed without any mention of Black troops in the *Stars and Stripes*.

The silence was broken when a letter by army engineer P. Beasley was published at the end of October 1944. "I've been waiting . . . for more news of colored troops. I feel sure thousands of fellows share this interest with me," he said. In case the *Stars and Stripes* did not know where Black combat troops were fighting, Beasley let them know. "There are infantry in the Pacific, infantry and fighter-squadrons in Italy, engineers and artillery in France and Germany," and the *Stars and Stripes* could "ask some of the boys from Brest to tell you about a certain company up there." Beasley explained he had plenty of time to read the newspaper and gripe about its incomplete news because he was in a hospital in France being treated for battle wounds. And so, from his bed, he promised to "keep on looking" for stories about the eight hundred thousand Black troops in the army, "because I'm sure you know how much this will mean to us."

Slowly, the *Stars and Stripes* took its cue. In one story about Black longshoremen, the newspaper marveled that a unit unloaded 151 long tons of artillery ammunition in twelve hours at Cherbourg. "I've handled artillery shells until my arms were numb," Private Elmer Lockhart told the *Stars and Stripes*. Another article recorded how a new "Negro Artillery Unit" in the Third Army fought so gallantly that their commanding officer effusively bragged that these untested men had "made [him] proud" as they operated like troops who "had been in the line for weeks." And in the spring of 1945, the *Stars and Stripes* featured integrated units on its front page. "Negroes Fight Beside Whites on West Front," read the banner stretching across the newspaper. As Beasley had predicted, these articles were treasured by Black troops.

But it was not only Black troops who received a boost from inclusive coverage. *Yank* discovered that soldiers of all races felt pride to be part of an integrated army that repelled not only Germany's troops but also Hitler's ideas about an Aryan race.

———

Perhaps the most important letter to the editor that *Yank* dared publish came in April 1944, when Corporal Rupert Trimmingham shared a story about a cross-country trip he took with eight other Black soldiers on army business. They traveled from their home base of Fort Huachuca, Arizona, to Camp Claiborne, Louisiana.

In Arizona, Fort Huachuca was a source of pride. As the *Arizona Republic* reported in 1942, the fort was "home of the splendid 93rd Infantry Division, [the] first all-colored division to be organized in World War II," and "one learns in a hurry at Arizona's Fort Huachuca" that "America's colored citizens . . . make some of the nation's finest and most efficient fighting troops." Trimmingham, used to Arizona's customs and attitude toward Black troops, was amazed by how differently he was treated by the Camp Claiborne community.

According to Trimmingham, after a one-night layover in Louisiana, he and his fellow soldiers discovered that "we could not purchase a cup of coffee at any of the lunchrooms" because, "as you know, Old Man Jim Crow rules." Trimmingham continued:

> The only place where we could be served was at the lunchroom at the railroad station but, of course, we had to go into the kitchen. But that's not all; 11:30 A.M. about two dozen German prisoners of war, with two American guards, came to the station. They entered the lunchroom, sat at the tables, had their meals served, talked, smoked, in fact had quite a swell time. I stood on the outside looking on, and I could not help but ask myself these questions: Are these men sworn enemies of this country? Are they not taught to hate and destroy . . . all democratic governments? Are we not American soldiers, sworn to fight for and die if need be for this our country? Then why are they treated better than we are? Why are we pushed around like cattle? If we are fighting for the same thing, if we are going to die for our country, then why does the Government allow such things to go on?

And so Trimmingham closed his letter to *Yank* by asking a question that "each Negro soldier is asking. What is the Negro soldier fighting for?"

When *Yank* published Trimmingham's story, a flood of letters poured into *Yank*'s mailbox. Nearly every message to *Yank* spoke to the indefensibility of treating enemy combatants with greater respect and courtesy than a fellow American. "Gentlemen, I am a Southern rebel," a letter by Corporal Henry S. Wooten Jr., began. "But this incident makes me none the more proud of my Southern heritage!" Wooten continued:

> Frankly, I think that this incident is a disgrace to a democratic nation such as ours is supposed to be. Are we fighting for such

a thing as this? Certainly not. If this incident is democracy, I don't want any part of it! . . . I wonder what the "Aryan supermen" think when they get a first-hand glimpse of our racial discrimination. Are we not waging a war, in part, for this fundamental of democracy? In closing, let me say that a lot of us, especially in the South, should cast the beam out of our own eyes before we try to do so in others, across the sea.

Hundreds of letters agreed with Wooten's sentiments.

Sergeant Arthur Kaplan complimented *Yank* for printing Trimmingham's letter and said, "It seems incredible that German prisoners of war should be afforded the amenities while our own men—in uniform and changing stations—are denied similar attention because of color . . . What sort of deal is this?"

"I'm not a Negro, but I've been around and know what the score is. I want to thank the YANK . . . and congratulate Cpl. Rupert Trimmingham," wrote Private Gustave Santiago.

One missive, signed by an entire outfit, laid bare the hypocrisy of the army's policy on racial segregation and the government's claim that this was a war for freedom. The unit explained, "We are white soldiers in the Burma jungles, and there are many Negro outfits working with us. They are doing more than their part to win this war. We are proud of the colored men here," they said, and "it is a disgrace that, while we are away from home doing our part to help win the war, some people back home are knocking down everything that we are fighting for." Ironically, this letter remarked that soldiers from other Allied nations had marveled at the racial diversity of the United States Army and how all troops worked cohesively together. Were they masquerading a lie? It angered them to know that German soldiers were being treated better at home "than the soldier of our country, because of race." The letter closed by stating, "Cpl. Trimmingham asked: What is the Negro fighting for? If this sort of thing continues, we the white soldiers will begin to wonder: What are we fighting for?"

Trimmingham's letter provoked such outrage that it commanded the attention of the home front. The *New Yorker* published a fictionalized account of Trimmingham's story in June 1944, which was reproduced repeatedly in the *New Yorker*'s books of "war stories" over the following decades. A dramatic skit about Trimmingham's story was aired on national radio. And when *Yank* produced a volume of its best stories, Trimmingham and the letters responding to Trimmingham's letter were included.

Months after his original letter was published, Trimmingham appeared in the pages of *Yank* again. "Allow me to thank you for publishing my letter," he began. Every day brought a fresh batch of letters from fellow soldiers, many from "the Deep South," who condemned the treatment he had received. "It gives me new hope to realize that there are doubtless thousands of whites who are willing to fight this Frankenstein that so many white people are keeping alive." If white allies would "stand up, join with us, and help us prove to their white friends that we are worthy, I'm sure that we would bury race hate and unfair treatment," Trimmingham said.

The success of racially integrated fighting forces and the publication of letters about racial inequalities in the army forced many to question the meaning of democracy and freedom. Changes to military policy followed. In July 1948, President Truman signed an executive order to end racial segregation and discrimination in the armed forces. "It is hereby declared to be the policy of the President that there shall be equality of treatment and opportunity for all persons in the Armed Services without regard to race, color, religion or national origin," stated the order. Declaring segregation and discrimination over was one thing. Effecting actual change was another. It would take the military decades to fully dismantle the race-based policies that permeated the ranks during World War II. And it would take the Civil Rights Movement of the 1960s to deliver powerful blows to the system of Jim Crow and segregation outside of the military. The work Trimmingham hoped would be done by his generation continues to this day. Despite this slow pace, many historians credit the Black soldiers of World War II for exposing the duplicity inherent in their democracy and starting mainstream conversations about the discordance between racism and freedom.

When FDR dedicated the first issue of *Yank*, he declared that soldiers were not only fighters but "delegates of freedom." As Black troops took up arms, they also took up their pens, precipitating some of the most meaningful discussions about democracy in the war. For writing his letter and sparking a worldwide dialogue on race, Corporal Rupert Trimmingham was perhaps the ultimate "delegate of freedom."

———

Another ostracized group in the army was the hundreds of thousands of women volunteers. After the attack on Pearl Harbor, many women felt a desire to serve the nation, but not by knitting socks or working on an assembly line in a war factory. They wanted to join the military. There was one person in Congress who seemed to understand this. In May 1941, Massachusetts representative Edith Nourse Rogers, one of only eight women serving in the House of Representatives in 1941, introduced a bill to create the Women's Army Auxiliary Corps, giving women "a chance to volunteer to serve their country in a patriotic way."

The bill was initially sidelined because it was introduced before the nation had declared war. However, after Pearl Harbor, Rogers renewed her efforts, fueled by thousands of letters from women demanding the opportunity to serve. In May 1942, Rogers gained enough support from her congressional colleagues, and her bill became law. The Women's Army Auxiliary Corps (WAAC) was formed.

However, the emphasis seemed to be on the word *auxiliary*. Women worked *with*, but were not *part of*, the army. Female volunteers were denied many of the benefits men received, like overseas pay and life insurance. When the Senate Military Affairs Committee considered amending the WAAC legislation so that women would be incorporated into the army, Helen Douglas Mankin, a Georgia attorney, was invited to testify. "I hate the word 'auxiliary,'" Mankin told the committee, "and I am speaking for the women in America in that. When I say that women are tired of being auxiliaries, I am speaking for them. If they do the work, why not call them a corps: why stick that word 'auxiliary' in there? Women do not like it; it is objectionable." Congress listened. In July 1943, President Roosevelt signed legislation that incorporated the WAAC into the army, and the word *auxiliary* was eliminated. From that point forward, women would serve in the Women's Army Corps ("WACs"), with all the rights and benefits enjoyed by the army's male soldiers, at least on paper. Unfortunately, a name change did not alter attitudes; most women in the corps never stopped being treated as inferior interlopers. A man in uniform was respected. A woman in uniform was disparaged.

Traditional values held that a woman's place was in the home. It was easy to stir dissent when a wide swath of America believed it was blasphemous to shepherd naive, young women into the male-dominated armed forces. How could they possibly remain virtuous and marriageable? In the words of a 1954 treatise on the WACs published by the Office of the Chief of Military History, "The Army had its share of a conservative element that had scarcely recovered from the shock of the mechanized horse when confronted with the militarized woman." There was something threatening about women wearing uniforms and performing "masculine" jobs. Was it a woman's place to work as an airplane mechanic? Wouldn't a woman's delicate mind be overtaxed trying to crack codes and ciphers? It defied societal norms for women to do the work the army had slated for them. Perhaps in response, noxious rumors about the WACs spread widely at home and overseas, making life miserable for the innocent women who had simply volunteered to serve their country.

One of the most damaging and prevalent rumors was invented in June 1943, when the *New York Daily News* published an article stating that a "supersecret agreement" had been reached between the War Department and the WACs so that "contraceptives and prophylactic equipment will be furnished to" the women so they could safely perform their patriotic duty. This article was republished across the United States. Soon, much of the nation was under the impression that the true "morale purpose" for the WACs was essentially army-sanctioned prostitution. The article was false—no contraceptives or prophylactics were ever issued to the WACs—but vehement denials from the White House and War Department, along with retractions of the original articles, did little to quell the damage. This falsehood was only the beginning of an onslaught of public attacks on the character and conduct of the army's women. According to one War Department study, in the summer of 1943, WACs were accused of an impressive array of bad behavior: they "drank too much; . . . they picked up men in streets and bars; . . . they were registered with men in every hotel and auto court, or had sexual relations under trees and bushes in public parks; . . . there was a nearby military hospital filled to overflowing with maternity and venereal disease cases," and "brazen" WACs were "touring in groups seizing and raping sailors and Coast Guardsmen."

In truth, WACs were better educated than "both the civilian average and that of Army men." They tended to be mature, twenty-five to twenty-seven years old, healthy, single, high school graduates, and proficient in a professional skill like clerical work. When it came to chastity, WACs had a venereal disease rate that was "almost zero," and the pregnancy rate among unwed WACs was one-fifth the rate of civilian women. Even though WACs tended to be above average in intellect and virtue, they were subjected to never-ending abuse. It was crushing. As one WAC described, when she was granted a leave home to visit her family, she held her head high as she walked through town in her uniform, but she knew "everybody was talking about me." "I was so humiliated," she said. The moment she arrived home, "I just burst out crying . . . I couldn't understand how my eagerness to serve our country could have brought such shame on us all."

Not only were civilians dubious about the WACs, but the army's research and intelligence divisions confirmed that most male troops harbored extreme animosity toward women in uniform. Even the Office of Censorship (which kept tabs on how often soldier mail referenced the WACs) reported that 84 percent of soldiers' letters referred to the WACs in negative terms. "You join the WAVES [the navy's Women Accepted for Volunteer Emergency Service] or WAC and you are automatically a prostitute in my opinion," one man wrote to a female relative who was considering joining the military. "About joining the Wacs, the answer is still NO. If they really need service women let them draft some of the pigs that are running around loose in every town," another man wrote to his wife. Divorce threats and actual divorces were also common. One soldier wrote his parents after learning that his wife had joined the WACs, "I cannot put this on paper how I feel and I am ashamed to tell my fellow officers. She cannot even consider herself as my wife from now on. I am stopping all allotments to her and am breaking off all contacts with her. Why she did such a thing to me I cannot understand. My heart is broken."

Although the *Stars and Stripes* and *Yank, the Army Weekly* could have used their platforms to showcase the significant contributions of the WACs and tackle the untrue rumors, they instead did little to rectify the rampant misunderstandings surrounding the army's women. While the *Stars and Stripes* could justify its inaction by strictly adhering to its editorial policy of focusing on combat (no women served in combat), *Yank* had no such policy to excuse its incomplete coverage. It is curious that when *Yank* expressed its policy toward Black soldiers, it quoted the Declaration of Independence, emphasizing "*all* men are created equal." However, when it came to the WACs, it seems that *Yank* transposed its emphasis from the word "all" to "men."

In August 1943, *Yank* published "WAACs Drop An 'A,'" which was an article about how women were going to officially join the army and receive all the rights and benefits of male soldiers. It was the first and last substantive article *Yank* published about the WACs during the war. The piece generated letters to the editor suggesting that it was not just an "A" that needed to be dropped; the entire idea of women in uniform should be abandoned. Rather than take a stand on behalf of the WACs, *Yank* instead downgraded its coverage from multipage feature articles to single-page collages of photographs of servicewomen. One piece showed images of WACs at Fort Belvoir, Virginia, and another featured the navy's WAVES. The photographs and illustrations depicted smiling women working as chauffeurs, clerks, air traffic controllers, weather forecasters, radio operators, and parachute seamstresses. Even this was too much for some servicemen, who begged *Yank* to stop printing "feminine propaganda."

"Why we GIs over here in the Pacific have to read your tripe and drivel about the Wacs beats me," Sergeant Bob Bowie wrote in a letter that was published in *Yank* in February 1944. "Who in the hell cares about these dimpled GIs who are supposed to be soldiers? All I have ever heard of them doing is peeling spuds, clerking in the office, driving a truck or tractor or puttering around in a photo lab." After suggesting that the true roles WACs played involved going to "dances, picnics, swimming parties and bars," Bowie believed that women wore uniforms simply to see "how many dates they can get." "We would like them a hell of a lot better, and respect them more, if they did their part in some defense plant or at home, where they belong." Bowie asked *Yank* to stay focused on *real* war coverage because it was "sickening to read about some doll who has made the supreme sacrifice of giving up her lace-trimmed undies for ODs."

*Yank* also printed a letter from Private William J. Robinson, who said, "I was disgusted when I opened the pages of a recent *Yank* and saw some silly female in GI clothes. I detest Wacs very thoroughly and I hope I never meet one. That is also the opinion of all my buddies." For a magazine that was supposed to build morale and unity, it is odd that *Yank* dignified these letters by printing them.

A few weeks later, *Yank* at least published responses from several WACs. "After reading Sgt. Bowie's disgusting opinion of the Wacs I must say that I think he's one hell of an American," Private Helen London wrote. "Many of these frilly females Sgt. Bowie blows his top about are a lot closer to action than a smug soldier who apparently has enough time at his desk . . . to write letters critical of the Wacs," Private Mildred McGlamery said. One anonymous letter from a "WAC Private" retorted, "I'll bet two months' pay that Sgt. Bowie was drafted. . . . We volunteered." And Technician Jane Nugent said, "Thanks for the bouquets, boys. Go right on sticking the knife in our backs. . . . When it's all over we'll go back to our lace-trimmed undies and to the kind of men who used their anger on something beside the Wacs."

For the remainder of 1944, the only times WACs made an appearance in *Yank* were in photographs in which they were always attractive, posing, and smiling (and never showcasing the serious work they did). Most male troops did not seem to take umbrage with these visuals. After all, every issue of *Yank* included a full-page photograph of an attractive, posing, smiling celebrity clad in a bathing suit, formfitting gown, or some other revealing costume. *Yank* was even credited with coining the term *pinup* to describe these photographs. Rather than shift the narrative about how women were diligent workers performing essential war work for the army, *Yank* instead cemented the prevalent view that women were objects of beauty and had little else to offer. Accordingly, when *Yank* devoted its front cover to a photograph of Private Grace Glocke, a WAC who was pleasantly smiling from an armchair at the army air base in Rapid City, South Dakota, no one seemed to object to the caption "The Army Could Use More Like Her." Troops knew what *Yank* meant. "That is worth fighting for," a private wrote to *Yank*. "I wonder if you could give me her address? . . . She might become our ship's pin-up girl," said Fred Bastian. "Yeow, why didn't I take up photography before I was drafted? Here's hoping to see more Wac pictures," said Private R. H. Fanning Jr. *Yank* understood what sort of pictures Fanning meant.

It was not just the army-wide publications that failed to defend the WACs. Unit and division papers produced by male troops regularly published cartoons portraying the WACs as silly and featherbrained. They were typically drawn as big-busted, wide-eyed nuisances who had no place in the army. For the WACs, it was depressing to work long days performing difficult jobs only to pick up a post newspaper and find a cartoon lampooning their contributions. Unsurprisingly, the recruitment of women plummeted in 1943. Why would women willingly risk tarnishing their reputations and subjecting themselves to ridicule and scorn?

Because the WACs were capably performing essential jobs throughout the army, the War Department was forced into damage control. Commanding officers went on the record to praise the work of the WACs. Civilian newspapers across the country published stories quoting famous generals on how women were admirably serving their country. General Dwight Eisenhower told the press that he was begging for more WACs to be sent to Europe and threatened that, if WACs did not arrive soon, he would turn to British servicewomen who were also known for their excellent work. In the Pacific, General Douglas MacArthur said the WACs were "good and faithful soldiers in the onward march to victory." For their work in the air force, General H. H. Arnold lauded the WACs' "outstanding performance." And from Italy, General Mark Clark reported, "I wish I had many more WACs serving with the Fifteenth Army." While this publicity campaign may have helped improve the induction rate of women, it did not change opinions within the army.

The morale of the WACs was not going to receive a boost through the sexist perspectives adopted by *Yank* or the nonexistent coverage in the *Stars and Stripes*. So women made their own periodicals, hoping that they might fall into the hands of chauvinist, male soldiers. This strategy was a good one. When the Army Library Service created its magazine sets for troops, it assembled a WAC magazine kit that consisted of the most popular periodicals for women, including *Harper's Bazaar, Ladies' Home Journal, McCall's, Mademoiselle*, and *Woman's Home Companion*. Although ten thousand packages of these magazines were shipped each month, the WACs rarely received them. The army's chief librarian, Ray Trautman, explained the problem. "Soldiers would grab the women's magazines before the gals had a chance at them," he said. "The men away from home wanted to read about women, what they were doing, what they were thinking. And they especially liked the fashion magazines, as they could see what the American girl looked like when she was all dressed up." Given male troops' appetites for women's periodicals, it was a sound conclusion that WACs would not be the only ones reading the magazines and newspapers that were being printed by and for them. And if more men read serious articles about the important war work the WACs were doing, the animosity most male soldiers felt for the WACs might dissipate.

And thus, in lieu of the *Stars and Stripes*, there was the *Service*

*Woman* newspaper, which covered stories about women serving in the army, navy, marines, coast guard, army nurse corps, and navy nurse corps. Its coverage was comprehensive and showcased the importance of the work being done by women—from saving lives in combat zones to enduring long periods of captivity as prisoners of war. Those in the European theater replaced *Yank* with *Overseas Woman*. This magazine reported on WAC scientists, female doctors, and women who were test pilots for the Army Air Corps. Articles explored what work might be available to women after the war and how the war might change traditional gender stereotypes. Rather than read what men thought women should do, *Overseas Woman* was an empowering periodical that did not underestimate the intellect or ambition of its readers.

There were also smaller-scale newsletters for individual posts, like Fort Des Moines' *WAC News*, which confronted the "malicious and untruthful reports about the Wacs." One issue included an interview with a civilian correspondent in Algiers, who insisted that "one Wac was doing as much work as two or three men soldiers could do," and that the correspondent was told by "General Eisenhower and various other officers . . . that the Wacs were so valuable to the American Army in North Africa that they wished they had ten times as many as were there." *WAC News* also had some fun with the army's double standards, reporting how WACs proudly hung photographs of "pin-up boys" in their bunks. And when the *WAC News* celebrated its second anniversary in print, Milton Caniff and Sergeant Sansone joined forces to create a congratulatory cartoon featuring their famous characters, Miss Lace and Wolf. Over six thousand copies of the paper were printed, and one thousand were mailed to posts across the world. If anything would lure male readers to this servicewomen's newsletter, seeing their favorite cartoon characters emblazoned on the front cover was an ingenious ploy.

According to statistics tracked by army censors in the Southwest Pacific, male attitudes toward women's services went from an all-time low of only 10 percent of soldiers having a favorable perception in 1944 to 70 percent on V-J Day. What exactly caused this change is difficult to pinpoint. Maybe male soldiers had a chance to witness the valuable work that WACs performed? Or perhaps victory brought a wave of relief that women would soon leave the military and return to their traditional role at home? But it is also possible that these servicewomen's periodicals helped change perceptions of women in uniform, converting male soldiers to the notion that women were helping win the war too.

Franklin Roosevelt went on frequent presidential cruises during the 1930s and became a regular reader of the crew-made shipboard newspapers. When Gen. George Marshall proposed troop newspapers during World War II, Roosevelt was an eager supporter.

General George C. Marshall was the visionary behind the army's troop newspaper program, an unprecedented experiment in giving all troops the freedom to print their own words while at war. Soldier newspapers were "essential" armor "in a democratic army," Marshall said.

Few GI newsrooms had furniture, electricity, and telephones, but the London office of the *Stars and Stripes* did. It was the first army-wide newspaper of World War II.

## ON ACTIVE SERVICE

**BENT.**—In March, 1944, killed on air operations, ARTHUR LEA BALDWIN (BERTIE), Flt. Lt., R.A.F.V.R., younger son of the late BALDWIN BENT and of Mrs. Bent, of Wray House, Lancaster.

**CRAIG.**—Died of wounds received in Burma in March, 1944, MAJOR P. B. CRAIG, Somerset Light Infantry, serving with the West African Force, dearly loved only son of the late Sir Maurice Craig, C.B.E., M.D., F.R.C.P., and Lady Craig (Manor House, Manor Road, Taunton, Somerset), brother of Monica Barry and Alison Kennett.

**CUNNINGHAM.**—On April 4, 1944, DOUGLAS CAMERON PRICE CUNNINGHAM, late R.A.F., beloved elder son of Mrs. D. G. Cunningham, 78, Roland House, Kensington, aged 23. Funeral Hampstead Cemetery, Saturday, April 8, at 11 a.m.

**HARDINGE.**—On April 3, 1944, after long illness nobly borne, THEODORE JOHN HARDINGE, Captain, R.N., of Pitney House, Taunton. Cremation private. Memorial service Langport Church, April 12, 3 p.m.

**HIGGINS.**—In Feb., 1944, CAPTAIN PETER HIGGINS, R.E., M.A., killed in action in Burma, second son of Sidney and the late Margaret Mabel Higgins, of Crumpsall and Knutsford.

**HOUGHTON.**—In Feb., 1944, in action, WILLIAM (BILL) HOUGHTON, Lieut., Queen's Royal Regiment, aged 22, dearly loved elder son of Mr. and Mrs. W. Houghton, The Elms, Little Blakenham, Ipswich.

**KELLETT.**—On April 1, 1944, at Royal Naval Hospital, Simonstown, LIEUT.-COMMANDER WILLIAM BASIL KELLETT, R.N., dearly loved husband of Audrey, of Beetham, Milnthorpe, Westmorland.

**LEE.**—In Italy, CLAUDE EDWARD LEE, Captain, Royal Artillery. Mentioned in Dispatches, aged 23, beloved husband of Joy, Gay's Daddy, and very dear son-in-law of William and Nance Robinson, of Thorpe Bay, Essex. For ever in our hearts and admiration as a very dear boy and a very fine soldier.

**MACLEAN.**—Missing, Sept., 1943, now reported killed, FLYING OFFICER IAN MACLEAN, D.F.C., R.A.F.V.R., eldest son of the late Rt. Hon. Sir Donald Maclean, M.P., and of Lady Maclean, husband of Mary and father of Alastair. Dearly loved. No letters please.

**STURT.**—In March, 1944, killed in action in Italy, MAJOR PHILIP CHARLES NAPIER STURT, Royal Artillery, beloved second son of Mr. and Mrs. Geoffrey Sturt, of 10, Perceval Avenue, Hampstead, N.W.3, aged 29.

**TYNDALE.**—In March, 1944, killed in action in Italy, WILLIAM BARNARD TYNDALE, only son of Mr. and Mrs. Geoffrey Tyndale, 76, Kensington Church Street, London, W.8.

**HELY-HUTCHINSON.**—In March, 1944, killed in action in Burma, PATRICK WALTER RICHARD HELY-HUTCHINSON, W/Sgt., R.A., son of Mr. and Mrs. John Hely-Hutchinson, Chippenham Lodge, Ely, Cambs.

**HIGGINS.**—In Feb., 1944, CAPTAIN PETER HIGGINS, R.E., M.A., killed in action in Burma, second son of Sidney and the late Margaret Mabel Higgins, of Crumpsall and Knutsford.

**HODDER.**—Now officially presumed killed over Germany, Sept., 1943, GROUP CAPTAIN FRANK HODDER, aged 37, most beloved husband of "Twinkle," and beloved father of Michael and Christopher, Ash Cottage, Brockenhurst, Hants.
  "Greater love hath no man than this."

**RODDY.**—In March, 1944, on active service, overseas, LIEUT.-COLONEL FRANCIS AUGUSTUS RODDY, R.A.M.C., 32, Fauconberg Road, Chiswick; husband of Mary Roddy, and eldest son of the late Michael and Mrs. Ellen Roddy, Leinster Road, Dublin. R.I.P.—Mary Roddy, Knock House, Knock, Belfast.

**SMITH.**—In March, 1944, in action in Italy, BRIGADIER IVAN VICTOR RUSSELL SMITH, Royal Artillery, beloved son of the late Dr. K. R. Smith and Mrs. Smith, of Sutton, and deeply-loved husband of Wendy.

## MISSING

**GANDAR DOWER.**—Reported missing, believed drowned, Feb., 1944, KENNETH CECIL GANDAR DOWER.

**PHIPPS.**—LIEUTENANT ALAN, R.N.—Missing on Leros, Nov. 16, 1943. Any information gratefully received by his wife, the Hon. Mrs. A. Phipps, Clunes Mains, Kirkhill, Inverness-shire.

## ON ACTIVE SERVICE

**BROOKE.**—On March 4, 1944, following an accident whilst on duty, BASIL MALISE BROOKE, Lt., 11th Hussars (P.A.O.), aged 22, adored husband of Bunty (née Bateson) and dearly loved only child of Rear-Admiral Sir Basil Brooke and Lady Brooke, 3, Oxford Square, W.2. Memorial service to be held at King's Chapel of the Savoy, 11.30, Friday, March 10.

**BUSSELL.**—In Feb., 1944, killed in action in Italy, ROBERT ANDRÉ BUSSELL, Lieut., R.T.R., second son of Mr. and Mrs. Raymond Bussell, "Little Copse," Langley Vale, Epsom. "He died that we might live."

**CORDNER.**—On March 2, 1944, died whilst serving with Air Transport Auxiliary, J. HERALD CORDNER (U.S.A.), Flight Captain, beloved husband of Mrs. J. M. Cordner, of 544, East Washington, Pasadena, California.

**CRISPIN.**—In Feb., 1944, missing, presumed killed, LIEUTENANT HUGH TREVOR CRISPIN, Royal Navy, dearly loved only son of Captain G. Crispin, Royal Navy, and Mrs. Crispin, Combe Ridge, Chiddingfold, Surrey.

**DAVEY.**—In Jan., 1944, killed in action, JOHN BRETT DAVEY, Lieut., The (22nd) Cheshire Regt., only son of Lt.-Col. and Mrs. C. W. B. Davey, of The Old Parsonage, Broughton, near Chester, aged 25.

**HARRINGTON.**—On March 2, 1944, killed on ferrying duties in England, JANICE MARGARET HARRINGTON, Flight Engineer, Air Transport Auxiliary, beloved daughter of Mr. and Mrs. A. G. Harrington, of "The Orchard," Putnoe Lane, Bedford.

**HEALD.**—In Feb., 1944, killed in action in Italy, CAPTAIN STANLEY ALASTAIR HEALD, Royal Artillery, late H.A.C. (11th Regt., R.H.A.), beloved eldest son of Mr. and Mrs. Stanley Heald, British Guiana, and dear brother of Barbara, Peggy, and Teddy, aged 28 years.
  Quo fas et gloria ducunt.

**HILL.**—In Feb., 1944, NORMAN GRAY HILL, M.C., Lt.-Col., R.A.M.C., 2nd Baronet of Stockbridge, only son of the late Norman and Mary Hill, of Green Place, Stockbridge, Hampshire, in his 50th year.

**LANG.**—On March 2, 1944, whilst ferrying his Majesty's aircraft in England, DORA LANG, First Officer, Air Transport Auxiliary, beloved wife of H. A. Lang, of 57, Sidney Street, London, S.W.3.

**LECKIE.**—Killed in action, in Feb., 1944, JAMES LECKIE, B.A.Cantab (Fettes and Emmanuel), Lieutenant, The Gordon Highlanders, elder son of Mr. and Mrs. Leckie, Craggan House, Callander, aged 27.

**LOEWI.**—On March 4, 1944, passed peacefully away, FLIGHT LIEUTENANT GEORGE F. LOEWI, R.A.F.V.R., son of the late Paul R. Loewi, and of Mrs. Loewi, Highwood, Gerrards Cross, aged 32. Cremation Golders Green, to-day (Tuesday) at 1.30 p.m. No flowers, please.

**MAGAWLY.**—In Feb., 1944, killed in action in Burma, MAJOR ERIC V. MAGAWLY, The Wiltshire Regiment, dearly beloved only son of Mr. and Mrs. W. J. H. Magawly, Portesham, Dorset, and dearly loved brother of Kathleen and Joy, aged 25.

**MILES.**—Officially reported missing, presumed killed, whilst on war service, ABLE SEAMAN GERALD VALENTINE MILES, R.N., only son of Charles V. Miles, prisoner of war in Singapore, and of the late Mrs. J. M. D. Miles (née Mustiston).

**MUNBY.**—In Feb., 1944, officially reported missing, now presumed killed, the REV. PETER MUNBY, Chaplain, R.N.V.R., Vicar of Wribbenhall, Bewdley, and husband of Ruth (née Provis).

**NORCOCK.**—In Feb., 1944, killed in action, MAJOR R. NORCOCK, O.B.E., Bedfordshire and Hertfordshire Regt., dear husband of Alison Freda (née Hulton), and elder son of Major and Mrs. H. Norcock, Haslemere, Surrey.

**URE.**—In Feb., 1944, killed in action, CAPTAIN ROBERT REID URE, R.A., dearly loved husband of Eleanor (née Smyth), of Bicton Heath, Shrewsbury, and only son of the late J. J. Ure and of Mrs. Ure, of Hampstead, aged 28. No letters, please.

**WALDEGRAVE.**—COMMANDER the HON. JOHN M. G. WALDEGRAVE, D.S.C., missing, presumed killed while on active service, the dearly loved husband of Lady Hersey Waldegrave, and only son of Lord Radstock and the late Hon. Mrs. Montagu Waldegrave.

**WOLLOCOMBE.**—On March 3, 1944, at a Royal Naval Hospital, COMMANDER HENRY BIDLAKE WOLLOCOMBE, R.N.

Once overseas, Germany's paper bullets pummeled American troops. Aiming to demoralize, scare, and persuade soldiers to surrender, Germany printed hundreds of unique leaflets in a campaign to undermine US resolve.

# 45ᵀᴴ Division News

October 14, 1943      NAPLES, Italy      Vol. IV, No 14

## Now Where Did I Put My Gun?

What to do when suddenly confronted by enemy soldiers may sound simple of solution, but its rather confusing when it actually occurs.

Take, for instance, the case of 2nd Lt. Max Wehren. He was only 100 yards from one of the infantry baittal on CPs, having just finished a study of a map with one of the officers, when he saw three soldiers aproaching him, carrying a light machine gun. Soldiers were rather numerous in that area, so he paid no particular attention to them.

When they got closer, however, he paid more attention. They also gave him a close look. The lieutenant noticed that the fatigue hat worn by one of the men wasn't like any he had ever seen, so he went into actiour, the Germans doing the same.

Wehren reached desperately for his automatic at his hip; couldn't find it, and reached again, this time circling his body in search of it About the time he realized he had it in a shoulder holster, the Germans got their gun set up.

Wehren killed one of them and captured another. The third escaped.

## Like Namesake The Dog's Crazy

They call him « Schickelgruber », that elongated pal of Cpl. David Werbin, New York City, and Pfc. Sanford Davidow, Patchogue, N. Y.

The dachhundt started tailing the engineer outfit as soon as they landed and has been with them ever since. His master claims he's GI, too, in every respect but one-his overwhelming preference for K-rations.

To Schickelgruber the world's greatest delicacy is veal and pork.

# Soviets Take M/C
# Gomel Suburbs

The Russians have entered the outskirts of Gomel, and the fighting for the city seems to be in its last stages.

Russian troops, tanks and war materiel are crossing the Dnieper every day in increasing number in an effort to enlarge their bridgeheads west of the river, while the Moscow Radio has announced that the Red forces have formed a wedge in the Germans' lines around Kiev. On the southern front, bitter fighting is in progress against Melitopol and Nevel.

*Here in Italy, the Allied Armies are strung out along the Volturno River. Patrols are being sent across in increasing numbers testing the German resistance. Supporting the ground troops, the air forces have been hammering away at German installations.*

*In New Guinea the Australians are still pushing forward, while isolated groups of Japs are being mopped up in the Finchhafen area.*

*Details of a naval attack last week on Wake Island were revealed. The raid was made by an aircraft carrier task force, dropping 320 tons of bombs and destroying 61 planes. We lost 13. This is the third attack on the island since the Japs occupied it.*

*In Denmark, Germans are looting Jewish homes of* *furniture which is being sent back to refurbish bombed out German homes. Following the outbreak of anti-Jewish measures in Denmark, Sweden offered haven to the Danish Jews. So far, Germany has not replied to the offer.*

*Delayed action bombs are still going off in Naples.*

*Prime Minister Churchill, in his Columbus Day address to the House of Commons, told the members that more than 100 Italian warships are now in Allied hands.*

*President Roosevelt sent a message to Congress requesting repeal of the Chinese Exclusion Act, and placing China's immigration quota on a par with other countries. The president explained, «Nations as well as individuals make mista-*

(Continued on Page 4).

---

In Italy, the Forty-Fifth Division's newspaper discovered that the Italian alphabet lacks the letters *w*, *y*, and *k*. To get by on the limited supply of these characters, typesetters swapped font sizes and styles, as seen in the articles in the left-hand column.

The chief librarian of the army, Col. Ray L. Trautman, was responsible for the distribution of nearly one billion domestic magazines to troops across all fronts. It was a sensational achievement that revolutionized the postwar magazine industry.

"Somewhere in North Africa," a private relaxes by reading a magazine in a tent called "Chaplain's Library." When short on time, soldiers favored magazines over books because they could finish a story before moving out.

When domestic magazines did not arrive on time, imitation proved to be the sincerest form of flattery. The Seventh Amphibious Force and USS *Iowa* each created their own GI version of *Time* magazine.

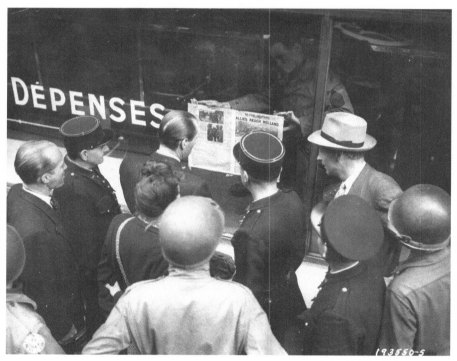

When the *Stars and Stripes* opened offices in Paris, news-starved US soldiers, French officers, gendarmes, and civilians flocked to the window to read objective updates about the war.

*"Radio th' ol' man we'll be late on account of a thousand-mile detour."*

Though Bill Mauldin was awarded a Pulitzer Prize in 1945 for his wartime cartoons, General George "Old Blood and Guts" Patton was not a fan of Mauldin's penchant for mocking military discipline. Here, Mauldin takes aim at Patton's rigid requirements for appearance in a combat zone.

## Merry Unrra Executives investigated

*Madrid.*

In consequence of complaints lodged by British military men the private lives of numerous members of the UNRRA in London are to be the object of an inquiry. One of the causes of complaint was the founding of a society of the «Friends of Vegetarianism» and of an «Anti-hunger Club», in which the members of the UNRRA led a life of perpetual gluttony. An inquiry will be made into how many of the members of the UNRRA can be dispensed with who have received high salaries without having any work to do. These are to be sent back to the U.S.A.

## It's time to fold up !

### The U.S. war aims have been reached

As even the American Government has admitted that the war aims propagandized at the beginning of this most murderous brain typhoon, called World War II, were not genuine, you have the right to ask WHY you are still in it. Stripped of all propaganda, the true reasons why America joined this war are:

1. Supremacy in the western hemisphere. That has been accomplished. Neither Britain, nor Germany, nor any other country can now interfere with the American political game in South America or Canada.

2. Increase of American exports. That also is now assured as America has built the largest commercial fleet in the world. She is now building in one year more ships than the whole British merchant navy amounted to before the war. These ships can carry American goods to the four corners of the world under the protection of the world's strongest navy.

3. Supremacy in the air traffic of the world. It has become a reality. America has built the largest air fleet. Her 2000 passenger and freight planes are quite sufficient to tackle the job of being the master of world air travel. The planes are there and more can be built easily to meet any requirements. The treasures of India and Africa, whether they are still British or not, are waiting to be shipped in American airplanes and ships as other nations have hardly any left.

4. German competition in the markets of the world is extinct. There will be no change even if the Germans survive this war. They will be busy for decades repairing their war destructions and their commercial interests definitely lie in the East of Europe.

The Americans thus have won everything that can be won in this war!

That is a fact. What remains are ideological reasons and they shouldn't count.

## German V-offensive against London

*Madrid, Jan. 24*

A member of the diplomatic corps who recently arrived in Spain after a stay of many years in England stated how relieved he was not to have to return to London any more. Since the middle of June he had experienced the German V-offensive. Then there had been a short pause, which people had foolishly thought was the end of the bombing. But during the last 80 days the enormous intensification of the bombing through the addition of the terrifying «V-2» had made life in London absolutely unbearable. He himself had come to the end of his physical and mental resistance. It was incomprehensible to him that there were still human beings left who could stand the life in London. For about 80 days hundreds of V-bombs had been falling on this biggest armament center in England. Alarm signals were no longer sounded. In those districts in which the coming bombs were expected to explode, red tracer bullets were fired off, whereupon everyone sought shelter as quickly as possible. With cynical humor people in (To be continued on page 2)

The *Home Telegram* has the appearance of a GI newspaper by and for American troops, but it was an elaborate attempt by Germany to create a propaganda leaflet that US soldiers would read and trust. The paper's main theme was to stop fighting.

# RAINBOW REVEILLE

VOLUME 3     WITH THE SEVENTH ARMY, GERMANY, THURSDAY, 19 APRIL 1945     NUMBER 21

## Rainbowers Salute Their Fallen Chief Among Schweinfurt's Ruins

Standing with bowed heads amidst the rubble of the city of Schweinfurt which they had captured only two days before, 1,000 Rainbow Infantrymen paid tribute on 13 April to the memory of Franklin Delano Roosevelt, their Commander in Chief. Facing the Division's 48 State flags, the men offered a silent one-minute prayer for their deceased commander.

## Doughs Root Out Nazi War Plant

When the Division's three regiments gave Schweinfurt the old one-two-three, they found a town battered to rubble, much of the famous ball-bearing factories destroyed—and underground factories still intact.

After the Air Force managed to smash large parts of the factories during the past two years, precious building materials were used to rebuild them, to put them underground. When the 42d took the town, it found concrete entrances to the underground factories with the wooden moulds still in place around them. The only trouble was, the Nazis had run out of concrete.

In the sprawling, silent

(Contd. on P. 3)

## Quick Work Picks Off Jerry Truck and Tank

While a Co F, 222d, LMG section was firing across the Main River into Wurzburg from a house above a church, section leader S-Sgt. George Merlock spotted a Kraut tank followed by a truck, pulling into the park across the river. After informing the TDs, his gunners opened up on the truck, hitting the driver. The truck stopped, and the TD 90 mm. got a direct hit on it.

Three minutes later the tank backed up, turned round to escape. "There she goes!" yelled Merlock. In the nick of time the TDs landed a direct hit on the tank. Firing at a distance of 900 yds the TDs and Merlock's men, Pfcs. J.C. Sales and Bill Walker, accounted for 18 dead krauts around the tank and truck.

## 222d Spearheads Wurzburg Assault

The Fighting 42d added one more city to its string of conquests in its smashing drive into Bavaria when the men of the 222d Inf Regiment swept across the Main River to spearhead the assault on the shell-wracked city of Wurzburg.

In anticipation of a bitter battle in its defense, the Germans had cut subterranean caverns and passageways connecting distant parts of the city to make possible surprise attacks

(Contd. on P. 8)

## Rainbowers Capture 1000 PWs A Day In Nine-Day Drive Along Main River

Two cities, Wurzburg and Schweinfurt, fell to the Rainbow in nine days' time, 9,278 prisoners poured into the Division's PW cages, and 18,000 forced laborers were liberated. To date, the Division has just about captured its weight in Supermen—14,263 in all.

### GI Gets Grim News From Freed Pole

Chatting with an 18-year-old Polish kid, Cpl. Bill Sak, Hq Btry, 542d, learned the boy was from the same town in Poland his father came from. He asked eagerly what the town was like.

"The Germans were there," said the Polish kid. "So now there isn't any town."

First to cross into Wurzburg was the 222d Infantry, the first elements of which crossed the Main in a rowboat before assault boats were brought up or a Bailey bridge span had replaced the blown-out center span of the South Bridge. Once over, the brunt of the fighting was borne by the 232d. The city was assaulted on 3 April, and on that and the following

(Contd. on P. 8)

The *Rainbow Reveille* followed the Forty-Second Rainbow Division from training in the United States through the liberation of the Dachau concentration camp and beyond. Troops chronicled their experiences and mailed the paper home to educate their families.

Civilian and GI war correspondents attend a secret press conference in France. Among the news organizations represented are the Associated Press, Reuters, *Yank*, the *New York Times*, the *Stars and Stripes*, BBC News, and the *London Daily Telegraph*.

A group of marines bide their time on a troop transport by turning out the *Pacific Press,* a daily newspaper. Their makeshift office was luxurious compared to printing conditions on land.

In the words of Andy Rooney, some members of the GI press "learned to fight and some learned to die." In the Pacific, an injured photographer continues his work after medics bandaged his head wound.

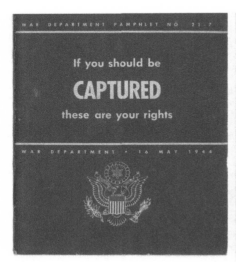

Germany pursued a relentless drive to outwit the US Army's efforts to combat Nazi propaganda. This included a leaflet that replicated a War Department booklet, with Germany's version promising that "If you should be CAPTURED you will be safe."

# TWO WAYS TO END THE MANEUVER

Men of the 84th --

After two days of back-pedaling and hill-chasing, you've gotten an idea of how this maneuver is going.

Your front is caving in on you. You've been flanked time and again.

You can go on climbing hills and digging valleys if you want to. You can have two more days of it.

Or you can end this maneuver right now. Cross the lines with this leaflet. You'll be taken to the rear to wait out the rest of the maneuver.

You've got two ways to spend the next two days. Spend them the easy way.

Some German propaganda leaflets were addressed to specific divisions and then scattered into Allied foxholes with unsettling accuracy. This leaflet for the Eighty-Fourth Division's Railsplitters was dropped directly on their position.

# THE Railsplitter

VOLUME 3     SOMEWHERE IN GERMANY, MAY 8, 1945     NUMBER 4

# VICTORY!

Americans threw confetti and telephone directories out the windows of New York's skyscrapers and Englishmen danced in London's ancient, bomb-pocked streets Monday night as the world was told that Nazi Germany had surrendered unconditionally and that Tuesday had been proclaimed Victory in Europe Day.

President Truman was to speak to the people of the United States and Prime Minister Churchill to the people of Britain Tuesday afternoon. While it had not been announced, it was expected that Marshal Stalin would address his countrymen at the same time. Tuesday night King George will speak to the people of the British Empire.

## All Enemy Action Ends in Div. Area

As the Railsplitters expanded their zone to more than 2000 square miles of German soil, all enemy action in the area had come to an end Monday.

With the Railsplitters and the Russians now neighbors across the Elbe, the 334th Infantry established a ferry service with the Russians and maintained liaison between unit commanders of the Red Army.

Lt. Col. Lloyd H. Gomes, whose 333rd Infantry increased its river boundary to 40,000 yards, was presented a horse by an officer of the 32nd Cossack (Smolenski) Division.

### Gets 350 PWs

In the meantime the 335th Infantry, continuing security missions in its area, corralled 350 more prisoners.

(continued on Page 8)

The historic surrender ending nearly six years of the bloodiest warfare the world has ever known was signed at 2:41 a. m. Monday, London reported, in the school house in Rheims, France, which is General Dwight D. Eisenhower's headquarters. Colonel General Joedl, new German chief of staff, signed the surrender instrument for the Germans and Lieutenant General Bedell Smith, General Eisenhower's chief of staff, for the Allies.

The Germans were asked if they realized the seriousness of what was taking place and they said they did.

General Eisenhower was not present for the signing, but appeared at his headquarters a short time later.

No official announcement was forthcoming, other than that Tuesday would be Victory in Europe Day, but the Czech patriot radio in Prague said that what actually happened was that a truce had been declared and that the surrender would become effective at midnight Wednesday.

### Struggle in Prague

All hostilities had ceased throughout battered Europe, save possibly for the struggle between the German garrison in Prague and the city's patriots. The situation there was confused. The Ger-

man-controlled station in Prague said Monday that the Germans would fight in Bohemia and Moravia until "troops in the East were saved" and a way was cleared for the troops in Prague to return to the Reich. Later there was a report that the Germans had been ordered by their commander to cease fire except in defense.

In any event, troops of Lt. Gen. George S. Patton's Third Army were nearing the Czech capital and there was little likelihood that German resistance, if such exists, would last very long.

(continued on Page 8)

## 2,000,000 to be Discharged; 15th Army Stays in Europe

Here's the dope you've been waiting for. —

The army plans to discharge 2,000,000 men beginning with the fall of Germany and intends to send 6,000,000 picked troops against Japan.

The men to be discharged will be those with the most dependents and the longest and most active records of service.

Of the approximately 8,300,000 men now in the army, between 300,000 and 400,000, comprising the Fifteenth U. S. Army, will be left abroad to occupy Germany and 2,000,000 others will be separated from the service within one year of V-Day in Europe with the speed of mustering out depending on the availability of shipping.

The Air Transport Command said it is will be ready to move 50,000 men a month within two months of the victory, but the army emphasized that these plans were tentative.

## Krauts Not So Cocky When They're Behind Rake or Broom

Not quite as cocky when they're behind a rake or a broom as they once were behind a panzerfaust or burp-gun, is the reaction of most doughs privileged to see the 600 some-odd Kraut prisoners on work details at the camp of the Second Battalion, 334th Infantry.

Prize prisoner is a short slight self-reported school teacher who tried to skip into France in a French PW's uniform. He was nabbed by a suspicious French NCO and turned over to MPs. This demagogue alleged his plan was to present a program to be called "New Germany". A little questioning revealed that his plan was strangely similar to that first presented by his Nazi overlords.

"Provost Marshal" of the stockade is 1/Lt Bruce Hutton of Freeport, Ill. He is assisted by an interpreter, T/Sgt Joe Green, Astoria, L. I.; T/Sgt. Ray Washmiera, San Francisco, Calif.; T/Sgt. Joe Childers, JoNancy, Ky., and Pfc. Arthur Mahler, New York City. All men are members of Headquarters Company, Second Battalion, 334th.

To combat Germany's "war of words," the Eighty-Fourth Division resumed printing its newspaper, the *Railsplitter*, after the Battle of the Bulge. The May 8, 1945, edition was the one the division had long been waiting for—"Victory!"

A young photographer stands amid the wreckage of a Pacific battle. Some of the most important images and stories of the war emerged because of the bravery and fortitude of the GI press.

Though more than 4,600 individual newspapers were created by troops in World War II, there were never enough copies to go around. Sharing was ubiquitous.

Milton Caniff's cartoon character Miss Lace was one of the most popular of the war. To dignify the strip's deactivation, Caniff created this special panel with Miss Lace standing on the shore of the United States, welcoming a soldier home.

# CHAPTER TEN
## NOW—WHERE WERE WE?

*"A 92nd Seabee's Yuletide Prayer"*

Please send us home, please!
It's not for myself I'm asking.
Who wants to go home to nothing but
beautiful women, plenty of whiskey,
and inner-spring mattresses?
Who wants to be awakened by a gentle nudge
instead of the blasts of a full-blooded bugle?
Who wants to leave this "healthful oceanic climate"
to go back to the States and taxes?

No, it's not for me I'm asking . . .
[T]hink of Homer Wheeler who wants to have another baby
and Ernie Ricou who wants to marry one . . .
Please . . . give Cy Plough and Sam Allen
a chance to earn an honest living again.
And give "Red" Lawrence a chance, period.
And if it's not asking too much please let
Fischer reach high "C" on his trumpet—
just once please!
And just one more thing,
please make me 42 years old.

—Kaplan, December 23, 1944

From the moment a military uniform hit their backs, many troops dreamed of the day when they would wear civilian clothing again. While in training camps, they prayed for furloughs and weekend passes, so they could escape the military, even if only for a few hours. Once overseas, "home" was a place they visited in their dreams, thoughts, and conversations. As months turned into years, troops never tired of making plans for their future lives back in the States. They imagined seeing their parents, getting married, buying homes, and securing lucrative jobs. Others were content fantasizing about simple pleasures, like having a roof over their heads when it rained, eating meals served on plates, and not sleeping on the ground. Home was a topic that never grew old.

Yet, when it finally came time to return home, troops were beset with a complex cocktail of emotions. As much as they complained about the army—and the litany of indignities and absurdities they were forced to tolerate—it had become part of them. They had gotten used to the war's rhythms and terrors; they forged indestructible bonds with the men with whom they had trudged into battle; they enjoyed late-night bull sessions with their buddies, especially if their beer ration had materialized for the occasion. As much as they had idealized home, when confronted with leaving the army, troops realized there was beauty and romance to their days at war. There were aspects of the army that they would miss.

Veterans of the Great War perfectly understood this phenomenon. Alexander Woollcott, who was a reporter for the *Stars and Stripes* in 1918 and 1919, candidly admitted how difficult it was for him to leave the war behind and become a civilian again. In France, he had spent most of his time at the front, where he witnessed how brotherhoods developed as troops shared hardships, triumphs, and all that went unspoken. As horrible as war was—scrunching his body into muddy foxholes, freezing in the cold, flinching at shell bursts, and cringing at the unimaginable chaos—Woollcott felt a sense of belonging he would never feel again. When he returned to New York after the war, he was consumed by "a sort of fog of the soul." He missed his friends "who slept in the adjoining bunks on the transport or stood in front of or behind me in the mess line." He had difficulty relating to those who had not gone to war and witnessed humanity in one of its most profound struggles. Friends of Woollcott joked that, while they were celebrating the Armistice, Woollcott was "in a corner, crying his eyes out."

Many American troops facing a trip home in 1945 related to Woollcott's feelings. As absurd as this would have seemed when they were inducted, troops facing demobilization craved a connection to the friends and memories they had made during the war. On the outside, they faced an outfit change, but on the inside, many troops would continue fighting for the friendships they wanted to keep, for the democracy that they treasured more than ever, for the peace they won, and for the buddies they had lost. Troop newspapers had helped them adjust to the army and chronicle their daredevilry overseas. Now, troops turned to their GI gazettes to guide them through their transition back to civilian life.

———

Most troops believed that victory would equate with a timely boarding pass for a ship headed to New York or San Francisco. In reality, tickets home were not doled out quickly. For those in Europe after V-E Day, the army announced it did not plan to discharge many men. In fact, on May 10, 1945, the War Department announced that of the 3.5 million American troops in Europe, 3.1 million would be redeployed to the Pacific. This news did not go over well. As the *Yankee Doodler* (an air service group's newspaper) put it, asking troops if they wanted to go home immediately or after a redeployment was "like asking a child if he wants an ice cream cone now, or after it melts!" Despite all the expletives directed at the army's redeployment plan, few troops ever made the trip to the Pacific. V-J Day came first. Yet August 1945 came and went, and still, most troops continued to wait for their trip home. It had taken years for the US military to ship millions of Americans to posts around the world, and it would take months to arrange passage for millions to return to the United States.

The waiting game provided many divisions an opportunity to prepare for their eventual departure and separation. One GI newspaper polled its readers, asking how their time in the army had been "benefi-cial to you as an individual." It received a range of answers. "My Army service has taught me a great deal more about humanity and coun-tries other than my own," an infantry platoon leader replied. A section chief in a chemical warfare unit appreciated "the chance to travel—an opportunity that I wouldn't have had otherwise." A dispatcher for a quartermaster company said that the "primary benefit is that I have re-ceived [a] sight-seeing tour of Europe." A rifleman said that "the Army has smartened me up in more ways than one, although I wouldn't want to go through it again." An infantryman had the least rosy response: "I haven't learned anything in the Army . . . it has been so much wasted time."

Regardless of how they felt about the military itself, many troops grew nostalgic for what they had achieved. Troops witnessed the lib-eration of concentration camps, endured the terror of combat, and felt the elation of civilian populations as their villages and countries became free of Nazi occupation. They experienced the heartfelt grat-itude of entire communities as troops freed European presses so that truthful stories could be printed, free of propaganda and indoctrination. And they gained a new awareness of the role independent newspapers played in a democracy. Troops had paid a price for the freedoms they were going home to, and they were loath to simply disperse into civil-ian society and return to "normal." They wanted to keep their stories alive and participate in the government that they had helped preserve. Many divisions used their final weeks and months to organize postwar groups. Just as they would transform from soldiers to civilians, many made plans to demobilize their wartime newspapers and convert them into home-front newsletters.

One typical example was the Eighty-Fourth Division's *Railsplitter*. It had carried the division from the heels of the Battle of the Bulge to V-E Day. While the civilians of Europe celebrated their freedom, the *Railsplitter* surveyed its readers to gauge whether they were interested in creating a club, so they could keep tabs on one another once they were civilians again. There was near unanimous support. "The spirit which has led the victorious Railsplitters through the pillboxes of the Siegfried Line, the snow banks of the Ardennes, and over the Roer, Rhine, and Weser should not be allowed to die," one Railsplitter said. "It should continue to act as an inspiration to everyone who has ever had any association with the division," he added. Over the summer and fall of 1945, everyone from low-ranking privates to the division's commander, General Bolling, registered to join the group and provided their civilian mailing addresses. Some battalions even published address booklets to ensure troops would be able to contact one another.

In December 1945, the *Railsplitter* printed an enormous headline: "DIVISION GOING HOME." They had waited so long for this news that some troops refused to believe it was true. "By the time we get back they will have . . . rocket ships," one man had joked. As exciting as this news was, it also created tremendous anxiety. To mollify the uneasiness many men felt, the *Railsplitter* did what it had always done: it attempted to give soldiers the big picture. "Here's A Play By Play On That Trip Home," a lengthy article promised. It explained the litany of inspections, baggage checks, and forms that needed to be completed. It detailed when live ammunition had to be surrendered and what gear to pack in one's duffel bag. From M-Day (Moving Day), when troops would leave their assembly area in Weinheim, Germany, and travel to the port of embarkation, to the boarding of an American liner for home, the *Railsplitter* provided a road map through the entire process.

As the division began to move out of Weinheim, a final European edition of the *Railsplitter* was printed. The infantrymen dedicated the issue to Major General Bolling. Like George Marshall, Bolling had always concerned himself with the morale of his men, and the infantrymen of the Eighty-Fourth Division wanted to express their gratitude. "Many qualities make for greatness—the quality that made General Bolling great in the eyes of all Railsplitters was his warm understanding and sympathy for the men who fought under him," the paper explained. "His thoughtfulness was manifested in many ways," including his display of confidence in his men by allowing them to publish the *Railsplitter*, even during the division's darkest days.

In late December 1945, the Railsplitters set sail from Le Havre. Just before their ship reached home, a final wartime *Railsplitter* was published. This time, Major General Bolling wrote an emotional farewell to his men as they were poised to leave his command. "I cannot help but feel that it will take much more than a mere paper transaction of inactivation to disperse the spirit of the 84th Infantry Division," he said. "You have been fine soldiers, great soldiers, and it has been my good fortune to have served with you. I am, as I am sure you are, proud to be a Railsplitter," Bolling said. The feeling was mutual. Bolling's men left the army proud, card-carrying members of the Railsplitter Society.

Months after they were issued honorable discharges, hundreds of veterans of the Eighty-Fourth descended on Cincinnati, Ohio, for their first annual convention. Greeting each man was their first postwar *Railsplitter*. Just as the army would have liked, it "oriented" veterans by giving them the schedule for the convention's activities. Inside, the paper had barely changed. There were war stories, poems, gripes, and a cartoon. It was a perfect tribute.

―――――

Many other divisions and smaller units went through a similar process as the Eighty-Fourth Division. The vast majority of troop newspapers across all services offered moral support to readers as they transitioned from combat troops to occupation forces, and from homebound veterans to civilians. Most did so with a dose of humor.

One popular send-off published on a liberty ship mocked the War Department's plethora of orientation guidebooks by printing its own. "A Soldier's Guide to the United States of America" promised to help soldiers acclimate to their next mission. "In view of the fact that some soldiers now overseas have been obligated to accept an assignment to the United States, we are publishing this short, practical guide to that foreign country," it began. This guidebook informed readers that the Mississippi River bisected the nation, and "everything east of the river is known as New York, while everything West is simply called Texas."

As for culinary customs, it stated that "food is generally plentiful, but in some localities, powdered eggs are almost impossible to obtain. You will probably be obliged to eat the old-fashioned shell-covered kind on most occasions. Remember: DO NOT EAT THE SHELL." It cautioned readers that a delicacy at many restaurants was "steak," which "doesn't measure up to the delicious delectability of our own 'SPAM.'" It warned that staying hydrated could be a challenge. "Water comes out of a fixture called a faucet, and is barely chlorinated. Remember, it is wise to carry a small packet of chlorine with you. To make sure of the safety of drinking water, place it in a lister bag before using," the guidebook counseled. As for language and politics, the main dialect was said to be "Brooklynese" and the "country is run by Democrats, Republicans, and Frank Sinatra." The guidebook's final words of advice were, "Keep on your toes, and you will get along okay."

While humor helped disguise anxiety, there was no easy way to ameliorate the heavier feelings that emerged as troops prepared to scamper up a gangplank and leave the quieted battlefields behind. For many, one of the hardest parts of boarding a transport was the realization that they, who had survived the war, were now going to be thousands of miles away from their buddies who had not. During the war, there was an unspoken understanding that a wounded or dying man did not want to be left alone. With an ocean separating them, it would be difficult to visit a buddy's grave and keep him company from time to time. Many troops felt the need to whisper final words—just one more time—and try to make sense of what had been gained through the loss of so many young lives.

To unload their grief and survivor's guilt, troops took up their pens and wrote touching tributes to the fallen and heartfelt promises to continue the fight for a better world at home. The most appropriate place to share these words was in the hallowed pages of the newspapers written by and for soldiers. One rousing poem, "To the Unknown," beautifully captured the feelings of many homebound troops:

> We salute you dear buddies who gave so much,
> As we weigh your valor, your deeds and such.

We wonder what your thoughts were when you made that
    charge
As you landed in Africa after leaving the barge.
Were you thinking of the wife and the kiddies behind,
Or your girl and your mother with plans so fine.
Were you thinking of the flivver with a worn out tire,
Or the way your girl looked, just sitting by the fire.
Were you wondering very much of what lay beyond,
The life you know of which you were so fond.
Did it trouble you much to think it might end,
So abruptly and sharp with pain no end.

We salute you dear buddies, who are still lying there,
As our armies moved forward no time for prayer.
All across Africa and Sicily too,
You were left there silently, but your job was through.
The fears you faced drove your thoughts away,
From the home you left some yesterday.
No room for thoughts of the future to come,
For there was death in the air as you heard its hum.
You staggered on forward doing your best,
With a saddened heart and blood on your chest.
Did it trouble you much to think it might end,
So abruptly and sharp with pain no end.

We salute you dear buddies who gave so much,
For the future of America, as well as the Dutch.
Some day, God grant us the chance to explain,
How you died in victory, and not in vain.
But if we fail in our duties where you gave your best,
When the peace we're planning is given the test.
And we find our dreams and hopes not reached,
We'll think of that promise we have breached.
We'll hang our heads in sorrow and shame,

We'll wonder then if it is the same.
Will it trouble us much to think it might end,
So abruptly and sharp with pain no end.

―――――

"Your mess kit days are almost over," the *Alhamabra Echo* declared as this victory ship approached New York Harbor in July 1946. Once they disembarked, troops would scatter in all directions. Wherever a soldier had been inducted was where he would be officially discharged. From the ports of debarkation, each soldier received a train ticket and the address of a separation center where he would face army processing for the final time. After a medical examination and exit interview, troops received their mustering-out pay, an explanation of their rights and benefits under the GI Bill, and counseling. They stumbled out of these centers as civilians.

The end of the war marked the end of many military careers, from privates to generals. Among those who left was George Marshall, who retired as the army's chief of staff in late 1945 only to be appointed US ambassador to China before the year ended. Never one to claim the limelight or clamor for recognition, the bulk of Marshall's unique ideas on building soldier morale received little publicity and praise. As troops were demobilized and their troop newspapers ceased publication, the tradition of granting GIs the freedom to print their own newspapers again fell into obscurity.

Never again would the US Army attempt a newspaper program like George Marshall's. Although some troops undertook the effort to continue printing their trusted division or unit newspapers in peacetime as a way to keep connected and plan social events, most did not. Occupation troops carried the torch, printing newspapers through the late 1940s. However, they no longer enjoyed the protection of Marshall and his protégés. In April 1946, the War Department adopted new regulations on army newspapers that sanitized content. "Army newspapers . . . must avoid publication of anything violating good taste," and the "value

and effectiveness of an Army newspaper depend on the maturity, professional experience, good judgment, and capabilities of the editor and his
staff," they provided. Some of the most popular features of World War II
troop newspapers would likely fall outside the War Department's ideas
of what was in "good taste" and "good judgment," like Bill Mauldin's
critical cartoons, Scott Corbett's comedic descriptions of his un-army-
like propensities, and practically every pinup ever printed. While George
Marshall was willing to grant troops the freedom to print the material
their readers wanted, the army's pendulum began to swing in the other
direction once new leadership was at the helm.

Not only did the War Department adopt regulations that would stifle
the content of troop newspapers, but with over 90 percent of the army's
soldiers facing demobilization, it also determined that large-scale troop
periodicals were no longer needed for morale. With the exception of the
*Stars and Stripes*, the army-wide periodicals that Marshall had champi-
oned were disbanded. At the end of 1945, the last issue of *Outfit* was
distributed to military hospitals, and GI editors were informed that their
monthly trade magazine on army publishing, *GI Galley*, would cease
publication. *Yank, the Army Weekly* also folded, albeit ceremoniously.
To break the news to readers, *Yank*'s final issue featured a front-page
certificate of honorable discharge made out to *Yank*, thanking it for its
"Honest and Faithful Service to this country." The certificate was signed
by the army's new chief of staff, Dwight Eisenhower. Though it was a
dignified end, readers still lamented the discontinuance of their favorite
wartime magazine. As one soldier wrote to the editor, "You probably will
never fully know how much *Yank* has meant to millions of soldiers . . .
I, for one of many, am truly sorry to see you demobilized, yet equally
glad that you can be." It would never again be printed as an army-wide
periodical.

The last Marshall-era holdout was the Camp Newspaper Service *Clip
Sheet*. Almost every military newspaper, no matter how big or small,
relied on the *Clip Sheet*'s cartoons to keep their readers happy. But in
February 1946, military newspapers received their last *Male Call* cartoon. Editors, journalists, and readers grieved this loss. "You lightened

many a dark and forlorn hour for all of us by the adventures of Miss Lace, and those who know her will join me in mourning the passing of *Male Call*," one man wrote to Caniff.

Because Lace was such a cherished part of their military service, Caniff honored the end of her tenure by creating a special, single-panel cartoon that hundreds of troop newspapers saved for their final issues. Lace had always been a reminder of civilian life, and Caniff wanted her to welcome troops home. The cartoon depicts Lace standing on the shore of the United States. She is wearing her usual formfitting evening gown, her arms outstretched toward a soldier returning from overseas. Still dressed in a uniform and combat boots, the grinning GI takes his first step onto American soil and says to Lace, "Now—where were we?"

# AFTERWORD

War is a stupid thing. We cannot afford another in our lifetime, or in the lifetime of our children. It's a waste of life, of wealth, and of time and anything that can bring us to another war must be avoided like the plague . . .

The price of peace is eternal vigilance, [and] we must be well informed, and keep informed as to what's going on at home and in the world . . . In the time to come . . . let's pledge to do our part, to keep informed, and to keep the best country in the world out of another war.

—*Sea Devil Sentinel*, "Farewell Edition"

Traditionalists might say that the currency of war is bullets, mortars, and bombs—the weaponry that forces one side of a conflict into submission. But the troops of World War II learned through experience that ideologies cause war, and conventional arms do not defeat ideas. Battlefield victories alone would not bring lasting peace and harmony. To end the war, the dogmas that drove the world to the brink needed to be fully extinguished. Ideas could only be fought with words.

As troops witnessed the Nazis' repressions across Europe and how enemy propaganda weaponized language to intentionally misinform and confuse, they realized that one of the most meaningful ways to fight was to practice their freedom of expression. In hate's stead, they needed to build understanding. To blunt the effects of propaganda and indoctrination, they needed to present the honest facts. Newspapers offered a space to achieve these objectives. And so troops printed GI gazettes despite the endless complications and impracticalities of doing so. In their newspapers, troops dismantled hate, explored the causes of the hostilities, exposed the imperfections of their democracy, and recorded their experiences. In the process, they saw how publishing free words was the most powerful counterattack they could unleash.

When the Nazis enacted the 1933 Editorial Control Law and began to taint Germany's newspapers with daily propaganda, the United States was embedded in a deep fog of isolationism. Most Americans justified their indifference by convincing themselves that Europe was too far away to matter. It was not. Today, the world has grown smaller through globalization and technology, and threats to democracy can arise from any quarter. But if there is a lesson to be learned from World War II, it is that democracy's best defense is an informed citizenry. It is up to all Americans to seek facts, understand and listen to different points of view, and engage in dialogue with one another. That is what *Yank, the Army Weekly* and the *Stars and Stripes* so deftly achieved through their editorial pages. These publications published a range of perspectives, and troops read and pondered the opinions of their fellow fighters. In these pages, troops disagreed, refuted one another, raised counterpoints to arguments previously aired, criticized the military, cursed, fumed, and *listened*. While the Axis bred intolerance, quashed dissent, and relied on communal ignorance to hide abuses and inconvenient truths, the Allies defended themselves by doing the opposite. And it was not just the American armed forces that paved the way for peace by publishing free words. As Allied troops encountered civilian populations across Europe that had been subjected to Nazi-controlled presses for years, efforts were made to refurbish publishing equipment sabotaged by the Nazis, reopen printing facilities, and restore power so that these newly liberated populations could practice freedom too. Factual information and the freedom to express differing opinions were not taken for granted.

Unsurprisingly, troops who subsisted on a diet of periodicals during the war returned home with a hankering for news. The greatest rise in magazine circulation rates in publishing history occurred after World War II. *Time* magazine, which was provided to troops between 1943 and 1946, reported a 154 percent spike in subscriptions after the war. Between 1946 and 1949, the number of magazine titles with a circulation of at least one million copies per issue surged from thirty-one to forty-four, and these rates would continue to climb through the 1950s. Meanwhile, newspaper circulation rates also soared, from forty million issues per day in 1940 to over fifty-two million in 1949. Considering that the United States had a population of approximately ninety-eight million adults in 1949, and most households consisted of at least two adults, these numbers show that the entire country was reading newspapers and magazines. If the price of peace was information, these periodicals were worth every penny.

Although the end of the war marked the dissolution of most troop newspapers, civilian publications met the growing demand for news by hiring experienced journalists who had learned the trade in jungles, deserts, trenches, and caves. Of the tens of thousands of troops who contributed to military newspapers, many earned graduate degrees in English or journalism under the GI Bill and made civilian careers of reporting the news and delivering laughs. Among those who became a household name was the *Stars and Stripes'* Andy Rooney, who transferred his skills as a columnist into a flourishing television career as a broadcast journalist. As the longtime host of *60 Minutes*, Rooney was a trusted news source for generations of Americans. He also wrote over a dozen books, some about newspapering at war. Bill Mauldin returned home with a Pulitzer Prize for his cartoons. Well into the 1990s, he continued to make drawings with witty punch lines that took aim at issues plaguing the world. Mauldin believed his job was to be a "stirrer-upper," and he never lost sight of how the mightiest weapon he ever wielded was his drawing pencil. Some veterans left journalism but continued to make their mark by publishing. Scott Corbett, the beloved humorist of the *Rainbow Reveille*, became a novelist after the war, writing eighty-one books, one of which was made into the movie *Love Nest*, featuring Marilyn Monroe. These soldiers, along with thousands of others, dedicated their lives to spreading information and honoring the written word.

———

Today, technology has fueled the spread of ideas and information, with some sources presenting noxious falsehoods under the cover of "news" and others attempting to provide the objective truth. At times, it can be difficult to delineate facts from viewpoint-driven fictions. Further complicating matters is the cacophony created by the plethora of media platforms and the range of voices screaming to be heard. This does not lessen or excuse the duty to perform the work required to maintain a democracy. It is up to the public to inform themselves by turning to a variety of sources and reaching outside of their ideological comfort zone. Democracy challenges its participants to grapple with competing ideas, engage in respectful dialogue, listen to the perspectives of others, and amend personal viewpoints as new information and ideas are learned.

Staying informed requires effort. But so did lugging eighty pounds of equipment and a typewriter into a war zone, carving gummy mimeograph stencils with a straightened paper clip while mixing ink out of insect repellent and shoe polish, stubbornly hand-cranking newspapers on a mechanical press well after arms had gone numb, and trying to distribute papers to readers pinned down in foxholes or perched somewhere in a craggy mountain where little else reached them. World War II shows us that information and truth mattered. They still do. And they are worth whatever effort is necessary to seek them because they are the ingredients for democracy and peace.

# ACKNOWLEDGMENTS

It has taken several years to research and write this book, and I am extremely fortunate to have had an amazing team of people who have helped and supported me along the way. I'd like to especially thank my husband, Christopher Manning. It is not easy to juggle parenting, working, and writing, and I am grateful to be partnered with someone who is supportive of my projects and dreams. Always my first reader, I appreciate your willingness and bravery to provide critical feedback and help sharpen my writing. And to my daughter, Beatrice—I am thankful for your patience and wise words. I feel incredibly lucky to be your mom.

I owe special thanks to Professor Richard Hamm, who has mentored me for nearly two decades. As my thesis adviser in college, he taught me so much about researching history and finding stories. And today I continue to learn from him and am so grateful for his friendship. I sincerely appreciate his careful review of the manuscript and sage advice. I would also like to thank Judith Barlow, who refined my writing when I was a student in one of her outstanding college English courses and who generously edited this manuscript many years after those fateful days in the classroom.

Three of my very talented former students kindly read several drafts of the manuscript. Katya Dzyubenko, I am grateful for your sharp editing and astute comments; both were incredibly helpful to me. Anthony Geremonte, your zeal for history and poignant insights helped me tremendously, and I appreciate your wonderful suggestions. And Jade Weiner, your edits and ideas on how to best communicate the substance of the book were so thoughtful and invaluable. I am so grateful for the help you provided.

I have had the great privilege of working with two gifted researchers who have helped me find source material. I am deeply grateful for their help. Peggy Ann Brown deftly discovered essential records at the National Archives about the *Stars and Stripes* and *Yank*. Tal Nadan, an extraordinary librarian at the New York Public Library, has, once again, been an incredible help in tracking down material and suggesting related records and sources germane to my research. It is always a pleasure to visit the archives at the New York Public Library and have the opportunity to work with Tal. Thank you!

I would also like to thank the US Army Heritage and Education Center and the Ridgway Committee for their generous support in selecting this project for a 2016 General and Mrs. Matthew B. Ridgway Military History Research Grant. I am grateful for the time I was able to spend reviewing the extensive collection of material on troop newspapers and working with the center's exceptional staff members. I am also incredibly grateful for the FDR Presidential Library's generous 2016–2017 research grant. My days spent at the FDR Presidential Library enabled me to make connections between FDR and George Marshall's troop newspaper program and discover FDR's fondness for shipboard newspapers.

Throughout this entire process, I have been incredibly fortunate once again to work with E. J. McCarthy, my extraordinary literary agent. Words are entirely insufficient to describe how much I appreciate his encouragement, passion, and dedication. From the days when this book was merely an idea, to navigating the publishing process, E. J. has generously offered excellent suggestions and advice. It is a privilege to work with such a talented agent and friend. I hope we go through this process with many more books in the future.

Finally, I would like to thank my team at Blackstone Publishing. I am grateful for the vision and enthusiasm of Naomi Hynes, who believed in this book as soon as it crossed her desk. I am fortunate for the guidance of Vikki Warner, who has been instrumental in overseeing the manuscript's smooth journey to publication. I am so appreciative of the enthusiasm and expertise of Sarah Bonamino and Francie Crawford, who have spearheaded an outstanding publicity and marketing plan. I would like to thank Holly Rubino for her excellent edits and suggestions as we refined the manuscript. I am grateful for the sharp eyes and ideas of Caitlin Vander Meulen, who was a fantastic line editor. Caitlin was such a huge help in polishing the manuscript and was a joy to work with. And I appreciate the help and assistance of Josie Woodbridge and Megan Bixler in preparing this book for publication.

# APPENDIX OF TROOP NEWSPAPERS

## SELECTED LIST OF GI NEWSPAPERS

? You Name It ?

! The Busy Bee !

13th AFSCAP

27th Division News

29 Storries

32nd Division News

35th Seabreeze

42d Rainbow Infantry Division
World News

45th Division News

49er's Buzzin' Briefs

56th Engineer

59th Latrineogram

65th Pulse Beat

66th Maroon & White

70th Division Trailblazer

72nd and 74th Signal Specials

89th Square Knot

92nd Island X Press

104th Battalion Bulletin

106 Battalion Scuttlebutt

124th Calvary News

124th Infantry Alligator

323rd Observer

349th Propwash

385th At Ease

495th Muzzle Blast

615th Bakery Weekly

815th Times

A La Moad

AA Barrage

Advance Base Breezes

Aerie

Aero News

AFS Letters

Ahoy

Aiean

Ailerson

Ain's Pains

Air Base Beacon

Air Base News

Air Corpsman

Air Foil

Air Gram

Air Pulse

Air Scoop

Airbase Echoes

Airman

Alabam

Alahambra Echo

Alaska Service Record

Alert

Alexair

All American Paraglide

All Hands

Altus Word

Amarillo Jet Journal

Ambassador-Beam

America's Alertmen

Americal

American Traveler

Amphibian

Andrews Ambassador

Anti-Tank Weekly News

Apache Sentinel

API Digest

Arizona Contact

Armodier

Armored Castle

Army Flier

Armored Force News

Armored News

Army Amateur

Army News

Army Reporter

Army Times

Arsenal News

Artillery Cannoneer

Ascomo Daily News

Ashford News

Aspirin Tablet

At Ease

Atomic Blast

Atomic Flyer

Auburn Press

Avenger

Baedeker for Guinea

Bamboo Bulletin

Banana Peelings (Banana
    River, FL)

Bankstatement (Ft. Banks)

Barbarian

Barksdale Bark

Barksdale Field News Bulletin

Barmum Bugle

Barracks Bag

Barranacas Breeze

Base "K" I&E Banner

Basha Breeze

Bat

Bau Banner

Baxter Bugle

Bayonet

Bayou Blast

Beach Buster

Beach Times

Beachhead Bugle

Beachhead News

Beachmaster

Beacon

Beam

Bear Facts

Bee Lines

Bell Tech Bulletin

Belvoir Castle

Benning Herald

Berlin Sentinel

Bermuda Skyliner

Bi-Monthly Bitch

Big T

Big Time

Bilge Bunk

Black Hills Bomber

Black Panther

Blazzer

Block Buster

Blood and Fire

Blue Devil

Blue Twain

Bomb Bay

Bomb Bay Messenger

Bombs Away

Bombshell

Bombsight

Bonjour

Booster

Boot Hill Marauder

Border Airman

Borinquen Bomber

Boston Navy Yard News

Bowman Bomber

Bridgehead Sentinel

Brief

Brigadier

Broadcaster

Broadcaster News

Broadcaster: Recreation &
 Athletic News

Brookley-Bay Breeze

Brooks Field Observer

Buckley Armorer

Buffalo

Bugle

Bull Sheet

Bull's Eye

Bulldozer

Bullet

Bulletin

Bulletin Board

Bureau of Naval Personnel
 Training Bulletin

Cactus Review

Cadet News

Caduceus

Camp Adair Sentry

Camp Ames News

Camp Barkeley News

Camp Bowie Blade

Camp Butner News

Camp Caltsop Chronicle

Camp Carson Mountaineer

Camp Cedar News

Camp Chaffe

Camp Claiborne News

Camp Crier

Camp Crowder Message

Camp Dix News

Camp Edwards News

Camp Ellis News
Camp Haan Tracer
Camp Howze Howitzer
Camp Hulen Searchlight
Camp Lamoni News
Camp Lejeune Globe
Camp Lyre Seabee
Camp McCoy News
Camp Parks Log
Camp Pickett News
Camp Roberts Dispatch
Camp Roberts Trainer
Camp Rucker Reporter
Camp Skokie Valley Review
Camp Static
Camp Wallace Trainer
Camp Wolters Longhorn
Camp Woodson News
Cannon Report
Cannoneers Post
Cardinal
Caribbean Breeze
Caribbean Sentinel
Carolina Chameleon
Carrier
Casemate
Castle Horizon
Casual News
Casual Observer
Cat's Meow
CCC Supplement
Cebugle
Cecil Field Beam
Centinela Alerta

Chaplains' Bulletin
Chaplain's Herald
Chesapeake Bay Defender
Chevron
Chicago Schools' Skylines
Chin Strap
Chin Up
Christmas Rush
Chronicle
Citrus Flyer
Civilian Front
Clarion
Clark Field Prop Wash
Cloudbuster
Cochran Communique
College Marine
Combat Construction
Combateer
Command Courier
Commando News
Communicator
Communique
Contact
Control Tower
Cooke Clarion
Coral Cryer
Coral Sea Barnacle
Corrected Data
Courier
Covered Wagon
Craig Field Journal
Credibilis
Crossroads
Crow's Nest

Cru-Des-Pac News

Crusader

Culvert

Cycloner

Daily Beacon

Daily News

Daily Okinawan

Daily Pacifician

Daily Stetsonian

Daily View

Dale Mabry Observer

Daniel Field Notam

Deep Six

Demobilizer

Depot Informer

Depot Times

Desert Maneuver

Detonator

Devil's Digest

The Digest

Dispatch

Ditsa and Dotsa

Dix Cue-Em

Dixie Tab

Dodo

Dope Sheet

Double Deucer

Dragon's Tale

Drew Field Echoes

Dry Dock

Dry Run

Duck Board

Duration Daily

Eaglet

Eastern Provider

Echoes

Eglin Eagle

Eight Ball

Eighty-Third Spearhead

Engineerful

Ernst Enquirer

Evening News

Eve's Dropper

Exceptional Release

Extractor

Falcon

Farragut

Ferret

Ferrogram

Ferry Tales

Ferry Wheel

Field News

Fifth Corps News

Fighter Post

Fightin' 502d News

Fiji Times and Herald

Finney Findings

Fireball Express

First Armored Division Bulletin

First Call

Flame

Flaming Bomb

Flexigun

Flight

Flight Dispatcher

Flight Jacket

Flight Prelude

Flight Time

Floating Time

Flyer

Flying "V"

Flying Sioux

Flying Times

Fog Horn

Form One

Fort Bliss Cavalcade

Fort Bliss News

Fort Bragg Post

Fort Custer News

Fort Devens Digest

Fort Dix Post

Fort George Wright Wing Tips

Fort Hamilton Post

Fort Logan News and Views

Fort Mason Guard

Fort Meade Post

Fort Meade Scout

Fort Moultrie Defender

Fort Niagara Drum

Fort Niagara Newsletter

Fort Ord Panorama

Fort Riley Guidon

Fort Screven Echoes

Fort Sheridan Target

Fort Sheridan Tower

Fort Sill Army News

Fort Sill Guidon

Fort Sill Replacement Center
    Recorder

Forty-First News

Forward Observer

Foster Field Fighter

Fourth Cavalry Scout

Front Lines Daily 0900 News

FRTC Ledger

Ft. Snelling Bulletin

Ft. Wood News

Ft. Wood Sentinel

FUBAR

Gangplank Gazette

Gator

George Field News

GI

GI Galley

GI Gazette

GI Rag

Golden Arrow

Golden Gate Guardian

Golden Gator

Goodhue Invader

Gooney Tales

Gosport

Gowen Beacon

Grapeleaf

Grapevine 26th Infantry
    Division

Great Bender

Great Lakes Bulletin

Green Riverite

Gremlin

Gremlin Gazette

Grenier Field Beacon

Griffin

Grooper

Guinea Gold

Guinea Pig

Gulfport Field Post

Gunter Aero-Gram

Halyard

Hampton Roads Defender

Hangar Dust

Harbor Defense Digest

Harpoon

Hasette

Heaving Line

Hell on Wheels

Hellcat News

Hendricks-Herald

High Score

Hi! Sailor!

Hickham Highlights

High Score

Hi-Life

Hi-Lite

Hoist

Holabird Exhaust

Home Crier

Home Run

Homeward

Home-Wrecker

Horned Toad

Hornet Tales

Hospital Gauzette

Hour Glass of the 7th Division
    of the U.S. Army

Hub

In the Wind

Intransit

Invasion Bulletin

Iroquois

Island Breeze

Islander

Ivy Leaf

Iwo Jima Inquirer

Jeep

Journal

Jumper Journal

Jungle Echo

Jungle Jingle

Jungle Journal

Jungle Mudder

Jungle-Cat

Kay-Det

Kearns Post Review

Kee Kee Krier

Keep 'Em Flying

Keesler Field News

Kenny Letter

Key Outpost

Khaki Commentator

Kodiak Bear

Kodiak Cub

La Llave

Ladd Field Midnight Sun

Latitude Nine

Latrineogram

Lawson News

L'Chaim

Le Tomahawk

Leatherneck

Lejeune Moon

Leo is Waiting . . .

Leonitic

Lightning

Lightning Bug

Lightning Strikes Twice

Lincoln Aire

Lincoln Log

Litter Bearer

Lock Guard

Log

Loggin Times

Long Island Sound Defenses
    Digest

Longhorn

Look Out

Lukomunique

M. C. D. Bulletin

Mac Dill Fly Leaf

Maintenance Engineer

Malden-Breeze

Manila Chronicle

Man-O'-War

Marine Adder

Masthead

Mather Field Wingtips

Maxey-Times

McClellan Cycle

Meade Post

Medical Soldier

Medicos

Memflite

Message

Message Center

Miami Beach Daily Tropics

Miami Herald Service Parade

Midpacifican

Mississippi Dragon

Mitchel Beacon

Mock Up

Moffett News

Moore News

Mopwringer

Morale Bulletin

Morale Minutes

Morriscode

MP Blotter

Muzzle Blast

Name?

Narragansett Bay Defender

Nav-Static

Navy News

New Hebrides Buzzer

New Okinawan

New York Navy Yard Shipworker

Newport Recruit

News

News Bulletin

News of Germany

Nichol News

Ninety-Third Blue Helmet

NOB News

Now Hear This

NSD Bulletin

NSD Echo Throughout Okinawa

NYPE News

Oflag 64 Item

Okie City Times

Onaway

On the Way

One Hundred and Two Capers

One Hundred Sixth Calvary
News

Open Post

Ordnance Observer

Oregonian

Orlando Air Base Wing Tips

Otter News

Our War Army Service Force
Outfit

Overall Picture

Overs and Shorts

Overseas Woman

Pabloid

Pacific Citizen

Palisades

Panama Coast Artillery News

Panel

Paraiso-News

Parris Island Boot

Patient's Progress

Patterson Field Postings

Peary Scope

Peep Sight

Pelican

Pennant Parade

Photo Blub

Pilot

Pilot Reporter

Pine Bur

Plane Talk

Poler Tech

Police-Up Gazette

Pontoon Patter

Porpoise

Post

Post Marquise

Post Script

Post Star

Postscript of the Apache Sentinel

Powder Keg

Prairie Flyer

Preflight

Presque Isle Army Airfield News

Processor

Prop Wash

Proppaganda

Puck

QM Quipster

Radio News

Radio Post

Railsplitter

Rainbow Reveille

Ramp-Age

Range Finder

Rattler

Receiving Station Bulletin

Reception Center

Reception Center News

Reception News

Red Triangle

Redlander

Report

Retort

Reville

Rev-Meter

Ricochet

Rip-Chord

Rising Sun Review

Robins Call

Robius-Field News

Rock-n-Roll

Rohwer Outpost

Rotate Review

Roundup

Ruff Draft

Runway

Saber and Key

Sacramento Air Depot Priority

Sagebrush Rattler

Saipan Beacon

Saipan Daily Target

Salty Breezes

Salute

Salvo

Sand Point Static

Sandfly

Sandpounder

Sandy Hook Foghorn

Santa Fe Express

SBAD News

Scars and Gripes

School Daze

Scott Field Broadcaster

Screamer

Scuttle Butt Poop

Scuttlebutt

Sea Breeze

Sea Devil Sentinel

Sea V Ten

Seabee News Service

Seabees Coverall

Seagull

Seaweed

Seaweed Gazette

Selectee

Selective Service

Selfridge Field News

Semper Primus

Sentinel

Service Salute

Service Section

Service Woman

Seven Hundred Sixteenth
    M. P. Blotter

Seven Hundred Thirty Ninth
    M. P. Review

Seventeenth Reporter

Seventh Regiment Field Gazette

Seventh Zone Constructor

SHAEF

Shaw Field Flight Line

Shemya News Sentinel

Sheppard Field Texacts

Sheridan

Shield

Ship Craft News

Ship's News

Shoot 'Em Down

Shot In Shell

Sight Seer

Signal Corps

Signal Corps Message

Signal Specials

Singla

Sioux Sentinel

Skeeeter

Skunk Hollow News

Skyscrapers

Skylighter

Skywatch

Skywriter

Slip-Stream

SNAFU

Snarkyville Gazette

The Sniper

Sno Job

Snort'n Morton

Snowball

Sortie

Sorryburg Gazette

Sound Off

Soundings

South Pacific Daily News

South Wind

Spearhead

Special Service

Spectator

Spindrift

Spirit of '76

Sponge City Splash

Spotlight

Squadron Six Gizmo

Star Garter

Stars and Stripes

Steward Field Prop

Stinger

Stoneman Salvo

Straight Dope

Sub Base Gazette

Sunday Mud & Mildew

Sunrise Press

Super-Fort

SWPA Maptalk

Tailspin

Tailspin Topics

Tailspinner

Take Off

Tale Spinner

Talewind

Tally

TARFU

Target

Targetur Towline

Tarheel

Tent City Transcript

Tex-Press

Third Division Front Line

Third Division News

Thirty-Sixth Letter

This Is It!

Three Hundred and Fiftieth
   Fighter

Three O Forum

Three Sheets to the Wind

Thunderbird

Thunderbolt

Thunderhead

Ticonderoga Times

Tilton Talk

Time Table News Features

Time Zero

Times

To Keep Em Flying

Tomah Interceptor

Tomorrow

Topo Rag

Tough Sheet

Trainee Tribute

Trinidad News Tips

Troop Courier

Tropic News Lightning

Tropic Times

Tropic Topics

Tropical Daze

Truck Tracks

TTF

Turret

Turret Observer

Twelfth Weathers Poop Sheet

Tyndall Target

Upton Nooz

USAT

USS Leonis Radio Press News

USS Susan B. Anthony

Vigilante

Voice of Sangamon

Volcano

Waac-tivities

WAC News

WAC Newsletter

Warner Robins Beacon

Warren Clip

Warrior Schofield Barracks

Warweek

We Lead the Way

Weekly 127 Seabreeze

Weekly Log

Weekly Okinawan

Weekly Salute

Weekly Seabreeze

Weekly Wig-Wag

Weigh Off

Wellston Beacon

Westover Yankee Flyer

Westpoint Log

What's My Name

Wheel

Wheel Watch

Wheeler Windsock

White Cap

White Falcon

Wildcat

Wildcat Howitzer

Will Rogers Field News

Williwaws

Windsock
Windy City Journal
Wing
Wing Tips
Winged Star
Wings
Wingspread
Winter Field Snap Roll
Wire
Wolf Call
Wolfhound News
Wolters Blade
Wow Wow Ow

X-Isle

Yank
Yankee Doodler
YD Grapevine
Yukon Sentinel

Zombie
Zone One

# NOTES

## INTRODUCTION

1    *"perfect artillery shot"*: "Our Boys and Girls with the Colors," *Kilgore News Herald* (Kilgore, Texas), June 23, 1943, 4.
     *escape the inferno:* Lt. Dean F. Chatlain, *With Pen and Sword*, (Cuyahoga Falls, Ohio: F. W. Orth Company, 1945), 16.
     *Alone, Chatlain lay:* Chatlain, *With Pen and Sword*, 16.
     *Worried he would:* "Soldiers' Sacrifices Surpass Civilians, Chatlain Declares," *Salem News* (Salem, Ohio), June 6, 1945, 1.
     *he had married:* G. J. Koehnnderfer, "War Interrupted Education of This Mansfield Hi Grad," *New-Journal* (Mansfield, Ohio), December 2, 1956, 4.

2    *"That's what I think":* Chatlain, *With Pen and Sword*, VII.
     *"What did you":* Chatlain, *With Pen and Sword*, 16.

3    *rounds of surgeries:* "Hero Cuts Off Own Foot in North Africa Foxhole," *Akron Beacon Journal* (Akron, Ohio), September 1, 1943, 17.
     *honorably discharged:* Koehnnderfer, "War Interrupted Education," 4.
     *circulate in periodicals:* Lt. Dean F. Chatlain, "What Did You Do Today?" *92nd Island X Press*, March 8, 1944, 2.
     *the poem appeared:* "How Would You Answer This?" *San Francisco Examiner*, February 10, 1945, 12; "What Did you Do Today?" *Burlington Free Press*, February 23, 1944, 5.
     *Representative James Wadsworth:* 90 Cong. Rec. 2834 (Representative Wadsworth, March 21, 1944).

*CBS Radio program:* "WSOY All-Out in Bond Drive," *Herald and Review* (Decatur, Illinois), December 7, 1944, 11.

*book of poems:* Chatlain, *With Pen and Sword.*

4 *"When our work":* Terry Cordasco, "A Fighter's Lament," *Bonjour,* October 30, 1943, 2.

*"These papers come":* "The Navy Goes to Press," *All Hands,* July 1945, 14.

## 1. THE WORD FACTORY

6 *"Were it left":* Thomas Jefferson to Col. Edward Carrington, Paris, January 16, 1787, quoted in Mark Van Doren, *Man's Right to Knowledge and the Free Use Thereof* (New York: Columbia University, 1954), 32.

*Ranking first in:* Alexander G. Hardy, *Hitler's Secret Weapon: The "Managed" Press and Propaganda Machine of Nazi Germany* (New York: Vantage Press, 1967), 31.

*"intellectual influence upon":* Hardy, *Hitler's Secret Weapon,* 268 (1933 Reichsgesetzblatt, Part I, page 713, Editorial Law, October 4, 1933, Part Two).

*"tends to weaken":* Hardy, Hitler's Secret Weapon, 270 (1933 Reichsgesetzblatt, Part I, page 713, Editorial Law, October 4, 1933, Part Three).

*A guilty verdict:* Hardy, Hitler's Secret Weapon, 270 (1933 Reichsgesetzblatt, Part I, page 713, Editorial Law, October 4, 1933, Parts Four, Five).

7 *At these meetings:* Hardy, *Hitler's Secret Weapon,* 30–31, 50.

*"The receptivity of":* Hardy, *Hitler's Secret Weapon,* 17 (quoting *Mein Kampf*).

*greatest recurrence rates:* Hardy, *Hitler's Secret Weapon,* 31–32, 46–47.

*Hitler's warped ideas:* Hardy, *Hitler's Secret Weapon,* 41.

*"a complete blackout":* Hardy, *Hitler's Secret Weapon,* 31.

*"With the help":* Hardy, *Hitler's Secret Weapon,* 15.

8 *Typical headlines included:* Hardy, Hitler's Secret Weapon, 136–32.

*"the victor shall":* Hardy, *Hitler's Secret Weapon,* 117–18.

*After Germany's humiliating:* Guido Enderis, "Ceremony Is Brief," *New York Times,* June 22, 1940, 1.

*"psychological dislocation of":* Edmond Taylor, *The Strategy of Terror,* revised ed. (New York: Pocket Books, 1942), 62.

*The Nazis hired:* Taylor, *Strategy of Terror,* 63, 104.

*"whispering campaigns":* Taylor, *Strategy of Terror,* 61, 91.

9    *After months of:* Taylor, *Strategy of Terror,* 17, 143.

*Some makeshift newspapers:* Vincent Brome, *Europe's Free Press* (London: Feature Books Limited), 4–8.

10   *Lurking behind blackout:* Brome, *Europe's Free Press,* 6–8, 15.

*"The very act":* Brome, *Europe's Free Press,* 7.

*risk of death:* Brome, *Europe's Free Press,* 9, 14–16.

*Adopting patriotic-sounding names:* Michael Sayers and Albert E. Kahn, *Sabotage* (New York: Harper & Bros. Publishers, 1942), 137, 141.

11   *Facts in Review:* Sayers and Kahn, *Sabotage,* 170–71.

*The magazine described:* "German High Command Reviews First Six Months of War," *Facts in Review,* March 11, 1940, 82.

*The United States:* "Hitler's 'Frightful Weapon': Propaganda," *New York Times,* June 1, 1941, SM4.

*93 percent of voters:* Harvey J. Kaye, *The Fight for the Four Freedoms: What Made FDR and the Greatest Generation Truly Great* (New York: Simon & Schuster, 2014), 3–4; Hadley Cantril, "Impact of the War on the Nation's Viewpoint," *New York Times,* June 20, 1940, E3.

*"The free press":* Herbert S. Houston, "Blocking New Wars," *Furniture Worker,* October 1918, 364.

12   *State of the Union:* "For Four Human Freedoms," *Time,* January 13, 1941, 9.

*"The democratic way":* "President Roosevelt's Message to Congress on the State of the Union," *New York Times,* January 7, 1941, 6.

*"freedom of speech":* "For Four Human Freedoms," *Time,* 9.

*"first casualty of war":* Phillip Knightley, *The First Casualty, from the Crimea to Vietnam: The War Correspondent as Hero, Propagandist, and Myth Maker* (New York: Harcourt Brace Jovanovich, 1975).

*Knox's newspaper work:* "Knox a Crusader in Varied Career," *New York Times*, April 29, 1944, 8.

13   *Beginning in 1940:* Frank Knox to Arthur Hays Sulzberger, 31 December 1940, Arthur Hays Sulzberger Papers, New York Times Company Records, Manuscripts and Archives Division, New York Public Library, Astor, Lenox, and Tilden Foundations.

*British soldiers poured:* Arthur Hays Sulzberger to Frank Knox, 14 April 1941, Arthur Hays Sulzberger Papers, New York Times Company Records, Manuscripts and Archives Division, New York Public Library, Astor, Lenox, and Tilden Foundations.

*"seems only sportsmanlike":* Arthur Hays Sulzberger to Frank Knox, 8 April 1941, Arthur Hays Sulzberger Papers.

*"raised all hell":* Frank Knox to Arthur Hays Sulzberger, 12 April 1941, Arthur Hays Sulzberger Papers.

14   *As smoke billowed:* Theodore F. Koop, *Weapon of Silence* (Chicago: University of Chicago Press, 1946), 163.

*"All the suppression":* Arthur Krock, "In the Nation," *New York Times*, December 11, 1941, 56.

*"Knox is merely":* Arthur Krock, cable, 8 December 1941, Arthur Hays Sulzberger Papers, New York Times Company Records, Manuscripts and Archives Division, New York Public Library, Astor, Lenox, and Tilden Foundations.

*Office of Censorship:* 55 Stat. 838, 840 at Sec. 303 (December 18, 1941); Michael S. Sweeney, *Secrets of Victory* (Chapel Hill, North Carolina: University of North Carolina Press, 2001), 36.

*Byron Price: A Report on the Office of Censorship* (Washington, DC: US Government Printing Office), 4.

*Balancing journalists' need:* Peter B. Flint, "Byron Price, Wartime Chief of U.S. Censorship, Is Dead," *New York Times*, August 8, 1981; Koop, *Weapon of Silence*, 164.

*A five-page booklet: Code of Wartime Practices for the American Press* (Washington, DC: US Government Printing Office, 1942), 1–4.

*Admiral Ernest King:* "Admiral of the Fleet," *New York Times*, December 26, 1941, 12.

*Notorious for his:* "Admiral of the Fleet," *New York Times*; Michael S. Sweeney, *Secrets of Victory*, 68.

*"Highly successful action":* "Pacific Fleet Sinks Seven Enemy Warships," *El Paso Herald-Post* (El Paso, Texas), May 7, 1942, 1.

*US Marines' landing:* Byron Price Papers, 1901–1976, Archives Division, State Historical Society of Wisconsin, Madison, 6, 313.

15   *public-opinion polls:* Allan M. Winkler, *The Politics of Propaganda: The Office of War Information 1942–1945* (New Haven, Connecticut: Yale University Press, 1978), 54.

*At a private meeting:* Byron Price Papers, 1901–1976, 313.

*"date which will live":* "8 Battleships Hit," *New York Times*, December 6, 1942, 1.

*"The American people":* "The News Came Promptly," *Adrian Daily Telegram* (Adrian, Michigan), November 5, 1942, 4.

## 2. THE OBSCENITIES IN WASHINGTON

*"If I were":* Marion Hargrove, *See Here, Private Hargrove* (New York: Pocket Books, 1942), 1.

*They arrived wearing:* Gil Sandler, email message to the author, April 21, 2017.

18   *Orders came to:* James J. Fahey, *Pacific War Diary* (New York: Kensington Publishing Corp., 1963), 4; Frederick Simpich, "Around the Clock with Your Soldier Boy," *National Geographic*, July 1941, 5.

*placed in quarantine:* *The Bluejackets Manual* (Annapolis, Maryland: United States Naval Institute, 1940), 7–8.

*men ate outside:* Francis A. O'Brien, *Battling for Saipan* (New York: Ballantine Books, 2003), 10.

*"bare sandy lot":* O.C. McDavid, *My Name Is O.C.* (Gene McDavid, 2003), 59.

*In February 1941:* McDavid, *My Name Is O.C.*, 32, 55.

*"We looked terrible":* Sgt. Don Robinson, *News of the 45th* (New York: Grosset & Dunlap, 1944), 6–7.

*given dummy mortars:* O'Brien, *Battling for Saipan*, 10.

*Mop handles propped:* Meyer Berger, "American Soldier—One Year After," *New York Times*, November 23, 1941, SM3.

*Trucks were labeled:* O'Brien, *Battling for Saipan*, 10.

*"never fired even":* Simpich, "Around the Clock," 4.

19     *Up at 6:00 a.m.:* "Army Morale," *Life*, December 23, 1940, 55.

*ten miles per day:* Simpich, "Around the Clock," 1.

*"Hardening Process":* Hargrove, *See Here, Private Hargrove*, 2–3.

*"homesick and lonesome":* *The Bluejackets Manual*, 6.

*"guys in basic training":* Gilbert Sandler, email message to author, April 21, 2017.

*one in three:* "8,000,000-Man Army: Stepping Up the Draft," *United States News*, May 22, 1942, 11.

20     *twelve-month cap:* "Text of the Selective Service Bill as Passed by the Senate Yesterday," *New York Times*, August 29, 1940, 11.

*"Those obscenity obscenities":* "National Defense: Problem of Morale," *Time*, August 18, 1941.

*his disgust palpable:* Hanson W. Baldwin, "Longer Army Service Acts as Spur for Reform," *New York Times*, August 17, 1941, E3.

*"Snasu":* "National Defense," *Time*, August 18, 1941.

*many draftees' discontent:* Samuel A. Stouffer et al., *The American Soldier: Adjustment During Army Life*, vol. 1 (Princeton, New Jersey: Princeton University Press, 1949), 430.

*"suffers so deeply":* Paul Fussell, *Wartime: Understanding and Behavior in the Second World War* (New York: Oxford University Press, 1989), 96.

21     *Sworn in as:* Forrest C. Pogue, *George C. Marshall: Ordeal and Hope 1939–1942* (New York: Viking Press, 1966), 2, 81–82.

*"As an army":* *Biennial Reports of Gen. George C. Marshall, Chief of Staff of the U.S. Army, July 1, 1939 to June 30, 1943 to the Secretary of War* (Washington, DC: The Infantry Journal, 1943), 12.

*needed congressional approval:* Pogue, *Ordeal and Hope*, 1, 6, 47.

*"modernize our artillery":* *Biennial Reports of Gen. George C. Marshall*, 13; *see also* William Frye, *Marshall: Citizen Soldier* (New York: Bobbs-Merrill Company, 1947), 264.

*One senator described:* Pogue, *Ordeal and Hope*, 60.

*"My relief of mind":* Pogue, *Ordeal and Hope*, 59.

22 *"a lag of time":* Pogue, *Ordeal and Hope*, 16–17.

*fifty-seven airplanes:* Pogue, *Ordeal and Hope*, 18.

*"more deeply troubled":* Pogue, *Ordeal and Hope*, 36.

*71 percent of Americans:* Doris Kearns Goodwin, *No Ordinary Time* (New York: Simon & Schuster, 1994), 147–48.

*In September 1940:* Charles Hurd, "Need of Men Vital," *New York Times*, August 3, 1940, 1; "FDR Pledges Total Defense for Americas," *The New London (Conn.) Evening Day*, October 14, 1940, 8; Pub. L. No. 76-783, § 2, 54 Stat. 885, 885 (Sept. 16, 1940).

*On October 16:* "Procedure Smooth," *New York Times*, October 17, 1940, 1.

*Initial plans called:* "Sets Number 3,000 as Draftee Limit," *New York Times*, October 31, 1940, 8.

23 *"gladly played that":* "National Defense," *Time*, August 18, 1941.

*"burning incentive to":* "Army Morale," *Life*, 55.

24 *He had struggled:* Forrest C. Pogue, *George C. Marshall: Education of a General 1880–1939* (New York: Viking Press, 1963), 40; Frye, *Marshall: Citizen Soldier*, 48.

*"half of all":* Frye, *Marshall: Citizen Soldier*, 75.

*Secretly, Marshall ordered:* Frye, *Marshall: Citizen Soldier*, 81.

25 *"the poor devil":* Pogue, *Education of a General*, 160.

*"The army is":* Assistant press officer to chief of press division, re: establishment of an official newspaper for and by the American Expeditionary Forces, 8 November 1917, General Correspondence of the Office of the Stars and Stripes, 1917–1919, National Archives identifier 6634103, entry number NM-91 236, National Archives Building, Washington, DC (hereinafter "Gen. Corresp. S&S, Nat. Archives").

*Isolated and lacking:* Assistant press officer to chief of press division, 8 November 1917, Gen. Corresp. S&S, Nat. Archives.

*"small travelling press":* Frank Keppel, "Study of Information and Education Activities in World War II," 1946, 3, Frederick Osborn Papers, folder "Keppel, Frank—Study of Information and Education Activities," American Philosophical Society Archives.

*General Andrew Jackson:* "Information and Education in the Armed Forces," 1 December 1949, appendix A, Frederick Osborn Papers, folder "U.S. Army—Information and Education in the Armed Forces," American Philosophical Society Archives.

*The Civil War:* Ralph Canevali, "Soldier Newspapers in the Civil War," National Endowment for the Humanities, Division of Preservation and Access, May 23, 2016, https://www.neh.gov/divisions/preservation/featured-project/soldier-newspapers-in-the-civil-war.

26    *Talented newsmen were:* Bulletin no. 10, 8 February 1918, Gen. Corresp. S&S, Nat. Archives.

*"for a weary":* Samuel Hopkins Adams, *A. Woollcott: His Life and His World* (New York: Reynal & Hitchcock, 1945), 87; Alexander Woollcott, *The Command Is Forward: Tales of the A.E.F. Battlefields as They Appeared in The Stars and Stripes* (New York: The Century Co., 1919), ix.

*Through honest reporting:* Michael E. Unsworth, ed., *Military Periodicals* (New York: Greenwood Press, 1990), xxv.

*"was made in":* Pogue, *Education of a General*, 161.

*Because they generously:* Bulletin no. 26, 11 May 1918, Gen. Corresp. S&S, Nat. Archives; "Read the 'Stars and Stripes,'" 30 May 1918, Gen. Corresp. S&S, Nat. Archives.

27    *"I'm out here":* Theodore Wesley Koch, *War Libraries and Allied Studies* (New York: G. E. Stechert & Co., 1918), 54.

*An American working:* Koch, *War Libraries*, 55.

*Popular American magazines:* Koch, *War Libraries*, 54–56; John Jamieson, *Books for the Army* (New York: Columbia University Press, 1950), 13–14.

28    *"more shipboard time":* Gaddis Smith, "Forty Months: Franklin D. Roosevelt as War Leader, 1941–1945," *Prologue* 26, no. 3 (Fall 1994): 134.

*Sailors who were:* James Roosevelt, *My Parents* (Chicago: Playboy Press, 1976), 215.

*Roosevelt and members:* Roosevelt, *My Parents*, 202.

*on one cruise:* "Personnel," *Blue Bonnet*, October 16, 1935, 1, Franklin D. Roosevelt Papers as President, official file, box 16, cruise USS *Houston*, Franklin D. Roosevelt Presidential Library, Hyde Park, New York.

*Roosevelt submitted:* Roosevelt, *My Parents*, 202.

## 3. COMMA-FLAGE

30    *"What they really":* Gilbert Sandler, email message to author, December 5, 2015.

*"We sailed from":* Cpl. C. Claude Ramsey, "A Yank's Log," *U.S.A.T.*, June 1942, Souvenir Edition, 5.

*So Marshall asked:* War Department, memorandum, 7 September 1941, no. W210-6-42, re: publication of post, camp, and unit newspapers, available in *Army Editors' Manual* (New York: War Department, 1943), 67.

*motion picture kit:* *The Special Service Company*, FM 28-105 (Washington, DC: War Department, January 5, 1944), 24–26.

31    *newspaper field kit:* War Department, memorandum, 7 September 1941, no. W210-6-42, 67.

*Other incidentals for:* *The Special Service Company*, 57–58.

*For technical information:* *Army Newspaper Editors' Manual* (New York: Information and Education Division, Headquarters, Army Special Forces, September 1944).

32    *The Galley's solution:* "GI Galleybird," *GI Galley*, November 1942, 3.

*When an artist:* "Ye Gallie Roome," *GI Galley*, July 1943, 8.

*"Mimeograph manufacturers tell":* "Letter from McLaughlin, "Galley Room," *GI Galley*, May 1943, 16.

*"Don't criticize his":* "Listen to the G.I. Galley Bird," *GI Galley*, September 1942, 3.

*When Camp Roberts:* "Perfume (A la Ann Sheridan) Scents Paper," *GI Galley*, February 1943, 3.

*used a sewing machine:* "Side Stitching with Thread Binds Mimeo Sheet," *GI Galley*, July 1943, 1.

*"brass roosters":* "Vernacular of Own Base Sought by *Post Review*," *GI Galley*, September 1943, 3.

33   *"Better than no":* "Ink Spots," *GI Galley*, November 1942, 1.

*"litterchure":* "Candles," *GI Galley*, March 1943, 1.

*"working with spades":* "Flood Fails to Halt *Broadcaster*," *GI Galley*, July 1943, 2.

*editors in Alabama:* "Editors' Profanity Draws Protest from Methodists," *GI Galley*, May 1943, 5.

*These early experiments:* "Camp Papers Planned in All Theaters of Combat," *GI Galley*, January 1943, 2.

*"After 22 years":* "Galley Room," *GI Galley*, November 1943, 8.

34   *"Because of typhoonic":* "Tough Sheet," *GI Galley*, October 18, 1945, 1.

*"these Aviation Engineers":* "Tough Sheet," *GI Galley*, October 1945, 2.

35   *"tough sheet to get out":* Sht. M. Phillip Brady, "Tough Sheet," *GI Galley*, October 1945, 2–4.

*Celebrity publishers sat:* "Galley Room," *GI Galley*, September 1942, 8; "CNS Sponsors Paper Contest," *GI Galley*, December 1942, 1; "Trophies Bought for Newspaper Contest," *GI Galley*, January 1943, 1; "Judges Names for CNS Paper Contest," *GI Galley*, February 1943, 1; "*America's Alertmen* Takes Grand Prize," *GI Galley*, April 1943, 1.

*"After reading you":* "Galley Room," *GI Galley*, April 1943, 8.

*"high schoolish":* "Color and Art Make Christmas Issue of *Drum Sparkle*," *GI Galley*, February 1944, 2; "Galley Room," *GI Galley*, March 1944, 7.

36   *After announcing its:* See, e.g., "Galley Room," *GI Galley*, June 1943, 7; "Slick Stock and Photos Spark *Windsock*," *GI Galley*, April 1943, 3.

*"This may be":* Walt to "Ane," letter, 30 May 1944, private collection of author.

*Army regulations empowered: Military Intelligence Military Censorship*, FM 30-28 (Washington, DC: Government Printing Office, 1944), 6, 26–27.

*"information determined by": Military Intelligence Military Censorship*, 16.

*"the censor, who":* Letter from Farren, "Galley Room," *GI Galley*, April 1943, 8.

*cut and pasted: See, e.g. Camp Newspaper Clip Sheet*, September 20, 1942, January 24, 1943.

*"That column":* "Galley Room," *GI Galley*, October 1943, 8.

*"only wastes space":* "Galley Room," *GI Galley*, October 1943, 8.

37    *following Terry's story:* Robert C. Harvey, *Meanwhile…: A Biography of Milton Caniff* (Seattle, Washington: Fantagraphics Books, 2007), 387.

*Caniff received thousands:* Harvey, *Meanwhile…*, 384–87.

*"morale of soldiers":* Harvey, *Meanwhile…*, 388.

*Caniff reached out:* "Marvin H. McIntyre Rites," *New York Times*, December 16, 1943, 27.

*"The last war":* Harvey, *Meanwhile…*, 389.

38    *"Our paper comes":* Letter from PFC Lou Stevens, "Galley Room," *GI Galley*, July 1943, 8 (tense altered).

*Marshall offered Caniff:* Harvey, *Meanwhile…*, 390, 402.

*breach of contract:* Harvey, *Meanwhile…*, 394–95.

*"in good taste":* Harvey, *Meanwhile…*, 397.

*Male Call with realism:* Harvey, *Meanwhile…*, 404–05.

*"all the editors":* "Galley Room," *GI Galley*, August 1943, 8.

*"the girl whom":* "Lace Outstrips Competition," *GI Galley*, October 1943, 2.

*"comic strip sweetie":* "Galley Room," *GI Galley*, February 1944, 7.

*the Marauder:* "Gal Like Lace Found by Paper," *GI Galley*, April 1944, 1.

*"two-minute furlough":* Harvey, *Meanwhile…*, 409, 414–16.

39    *"girl-hungry GIs":* Harvey, *Meanwhile…*, 408.

*Sansone also won points:* Milton Caniff, foreword to *The Wolf,* by Sgt. Leonard Sansone (New York: United Publishers, 1945) (minor alterations made to original).

*tracing the cartoons:* "Pre-cut Art Mimeo Stencils Offered," *GI Galley,* March 1943, 1.

*"We were about ready":* Letter from Krasney, "Galley Room," *GI Galley,* June 1943, 7.

*"manna from heaven":* Letter from McLaughlin, "Galley Room," *GI Galley,* May 1943, 16.

*Within five months:* Lace cartoon, *GI Galley,* August 1943, 1.

40    *Newspapers sprouted up: Oflag 64 Item,* December 1, 1944.

*newspaper unto itself:* "Laundry Unit Publishes Sheet," *GI Galley,* August 1943, 5; "'Cookie' Edits Baker's Sheet," *GI Galley,* June 1943, 4; "Second Bakers' Sheet Started by 616th QM," *GI Galley,* July 1943, 2; "First Valentine Appears," *GI Galley,* March 1943, 2; "Vol. 1, No. 1 Appears at Jeffersonville QM Depot," *GI Galley,* March 1943, 2.

*534 specialities:* Bud Hutton and Andy Rooney, *The Story of the Stars and Stripes: A Paper for Joe* (New York: Farrar & Rinehart, Inc., 1946), 141.

*GI slang:* "Comma-Flage," *GI Galley,* May 1943, 10.

41    *troop newspaper names:* H. L. Mencken, *The American Language: Supplement II* (New York: Alfred A. Knopf, 1948), 596.

*patronizing titles:* "You Supply the Brains," *Tale Spinner,* April 10, 1943, 2; "It's Time to Think," *Tale Spinner,* April 21, 1943, 2; "There's a Reason, Mister," *Tale Spinner,* May 22, 1932, 2.

*"An eye for an eye":* "Hate Your Enemies," *Tale Spinner,* May 15, 1943, 2.

*Wreathed around:* "Chaplain's Corner," "Chaplain Germain Serves Personnel of the AAFCC," *Tale Spinner,* May 15, 1943, 2.

42    *"Seeing is believing":* "Cadets Can Now Enjoy Meals Under Changed Plan of Mess," *Tale Spinner,* May 15, 1943, 1.

*scribbled words:* "How Long Did You Say You've Been a Cadet," *Tale Spinner,* May 15, 1943, 12.

*"Just three short weeks"*: "44A's Waiting for Turnabout, Then for 44-B," *Tale Spinner*, May 15, 1943, 15.

*These tender words*: "A Mother's Prayer," *Tale Spinner*, June 5, 1943, 5.

43    *"From pride and foolish"*: "'Old Blood and Guts' Poet; 'God of Battles' Is Theme," *Greenville News* (Greenville, South Carolina), October 22, 1943, 7.

44    *"Why don't you"*: Mrs. Victor Konkol to Victor Konkol, 21 October 1943, private collection of author.

*"Can't write a thing"*: "Approved by Censor," *Hornet Tales*, August 19, 1944, 2.

45    *"Dear John"*: "My Girl and Me," *Bonjour*, October 2, 1943, 2.

46    *Suffocated by the:* "Lament of a Private," *The 49er's Buzzin' Briefs*, August 1, 1943, 11.

47    *"Do what you"*: *The Bluejackets Manual* (Annapolis, Maryland: US Naval Institute, 1940), 7.

*One bittersweet ballad:* "Strictly GI," *59th Latrineogram*, May 7, 1944, 4.

48    *"American democracy is"*: "The Nation: The General," *Time*, January 3, 1944, Pony Edition, 3–4.

*one man described:* G. A. Van Bovone, "You Are Welcome," *U.S.A.T.*, June 1942, Souvenir Edition, 2.

*"Save these for"*: *Sandfly*, February 24, 1945, 1, private collection of author.

*"Cursified Advertising"*: "Cursified Advertising," *Weekly 127 Seabreeze*, July 15, 1945, 6.

## 4. TEAR-STAINED PILLOWS

50    *"Morale is to matériel"*: "A Well-Deserved Promotion," *New York Times*, October 9, 1943, 12.

*Llewellyn stressed that:* Bud Hutton and Andy Rooney, *The Story of the Stars and Stripes* (New York: Rinehart & Co., Inc., 1946), 22.

51    *With Llewellyn at:* Hutton and Rooney, *The Story of the Stars and Stripes*, 22.

*In April 1942:* "The Stars and Stripes Reappears in London; Army Paper 8-Page Tabloid in New A.E.F.," *New York Times,* April 18, 1942, 17; C. E. Dornbusch, *Stars and Stripes: Check List of the Several Editions* (New York: New York Public Library, 1948).

*one million subscribers:* Dornbusch, *Stars and Stripes.*

*"decided there wasn't":* Andy Rooney, *My War* (New York: Random House Times Books, 1995), 42, 48.

52 *broke this rule:* Hutton and Rooney, *The Story of the Stars and Stripes,* 42.

*"Circulation Man Gets":* Hutton and Rooney, *The Story of the Stars and Stripes,* 67.

*"collection of possibly":* Hutton and Rooney, *The Story of the Stars and Stripes,* viii.

*"The editorial staff":* Hutton and Rooney, *The Story of the Stars and Stripes,* 138.

53 *"learned to fight":* Hutton and Rooney, *The Story of the Stars and Stripes,* viii.

*"to stay around":* Hutton and Rooney, *The Story of the Stars and Stripes,* 55.

*"Only those who":* Hutton and Rooney, *The Story of the Stars and Stripes,* 55–56.

*Frank Keppel:* Glenn Fowler, "Francis Keppel Dies at Age of 73; Was Commissioner of Education," *New York Times,* February 21, 1990, 22.

*"treating the soldier":* Frank Keppel, "Study of Information and Education Activities, World War II," 6 April 1946, 79, folder "Keppel, Frank," Frederick H. Osborn Papers, American Philosophical Society Archives.

*"the weapon rusts":* Keppel, "Study of Information and Education Activities, World War II," 58.

54 *Marshall recognized this:* Hutton and Andy Rooney, 207–08.

*a high-ranking official:* Hutton and Rooney, *The Story of the Stars and Stripes,* 231.

*low-ranking staff members:* Hutton and Rooney, *The Story of the Stars and Stripes,* 127.

*"the combat man":* Hutton and Rooney, *The Story of the Stars and Stripes,* 232.

55    *the unsigned editorial:* "So You Wanna Go Home, Eh?" *The Stars and Stripes,* September 25, 1944, 4.

*"we wanna go home":* M/Sgt. Herman E. Durdan, "Home—When We've Won," *Stars and Stripes,* October 16, 1944, 4.

56    *"Have you ever":* Pvt. Wesley G. Wilson, "Lousy Editorial," *Stars and Stripes,* October 16, 1944, 4.

*"German propaganda":* S/Sgt. Casey and sixteen GIs, "Congratulations," *Stars and Stripes,* October 16, 1944, 4.

*"editor's hairy chest":* T/Sgt. H. W. Mattick, "Written in a Vacuum," *Stars and Stripes,* October 16, 1944, 4.

*"most unfavorable reaction":* Hutton and Rooney, *The Story of the Stars and Stripes,* 235–36.

57    *"the ordinary staffers":* Hutton and Rooney, *The Story of the Stars and Stripes,* 233.

*As of 1939:* "About the 1940 Census," http://1940census.archives.gov/about; Theodore Peterson, *Magazines in the Twentieth Century* (Urbana, Illinois: University of Illinois Press, 1956), 53–55.

58    *Among those consulted:* Barrett McGurn, *Yank, the Army Weekly: Reporting the Greatest Generation* (Golden, Colorado: Fulcrum Publishing, 2004), 66.

*Yank also expertly:* "Sad Sack's One Forlorn Buck; His GI Pals Get All the Luck," *Charlotte News* (Charlotte, North Carolina), December 2, 1944, 2.

59    *"Let's say that":* Sgt. Harold Applebaum, *Solo and Other Poems* (New York: Creative Age Press, 1947), 3 (original formatting by Applebaum); *see also* Sgt. Harold Applebaum, "The Death of Pvt. Jones," *Yank, the Army Weekly,* July 21, 1944, 21.

*"present Army raincoat":* T/Sgt. E. J. Lambiotte, "GI Raincoats," *Yank, the Army Weekly,* September 29, 1944, 14.

*"I am one"*: Pvt. William Whitman, "Too Young to Vote," *Yank, the Army Weekly*, September 29, 1944, 14.

*"Monotony, monotony"*: Pfc. H. Moldauer, "Monotony," *Yank, the Army Weekly*, August 18, 1944, 14.

60     *"offered every serviceman"*: McGurn, *Yank, the Army Weekly*, 11.

*"from interference, particularly"*: Frank Keppel, "Study of Information and Education Activities, World War II," 79.

*Roosevelt urged Yank*: Franklin Delano Roosevelt, "To the Armed Forces of the United States," *Yank, the Army Weekly*, June 17, 1942, 2.

61     *two million paying*: C. E. Dornbusch, *Yank, The Army Weekly* (New York: New York Public Library, 1950), 4.

*"best damn weekly"*: H. Chamberlin, "Gripe on Gripers," *Yank, the Army Weekly*, July 7, 1944, 14.

62     *Marshall proposed Outfit*: "Letterpress Mag, Called *Outfit*, to Serve Patients," *GI Galley*, December 1944, 1.

*In November 1944: Outfit*, November 27, 1944.

63     *Private Alex Chavez*: "Guys Who Miss Their Buddies," *Outfit*, March 19, 1945, 2.

*Technician Howard Givens*: "'Red Arrows' Scarce," *Outfit*, January 29, 1945, 2.

*Corporal Henry C. Basinger*: "Ol' Dabbil Censorship Again," *Outfit*, March 12, 1945, 2.

*"the bang-up job"*: "A Boost for Negro Troops," *Outfit*, April 30, 1945, 2.

*Outfit worked around: See, e.g.*, T/5 Dick Loomis and T/Sgt. Chuck Voorhis, "Battle Biographies," *Outfit*, March 26, 1945, 16.

*celebrated the wounded*: "Fighting Faces," *Outfit*, February 5, 1945, 16.

*"What happens during"*: Charles G. Bolte, *The New Veteran* (New York: Reynal & Hitchcock, 1945), 15, 17.

## 5. HELLO, SUCKERS!

65     *"We shall not land"*: "South America. Awake at Last," *Time*, June 24, 1940.

*Red Cross volunteers:* Sgt. Don Robinson, *News of the 45th* (New York: Grosset & Dunlap, 1944), 51–52.

*climbed rickety gangplanks:* Robinson, *News of the 45th*, 52.

*waited for anchors-up:* See, e.g., "Headquarters 569th Antiaircraft Artillery Auto Wpns Battalion (Mbl), Fort Bragg, North Carolina" to "All Members of the 569th AAA AW Bn (Mbl)," memorandum, 9 August 1944, re: "Preparation for Overseas Movement."

66      *War Department language guides:* See *North African Arabic Language Guide*, TM 30-321 (Washington, DC: War Department, 1943); *French Language Guide*, TM 30-302 (Washington, DC: War Department, 1943); *Pocket Guide to North Africa* (Washington, DC: War and Navy Departments).

*troops could expect:* Robinson, *News of the 45th*, 116.

*"If the stuff":* Ernie Pyle, *Here Is Your War* (New York: Pocket Books, 1944), 60.

*"train carried freight":* Robinson, *News of the 45th*, 62.

*"Some Arabic sounds":* Pyle, *Here Is Your War*, 62.

*Tossing the guides:* Robinson, *News of the 45th*, 62.

*"Our troops made":* Pyle, *Here Is Your War*, 57.

67      *"Watch for next":* "My Africa Souvenir," propaganda leaflet, series A, no. 4.

68      *"too little training":* Samuel A. Stouffer et al., *The American Soldier: Adjustment During Army Life*, vol. 1 (Princeton, New Jersey: Princeton University Press, 1949), 79.

*German snipers eyed:* Pyle, *Here Is Your War*, 158.

*synthetic lemonade:* E. B. Sledge, *With the Old Breed at Peleliu and Okinawa* (New York: Ballantine Books, 2007), 37.

*Under a blanket:* Pyle, *Here Is Your War*, 142.

*baptism by fire:* Pyle, *Here Is Your War*, 137, 205

69      *"It seemed ironic":* Pyle, *Here Is Your War*, 34.

*They contained world:* See *Boston Herald*, October 11, 1943, Liberty Overseas Edition, courtesy of Jordan Marsh.

*Spear and Company:* See *Daily Mirror*, vol. 1, no. 17, Servicemen's Edition, courtesy of Spear & Co.

70    *service edition:* See *Sunday Providence Sunday Journal*, March 7,
      1943, Service Edition.
      *available by subscription:* See *Oregonian*, April 6, 1945, Service-
      men's Edition.
      *swiftest overseas delivery: Journal Herald* (Dayton, Ohio), March
      25, 1954, Overseas Edition.
      *"Oh, I long":* Ernest O. Norquist, *Our Paradise: A GI's War Diary*
      (Hancock, Wisconsin: Pearl-Win Publishing Co., 1989), 102.
71    *newsprint rationing stymied:* "Newsprint Cut 10 Per Cent
      by Order of W.P.B.," *Medford Mail Tribune*, December 31,
      1942, 1.
      *"It is designed":* "From Other Pens: The Purpose of Paper Ra-
      tioning," *Gallup Independent* (Gallup, New Mexico), November
      16, 1942, 2.
      *"react vigorously against":* "Newsprint 10% Cut to Fall Heavily
      on Bigger City Papers," *Pittsburgh Press*, December 31, 1942, 2.
      *"Your overseas edition":* Virgil Harry Woods, letter to the editor,
      "Misses Overseas Edition," *Courier-Journal* (Louisville, Ken-
      tucky), October 29, 1944, 30.
72    *officer, Ray Trautman:* "Just a Few Lines….," *Sunday Herald-
      Leader*, December 9, 1945.
      *opened his own:* "Named National Director of Army Library Ser-
      vice," *Baltimore Sun*, November 27, 1946, 11.
73    *degree in library science:* Ray L. Trautman, "Personal Data Tran-
      script," 1–2.
      *"We are crying":* Letter from Pat to publishers, undated, Council
      on Books in Wartime Records, 1942–1947, coll. no. MC038,
      20th Century Public Policy Papers, Seeley G. Mudd Manuscript
      Library, Department of Rare Books and Special Collections,
      Princeton University Library.
      *subject to paper rationing:* "Newsprint Cut 10 Per Cent," *Medford
      Mail Tribune*, 1.
      *Reader's Digest sold:* Theodore Patterson, *Magazines in the Twen-
      tieth Century* (Urbana, Illinois: University of Illinois, 1956), 217.

*reduced the size:* "Newsprint Cut 10 Per Cent," *Medford Mail Tribune*, 1.

74    *Trautman felt he:* John Jamieson, *Books for the Army* (New York: Columbia University Press, 1950), 133.

*Trautman's contracts with:* Trunx to Mr. Ross, memorandum, 13 June 1944, *New Yorker* records, Manuscripts and Archives Division, New York Public Library, Astor, Lenox, and Tilden Foundations.

*sold to the army:* Trunx to Mr. Ross, memorandum, 13 June 1944.

*turned to Newsweek:* "Let a 300-Mile-an-Hour Mailman Speed Your Letter Overseas," *Capital Times* (Madison, Wisconsin), April 12, 1944, 7.

*font was so minuscule: Newsweek* V-mail Edition, US Army Library Service, January 18, 1943, Trautman Family Archives.

75    *became the model: Newsweek*, January 18, 1943, Special Edition for the Armed Forces, marked "sample," Trautman Family Archives.

*army's Library Service:* John Jamieson, *Books for the Army* (New York: Columbia University Press, 1950), 133.

*Beginning in mid-1943:* Jamieson, *Books for the Army*, 130–35.

*Harold Ross learned:* Jamieson, *Books for the Army*, 20–23.

*never-ending complaints:* "Hell File," note, undated, *New Yorker* records, Manuscripts and Archives Division, New York Public Library, Astor, Lenox, and Tilden Foundations.

*"halftones took an":* H. W. Ross to Messrs. Shawns, Lebrano, Geraghty, Cook, Peppe, 13 September 1943; Ross to Shuman, 19 October 1943, *New Yorker* records, Manuscripts and Archives Division, New York Public Library, Astor, Lenox, and Tilden Foundations.

76    *over 156 million:* "Army Library Service, Office in Charge, Library Branch, SSD," job description, 1945, folder 2, Trautman Family Archives.

*"gobbled them up":* Gilbert Sandler, email message to author, December 26, 2014.

*"welter of detail"*: George H. Martin, letter to editor, "What Went On," *Time*, May 29, 1944, Pony Edition, 1.

*"I found myself"*: Gilbert Sandler, email message to author, December 26, 2014.

77    *"It is true"*: Speech at Trinity College, 15 June 1941, *The Papers of George Catlett Marshall*, ed. Larry I. Bland, Sharon R. Ritenour, and Clarence E. Wunderlin Jr. (Baltimore, Maryland: Johns Hopkins University Press, 1986), 536.

*given equal standing: The Special Service Company*, FM 28-105 (War Department, January 5, 1944), 2.

78    *"good newspapermen"*: Robinson, *News of the 45th*, preface.

*903rd Engineer Air Force:* "First Overseas Edition Makes Debut as North African Campaign Ends," *Engineerful*, May 1943, 1.

*"Take one draftee"*: "Here's a Favorite Dish Liked by Everybody," *Engineerful*, May 1943, 1.

*It also experimented:* "Officer of the Day," *Engineerful*, May 1943, 1; *Engineerful*, May 1943, 4.

*"begging for copy"*: E. de S. Melcher, "The GI Keyhole," *Bonjour*, September 25, 1943, 4; Sgt. L. Howard, "First Words from New Outfit," *Bonjour*, October 2, 1943, 1; "Consider the Pig," *Bonjour*, October 2, 1943, 2.

*"What certain dog"*: Larry Babine, "New Wideawake Slogan: In the States by Christmas," *Bonjour*, October 9, 1943, 1.

*"Will wonders never"*: "OFFICERS DO K.P.!," *Bonjour*, October 16, 1943, 4.

79    *"break his heart"*: "Germany Fights to Keep Foreign Soil Battle Ground," *Bonjour*, September 18, 1943, 1.

## 6. 45TH GIORNALE MILITARE

80    *"Here we go again!"*: "Good Luck! 1945," German propaganda leaflet, 374/12.

81    *he refused to:* Bill Mauldin, *The Brass Ring* (New York: W.W. Norton & Co., Inc., 1971), 90.

*"honey bucket":* Mauldin, *The Brass Ring*, 85–86, 90–91.

*"How can you":* Mauldin, *The Brass Ring*, 91.

*"irreverent quality":* Mauldin, *The Brass Ring*, 93.

*"our little colonel":* Mauldin, *The Brass Ring*, 102.

82    *In June 1943:* Flint Whitlock, *The Rock of Anzio* (Boulder, Colorado: Westview Press, 1998), 32.

*shore at Arzew:* Whitlock, *The Rock of Anzio*, 32–34.

*stuffed his haversack:* Whitlock, *The Rock of Anzio*, 39–40.

*"an inch deep":* Whitlock, *The Rock of Anzio*, 38.

*"You wouldn't believe":* Mauldin, *The Brass Ring*, 143.

83    *Landing craft deposited:* Whitlock, *The Rock of Anzio*, 42.

*savageries of war:* Whitlock, *The Rock of Anzio*, 36–37, 43.

*silently trudged forward:* Whitlock, *The Rock of Anzio*, 46–53.

*"It was D plus one":* Sgt. Don Robinson, *News of the 45th* (New York: Grosset & Dunlap, 1944), 72.

*"We decided the":* Mauldin, *The Brass Ring*, 149.

*British troops managed:* "Two Catania Papers Operated by Allies 4 Days After Arrival," *GI Galley*, October 1943, 2.

*found a printer:* Robinson, *News of the 45th*, 75–76.

84    *The last place:* Mauldin, *The Brass Ring*, 153.

*"couldn't resist":* Mauldin, *The Brass Ring*, 154.

*unsuccessful strafing runs:* Mauldin, *The Brass Ring*, 154.

*It took all night:* Robinson, *News of the 45th*, 76–77; *see also* Mauldin, *The Brass Ring*, 155 (photo of July 13, 1943 edition).

*"paratroopers who had":* Sgt. Don Robinson to "Galley Room," *GI Galley*, August, 1944, 7.

85    *division's mimeograph machine:* Robinson, *News of the 45th*, 81.

*like a ransom letter:* Robinson, *News of the 45th*, 83.

*"if anything newsworthy":* Mauldin, *The Brass Ring*, 157–58.

*One was rattling:* Mauldin, *The Brass Ring*, 166.

*Caltanissetta issue:* Robinson, *News of the 45th*, 86–88.

86    *"Our paper became":* Robinson, *News of the 45th*, 93.

*battle for Sicily:* Robinson, *News of the 45th*, 98.

*studied its topography:* Mauldin, *The Brass Ring*, 185.

*trench foot:* "Trenchfoot," https://www.healthline.com/health /trench-foot#causes.

*soldiers scattered:* Mauldin, *The Brass Ring*, 185.

*"Just about the only":* Mauldin, *The Brass Ring*, 185.

87 *"the last job":* "Color Comics Printed for GIs in Italy on Press Owned by Family of Count Ciano," *GI Galley*, April 1945, 1.

*the Italian mainland:* "News Published First Allied Paper in Sicily," *45th Division News*, July 10, 1945, 2.

*"Week No. One":* "News Published First Allied Paper in Sicily," *45th Division News*, July 10, 1945, 2.

*became more grizzled:* Mauldin, *The Brass Ring*, 188.

*his drawing board:* Mauldin, *The Brass Ring*, 193–95.

*"purge the Italian":* Mauldin, *The Brass Ring*, 201–02.

88 *"specially equipped Jeep":* Richard Severo, "Bill Mauldin, Newspaper Cartoonist, Dies at 81," *New York Times*, January 22, 2003.

*his tough love:* Martin Blumenson, *Patton: The Man Behind the Legend, 1885–1945* (New York: William Morrow & Co., 1985), 103–04.

*"iron discipline":* Blumenson, *Patton: The Man*, 104–05, 220.

*meeting with Mauldin:* Bud Hutton and Andy Rooney, *The Story of the Stars and Stripes: A Paper for Joe* (New York: Farrar & Rinehart, 1946), 194–95.

89 *profanity-laced diatribe:* Mauldin, *The Brass Ring*, 254–63.

90 *"teaching respect":* Mauldin, *The Brass Ring*, 263–64.

*sets foot in Third Army:* Mauldin, *The Brass Ring*, 255, 264.

*"Wrote the Editor":* Martin Blumenson, ed., *The Patton Papers 1940–1945* (Boston: Houghton Mifflin Company, 1974), 624 (italics added).

*propaganda was dumped:* Rick Atkinson, *The Day of Battle: The War in Sicliy and Italy, 1943–1944* (New York: Henry Holt and Co., 2007), 491.

*"roads to Rome":* "Paved With Skulls!" propaganda leaflet, A1-061-4-44.

*pithy statements:* "Why are you still fighting in Italy?" propaganda leaflet, T 37.

*"Our sacrifices are":* "I fought in Italy too . . . Your dead pal speaking . . ." propaganda leaflet, A1-067-5-44.

91 *"Thousands of German":* "Paved With Skulls!" propaganda leaflet, A1-061-4-44.

*The News observed:* "Baker Hears Sssssssss! But No Boom," *45th Division News*, December 4, 1943, 1 (Naples, Italy).

*"all slit trenches":* "By the Right Flank!" *45th Division News*, December 4, 1943, 2.

*"The Aryan spoke":* "A Little Story for the Nazis," *45th Division News*, December 4, 1943, 4.

92 *reconstruction of Foggia:* F. H. Bonesch, "Hi Ya, Vets!!" *Spectator*, October 28, 1944, 1.

*replaced by a single:* "Last Editorial," *Chronicle*, November 4, 1945, 1.

*fifty thousand Allied:* "From African Desert to Italy, Local Unit Kept 'Em Rolling," *Chronicle*, November 4, 1945, 3; "The Wolf," *Chronicle*, 2.

*sensational stories of bravery:* "Flier Completes Fifteen Mission Run of 15 Days," "Century Mark," "Flier Fails to Reach Base in 12 Out of 32 Missions," *Sortie*, March 18, 1945, 1–2.

*satirized the army's:* "Italian Lessons in Paper Teach GIs to Say 'Sergeant, Please Wake Me at Ten,'" *GI Galley*, January 1944, 2.

*leaflets were divided:* "Words Are Weapons," pamphlet, US Office of War Information Psychological Warfare Team, APO 465.

*American "news" propaganda:* "Words Are Weapons," pamphlet.

93 *"trends in enemy thinking":* James M. Erdmann, *Leaflet Operations in the Second World War* (privately published, 1969), 217–18.

*"malaise in Axis morale":* Erdmann, *Leaflet Operations*, 221.

*"general attrition and fatigue":* Erdmann, *Leaflet Operations*, 221.

*"safe conduct passes":* "Words Are Weapons," pamphlet.

## 7. A MONUMENT TO INTOLERANCE

94 *"For we had just":* Sam Dann, ed., *Dachau 29 April 1945, The Rainbow Liberation Memoirs* (Texas: Texas Tech University Press, 1998), 67.

*a multifaceted invasion:* Stephen E. Ambrose, *D-Day, June 6, 1944: The Climatic Battle of World War II* (New York: Simon & Schuster, 1994), 43, 120–21.

*first-wave casualties:* Ambrose, *D-Day*, 140.

*supreme on the battlefield:* Dwight D. Eisenhower, *Crusade in Europe* (New York: Doubleday & Company, 1948), 238.

*included athletic equipment:* Frederick Osborn Papers, folder "Osborn-Diaries-1943-45, Typescript," 25 April 1944 entry, 9, American Philosophical Society Archives.

*landing had been:* "Invasion Starts," *Invasion Bulletin*, June 6, 1944, 1.

95    *newssheets onto trees:* "Carbon Copies, Published in Invasion, Posted on Trees," *GI Galley*, May 1945, 4.

*hodgepodge of clippings:* "Newspicture Board Set Up at Ordance Post," *GI Galley*, October 1943, 2.

*via loudspeakers:* Pvt. Pat Ward, "Galley Room," *GI Galley*, October 1944, 7.

97    *publication ceased: See Camp Howze Howitzer*, January 8, 1943, 3; "The 84th and 'The News,'" *Camp Claiborne News*, November 18, 1943, 2; "It's Your Paper," *Railsplitter*, July 20, 1944, 1.

*on French soil:* Roscoe C. Blunt Jr., *Foot Soldier: A Combat Infantryman's War in Europe* (Rockville Centre, New York: Sarpedon, 2001), 40.

*past roadside graves:* Blunt, *Foot Soldier*, 45–50.

*shoot a nine-pound:* Jeff Donn, "Pardoned After 55 Years, Court-Martial Still Rankles," *Los Angeles Times*, March 4, 2001.

*contorting his body:* Blunt, *Foot Soldier*, 64–67.

*"incoherent rage of battle":* Blunt, *Foot Soldier*, 106–07.

98    *"Germans were everywhere":* Blunt, *Foot Soldier*, 133.

*infiltrating American positions:* Blunt, *Foot Soldier*, 108.

*screamed in red ink:* "THE P.O.W. WILL SAFELY RETURN!" propaganda leaflet.

*"After two days":* "Two Ways to End the Maneuver," German propaganda leaflet to the "Men of the 84th."

99    *"another in a long list"*: Blunt, *Foot Soldier*, 56, 61, 83, 97, 132.
      *same horrific scene:* Blunt, *Foot Soldier*, 137.
      *"very special event"*: Blunt, *Foot Soldier*, 177.
      *thirty-six-hour press blackout:* "Security Blackout Rapped by Writer,"
      *Lincoln Sunday Journal and Star*, December 31, 1944, 21.

100   *He demanded that:* "Reporter Hits War News Lag," *Press and
      Sun-Bulletin* (Binghamton, New York), December 30, 1944, 2.
      *"intermittent Allied successes"*: "Headline Victories—Again," *Brief*,
      January 16, 1945, 12.
      *headlines at home:* "Headline Victories—Again," 12.
      *"observed the numbers"*: Blunt, *Foot Soldier*, 140.

101   *Reich Radio's news:* Richard Lucas, *Axis Sally* (Philadelphia and
      Newbury: Casemate Publishing, 2010), 12, 73, 131.
      *"It's time to fold"*: "It's Time to Fold Up!" *Home Telegram*, no. 4, 1–2.
      *"prefer a living POW"*: "Germans Treat POW Well—Congress
      Finds," *Home Telegram*, no. 4, 3.
      *"completely fantastic stories"*: "Reporter Hits War News Lag," *Press
      and Sun-Bulletin* (Binghamton, New York), December 30, 1944,
      2 (internal quotation marks omitted).
      *"monotony is deadly"*: "If You Should Be CAPTURED These Are
      Your Rights," War Department, pamphlet, no. 21-7, May 16,
      1944, 3.
      *"Nazis Found Fair"*: "If You Should Be CAPTURED You Will
      Be Safe," code SKJ 2004, German propaganda leaflet.

102   *"As an ideal"*: A. R. Bolling, *The 84th Infantry Division in the
      Battle of the Ardennes, December 1944–January 1945*, Historical
      Section, 84th Infantry Division, Société d'Impression et d'Edi-
      tion Société Coopérative, Liége, April 1945, 5.
      *"will fight better"*: A. R. Bolling, *The 84th Infantry Division*, 5–6.

103   *without Nazi consent:* Vincent Brome, *Europe's Free Press* (London:
      Feature Books Limited), 37.
      *"silence is often worse"*: Brome, *Europe's Free Press*, 39.
      *La Libre Belgique:* Brome, *Europe's Free Press*, 36–38.
      *sabotage the Germans:* Brome, *Europe's Free Press*, 36–40.

*"weather was kind"*: Robert Pollak, "335th Recon Patrol Seizes Town, Gets Statement as Proof," "Four 909th Men Help Stop Nazi Advance from Hollonge Hotel," "Medics By-Pass Tiger Tanks, Rescue Three Wounded Yanks," *Railsplitter*, February 5, 1945, 2–3.

104    *paper printed a tribute*: Sgt. Gareth Hiebert, "Men We Won't Forget—" *Railsplitter*, December 25, 1945, 1.

105    *"You have accomplished"*: "Railsplitters Accomplished the 'Impossible,'" *Railsplitter*, March 10, 1945, 1.

106    *most frequently published*: "Here's Your New Railsplitter," *Railsplitter*, May 1, 1945, 1.

       *"easier to read"*: "Here's Your New Railsplitter," *Railsplitter*, 1.

       *Headlines encouraged troops*: "Nazis Giving Up to 84th as Resistance Collapses," *Railsplitter*, May 1, 1945, 1; "84th Takes 4 Nazi Generals," *Railsplitter*, May 5, 1945, 1; "VICTORY!" *Railsplitter*, May 8, 1945, 1.

       *"billfold girl of the week"*: Lt. Hugh C. Daly, *42nd "Rainbow" Infantry Division: A Combat History of World War II* (Baton Rouge, Louisiana: Army and Navy Publishing Company, 1946), 3.

       *"taste of combat"*: Pvt. Scott Corbett, "Combat Conditions Taste Like Wet Chicken After Rains on Range," *Rainbow Reveille*, October 28, 1943, 8.

       *"leaped to attention"*: Pvt. Scott Corbett, "Personal Glances," *Rainbow Reveille*, November 4, 1943, 2.

       *nighttime bivouac exercise*: Pvt. Scott Corbett, "Immaterial Witness," *Rainbow Reveille*, November 25, 1943, 2.

       *"tendency away from"*: Corbett, "Personal Glances," 2.

       *"a rough night"*: Pvt. Scott Corbett, "Immaterial Witness," *Rainbow Reveille*, March 2, 1944, 2.

107    *In November 1944*: Daly, *42nd "Rainbow" Infantry*, 13–14.

       *killed 50 percent*: Daly, *42nd "Rainbow" Infantry*, 26–36.

       *regrouping in Nancy*: Daly, *42nd "Rainbow" Infantry*, 36–37.

       *"This is a silly"*: Daly, *42nd "Rainbow" Infantry*, 42.

108    *in March 1945*: Daly, *42nd "Rainbow" Infantry*, 47–51.

*Top command recognized:* Daly, *42nd "Rainbow" Infantry*, 47.

*"Here's the kind":* "They Cried Uncle—Uncle Sam," *Rainbow Reveille*, March 8, 1945, 1.

*"There was a time":* Pvt. Scott Corbett, "The Immaterial Witness," *Rainbow Reveille*, March 8, 1945, 2.

*trumpeted their progress:* "Rainbow Smashes Siegfried Line," *Rainbow Reveille*, April 5, 1945, 1.

*"Heinrich Himmler would":* "GIs Find Nazi Dream Castle," *Rainbow Reveille*, April 5, 1945, 1.

*"a nice spot":* "GIs Find Nazi Dream Castle," 4.

109    *blossomed and evolved: See, e.g.,* "White Flag Day in Furth," *Rainbow Reveille*, April 26, 1945, 4–5.

*gossip and humor:* "Short Rounds," *Rainbow Reveille*, April 26, 1945, 7.

*drive to Munich:* Dann, *Dachau 29 April 1945*, 5.

*"ran into an installation":* Dann, *Dachau 29 April 1945*, 5.

*"take a reading":* Dann, *Dachau 29 April 1945*, 18–19.

*"signs of beating":* Dann, *Dachau 29 April 1945*, 18.

*The prisoners surrounded:* Dann, *Dachau 29 April 1945*, 19.

110    *"Nothing can adequately":* Dann, *Dachau 29 April 1945*, 44.

*the inhuman treatment:* Dann, *Dachau 29 April 1945*, 13.

*"We never wanted":* Dann, *Dachau 29 April 1945*, 44–45.

*immediate account of Dachau:* Dann, *Dachau 29 April 1945*, 47.

*Creasman's raw account:* James W. Creasman, "Dachau," *42d Rainbow Infantry Division World News*, May 1, 1945, 1–2.

112    *"captured the most":* "From Strasbourg to Salzburg—42d Adds to Past Glories in Dash Across Germany," *Rainbow Reveille*, May 11, 1945, 10.

113    *"don't mail a copy":* "Enough copies . . ." *Rainbow Reveille*, May 11, 1945, 1.

*told by the soldiers:* "This Was Dachau," *Rainbow Reveille*, May 11, 1945, 5–8.

*"the natural outcome":* "This Was Dachau," *Rainbow Reveille*, May 11, 1945, 7.

114   *"I have only been"*: Lt. William J. Cowling III to "Folks," in Dann, *Dachau 29 April 1945*, 24.

## 8. DON'T SEND ME IN

115   *"Have you ever"*: "FUBAR," *Leonitic*, July 2, 1945, 2.

116   *"I found it"* E. B. Sledge, *With the Old Breed* (New York: Ballantine Books, 2007), 255–56.

117   *"seemed more unlikely"*: Sledge, *With the Old Breed*, 246.
      *Lord's Prayer*: Sledge, *With the Old Breed*, 58.
      *seal his nomination*: Samuel A. Stouffer et al., *The American Soldier: Adjustment During Army Life*, vol. 1 (Princeton, New Jersey: Princeton University Press, 1949), 13.
      *study of eugenics*: Wolfgang Saxon, "Frederick Osborn, a General, 91, Dies," *New York Times*, January 7, 1981.
      *"racial preventative medicine"*: Frank Lorimer and Frederick Osborn, *Dynamics of Population* (New York: The Macmillan Company, 1934), 348.
      *Osborn openly admired*: Barry Alan Mehler, "A History of the American Eugenics Society, 1921–1940" (PhD dissertation, University of Illinois, Urbana, 1988), 223, 227–29, 244.
      *a rosy description*: Frederick Osborn Papers, folder "Osborn-Diaries-1943-45, Typescript," 14 May 1945 entry, 27–30, American Philosophical Society Archives.
      *"Badly quartered"*: Frederick Osborn Papers, folder "Osborn-Diaries-1943-45, Typescript," 24–25 May 1945 entry, 42, American Philosophical Society Archives.

118   *"entertainment and diversion"*: "Slump in U.S. Morale: Sign of Trouble," *United States News*, September 5, 1941, 9.
      *"I was much disturbed"*: "Memorandum for General Osborn," 24 December 1943, #4-178, George C. Marshall Papers, Pentagon Office Collection, Selected Materials, George C. Marshall Research Library, Lexington, Virginia.

119   *Little Rock Barracks*: Geoffrey Perret, *Old Soldiers Never Die: The Life of Douglas MacArthur* (New York: Random House, 1996), 12.

*He graduated first:* Perret, *Old Soldiers Never Die*, 45.

*"real promotions":* Perret, *Old Soldiers Never Die*, 77, 83, 85–86.

*well-publicized episode:* Perret, *Old Soldiers Never Die*, 105.

*MacArthur received:* Perret, *Old Soldiers Never Die*, 84–85, 94.

120 *"Nothing affected MacArthur":* Perret, *Old Soldiers Never Die*, 120.

*"If the policy":* Phillip Knightley, *The First Casualty* (New York & London: Harcourt Brace Jovanovich, 1975), 279.

*MacArthur banned correspondents:* Knightley, *The First Casualty*, 281.

*a sarcastic poem:* Perrett, *Old Soldiers Never Die*, 326.

121 *one soldier snapped:* Ernie Pyle, *Brave Men* (Lincoln and London: University of Nebraska Press, 2001), 424–25.

*"That was what":* Pyle, *Brave Men*, 425.

*"morale situation":* Perret, *Old Soldiers Never Die*, 394.

122 *"disinterestedness of my position":* Frederick Osborn Papers, folder "Osborn-Diaries-1943-45, Typescript," 17 January 1944 entry, 15–26, American Philosophical Society Archives.

*"a brass-hatted old bastard":* Perrett, *Old Soldiers Never Die*, 396.

*"too sensitive to slights":* Perret, *Old Soldiers Never Die*, 396.

*Osborn told Marshall:* Frederick Osborn to the chief of staff, memorandum, 14 February 1944, NA/RG 165 [OCS, 330.11], George C. Marshall Papers, Pentagon Office Collection, Selected Materials, George C. Marshall Research Library, Lexington, Virginia.

*"most favorable report":* *The Papers of George Catlett Marshall*, ed. Larry I. Bland and Sharon Ritenour Stevens (Lexington, Virginia.: The George C. Marshall Foundation, 1981–), electronic version based on *The Papers of George Catlett Marshall*, *"Aggressive and Determined Leadership," June 1, 1943-December 31, 1944*, vol. 4 (Baltimore and London: The Johns Hopkins University Press, 1996), 207.

123 *MacArthur begrudgingly approved:* Frederick Osborn Papers, folder "Osborn-Diaries-1943-45, Typescript," 17 January 1944 entry, 15–26, American Philosophical Society Archives.

*SWPA Maptalk:* Frederick Osborn Papers, folder "Osborn—Speeches—'The Soldier Gets His Bearings,'" 13 June 1944, American Philosophical Society Archives.

*There were no editorials:* See, e.g., *SWPA Maptalk*, May 30, 1945.

*Fortunately for troops: The Special Service Company*, FM 28-105 (Washington, DC: United States Government Printing Office, 1944), 32.

*"If we printed":* 59th Latrineogram, May 14, 1944, 2; *59th Latrineogram*, June 11, 1944, 2.

124    *"morale was shot":* "Fire Dept Commits Arson," "Soldier Tried to End Troubles," *59th Latrineogram*, June 11, 1944, 1.

*"In fond memory":* "Obitchuaries," *59th Latrineogram*, May 7, 1944, 2.

*a classified ad:* "Wanted!" *Tough Sheet*, August 17, 1945, 4.

*"What I want": Bamboo Bulletin*, September 1, 1945, 8.

*marines reported their feelings:* "Book Suggestions of the Week," *This is It!*, November 15, 1944, 6.

125    *"Let me float":* "Don't Send Me In!" *Otter News*, August 25, 1945, 11.

126    *"aid or comfort": Military Intelligence Military Censorship*, FM 30-28 (Washington, DC: Government Printing Office, 1944), 16.

*"bloodiest battles of the Pacific":* "Saipan Was Worse Than Tarawa," *Yank, the Army Weekly*, July 28, 1944, 4; George F. Horne, "Gain in Marianas," *New York Times*, June 18, 1944, 1; George F. Horne, "Saipan is Stormed," *New York Times*, June 16, 1944, 1; "We Take Saipan," *New York Times*, July 10, 1944, 14.

*suicide was preferable:* Rembert James, "Last Stand on Saipan," *New York Times*, July 11, 1944, 9; John Wukovits, "Horror on Marpi Point: A Crucial Foothold in the Marianas," January 24, 2016, www.warefarehistorynetwork.com.

127    *one officer instructed:* "Ribs by 'Rog,'" *Beachmaster*, December 5, 1944, 7.

*"Uncle Bob" Roberts:* "Have a Donut?" *This Is It!*, January 24, 1945, 1; "Mr. Roberts Going Home," *This Is It!*, February 28, 1945, 1.

*weekly mimeographed paper:* "To the Men of the Group," *This Is It!*, February 14, 1945, 2.

*"We wish to commend":* "Editorials," *This Is It!*, November 15, 1944, 2.

*Issue after issue:* "Censorship," *This Is It!*, October 25, 1944, 2; "A Report to the Folks at Home," *This Is It!*, November 8, 1944, 3.

*Japanese radio propaganda:* "Raid on Marianas," *This Is It!*, November 8, 1944, 2.

*Editorials also chided:* "Rumors," *This Is It!*, November 22, 1944, 2.

128   *poem by a corporal lampooning:* "To the Men of the Group," *This Is It!*, February 14, 1945, 2.

*"A paper for the group":* "This Is It—To Wit," *This Is It!*, February 14, 1945, 2.

129   *weekly "Problem Hour":* "Problem Hour for Men of Group," *This Is It!*, January 31, 1945, 1.

*impacted the trajectory:* "29's Clearing Road to Tokyo," *This Is It!*, December 6, 1944, 1.

*Ninety-First's assistance:* "Iwo," *This Is It!*, February 21, 1945, 1.

*When Okinawa was:* "Planes Hit Japan as Ryukus Given Invasion All-Out," *This Is It!*, April 4, 1945, 1.

*"home six months":* "Points," *This Is It!*, February 14, 1945, 1.

*"The Club Atoll":* "Officers Open Club," *This Is It!*, March 7, 1945, 5.

*to include pinups: This Is It!*, March 7, 1945, 7.

*"no one can locate":* "Rock Happy," *This Is It!*, April 4, 1945, 3.

130   *A "favorite friend":* "To Uncle Bob," *This Is It!*, February 21, 1945, 2.

*The 1945 battle:* Hanson W. Baldwin, "Iwo a Strategic Prize," *New York Times*, February 18, 1945, 4.

*"bloody and disagreeable":* John Lardner, "D Day, Iwo Jima," *The New Yorker Book of War Pieces* (New York: Reynal & Hitchcock, 1947), 462.

*Japanese defenses were:* "The Campaign," *Fighter Post*, October 13, 1945, 1.

*"Iwo Jima was"*: "The Curtain Is Down," *Fighter Post*, October 13, 1945, 10.

132 *"Whether you want"*: "Sound Off!" *Brief*, November 28, 1944, 2.
*profanity-laden protests:* "The Bitching Post," *Brief*, November 14, 1944, 13.

*"Gripe Club"*: "This Ain't the Army," *Brief*, November 21, 1944, 13.

*Nelson jotted down:* Clive Howard and Joe Whitley, *One Damned Island after Another* (Chapel Hill: University of North Carolina Press, 1946), v–vi.

135 *weekly column devoted: See, e.g., Brief*, V-J Issue, 2.

## 9. DEMOCRACY?

136 *"Let America be"*: Arnold Rampersad and David Roessel, ed., *The Collected Poems of Langston Hughes*, "Let America Be America Again" (New York: Vintage Classics, 1994), 189.

*segregated units:* Laura Ruminski, "Against All Odds," *Hawaii Tribune Herald*, July 21, 2021.

*they were assigned: See* 442nd Regimental Combat Team Legacy website, http://www.the442.org/home.html.

*Native Americans also:* Thomas D. Morgan, "Native Americans in World War II," *Army History*, no. 35 (Fall 1995): 22–24.

137 *Selective Training and Service Act:* 54 US Stat. 885, Sec. 3(a) (1940).

*four hundred thousand:* Morris J. MacGregor Jr., *Integration of the Armed Forces 1940–1965* (Washington, DC: Center of Military History, US Army, 1981), 24, 33.

*"racial intermingling"*: MacGregor, *Integration of the Armed Forces*, 18.

*"inflexible separation"*: MacGregor, *Integration of the Armed Forces*, 19–20.

*"prevailing public sentiment"*: MacGregor, *Integration of the Armed Forces*, 20, 22.

*"settlement of vexing"*: MacGregor, *Integration of the Armed Forces*, 21–22.

138 *army's inflexible policy:* MacGregor, *Integration of the Armed Forces*, 25, 36.

*"separate and very unequal"*: Mary Penick Motley, *The Invisible Soldier: The Experience of the Black Soldier, World War II* (Detroit: Wayne State University Press, 1987), 55–57.

*servile or menial jobs:* Maggi M. Morehouse, *Fighting in the Jim Crow Army: Black Men and Women Remember World War II* (Lanham, Maryland: Rowman & Littlefield Publishers, Inc., 2000), 14–21.

*"introduced Jim Crow"*: MacGregor, *Integration of the Armed Forces*, 35–36.

*"perpetuated segregation"*: MacGregor, *Integration of the Armed Forces*, 57.

*racial segregation policy:* MacGregor, *Integration of the Armed Forces*, 23.

*"sorry for brutality"*: MacGregor, *Integration of the Armed Forces*, 9.

*"America of today"*: Lisa Sergio, "The Importance of Interpreting America," *American Library Association Bulletin* 35, no. 9 (October 1, 1941), 487 (internal quotations omitted).

139   *by and for Black troops:* "Sgt. Leon Smith, Editor," *GI Galley*, May 1944, 6; "Honorable Mention List," *GI Galley*, June 1944, 4; "59 Publications Win Honorable Mention," *GI Galley*, June 1945, 4.

*"This doesn't mean"*: Sgt. Leon E. Smith, "A 'Perfect' Paper," *GI Galley*, November 1945, 6.

140   *"Over the Mediterranean"*: Irwin Shaw, "Negro Fighters' First Battle," *Yank, the Army Weekly*, August 6, 1943, 8–9.

*"Yank takes its views"*: "Negro Soldiers," *Yank, the Army Weekly*, December 17, 1943, 18.

*Black troops were:* MacGregor, *Integration of the Armed Forces*, 51.

*"poll of white officers"*: Samuel A. Stouffer et al., *The American Soldier: Adjustment During Army Life*, vol. I (Princeton, New Jersey: Princeton University Press, 1949), 589, 593.

*"the prospect of"*: MacGregor, *Integration of the Armed Forces*, 54.

141   *"It is an obvious fact"*: "A Common Cause," *Stars and Stripes*, October 5, 1944, 2.

*"I've been waiting"*: "No Color Line Up Front," *Stars and Stripes*, October 28, 1944.

142  *"I've handled artillery"*: Allan Morrison, "Negro Artillery Unit Shows Gallantry in Epic of Bastogne," *Stars and Stripes*; "GIs Handle 'Hot' Cargo—Hot for Nazis," *Stars and Stripes*, December 16, 1944.

*"Negroes Fight Beside"*: "Negroes Fight Beside Whites on West Front," *Stars and Stripes*, March 19, 1945, 1, 5.

*"home of the splendid"*: "Colored Citizens Are A-1 Soldiers," *Arizona Republic* (Phoenix), November 22, 1942, 45.

143  *"we could not purchase"*: "Democracy?" *Yank, the Army Weekly*, April 28, 1944, 14.

*"a Southern rebel"*: Cpl. Henry S. Wootton, "Democracy?" *Yank, the Army Weekly*, June 9, 1944, 14.

144  *"It seems incredible"*: S/Sgt. Arthur J. Kaplan, "Democracy?" *Yank, the Army Weekly*, June 9, 1944, 14.

*"I'm not a"*: Pvt. Gustave Santiago, "Democracy?" *Yank, the Army Weekly*, June 9, 1944, 14.

*One missive*: Pvt. Joseph Poscucci, "Democracy?" *Yank, the Army Weekly*, July 28, 1944, 14.

*New Yorker published*: Robert McLaughlin, "A Short Wait Between Trains," *New Yorker*, June 17, 1944, 27–29.

*A dramatic skit*: *The Best from Yank, the Army Weekly* (New York: E. O. Dutton & Co., Inc., 1945), 213.

*volume of its best stories*: *The Best from Yank*, 212–13.

145  *"Allow me to thank you"*: Cpl. Rupert Trimmingham, "Democracy?" *Yank, the Army Weekly*, July 28, 1944, 14.

*"It is hereby"*: "Texts of Rights Orders," "The Armed Services," *New York Times*, July 27, 1948, 4.

*fully dismantle*: Emily Ludolph, "The Long Project of Desegregating the U.S. Military," *New York Times*, July 21, 2019, sec. F, p. 6.

146  *"delegates of freedom"*: Franklin Delano Roosevelt, "To the Armed Forces of the United States," *Yank, the Army Weekly*, June 17, 1942, 2.

*"chance to volunteer"*: 87 Cong. Rec. 4531 (Representative Edith Nourse Rogers May 28, 1941).

*"I hate the word"*: 88 Cong. Rec. 4091 (May 12, 1942).

*Roosevelt signed legislation:* "600,000 Goal Set for Women's Army Corps Enrollment," *Hartford Courant*, July 6, 1943, 4.

*Women's Army Corps:* 89 Cong. Rec. 4992-93 (May 27, 1943).

147 *1954 treatise:* Mattie E. Treadwell, *United States Army in World War II Special Studies: The Women's Army Corps* (Washington, DC: Office of the Chief of Military History Department of the Army, 1954), xii.

*something threatening: A Book of Facts about the WAC*, booklet, War Department, 1944, 10.

*"supersecret agreement"*: John O'Donnell, "Capitol Stuff," *New York Daily News*, June 9, 1943, 4.

*"vehement denials"*: Ralph McGill, "One Word More," *Atlanta Constitution*, June 16, 1943, 6.

*"drank too much"*: Treadwell, *The Women's Army Corps*, 209.

148 *WACs were better educated:* Treadwell, *The Women's Army Corps*, 192–93.

*"everybody was talking":* Treadwell, *The Women's Army Corps*, 204.

*"You join the WAVES":* Treadwell, *The Women's Army Corps*, 212–13.

149 *policy toward Black soldiers:* "Negro Soldiers," *Yank, the Army Weekly*, December 17, 1943, 18.

*In August 1943:* Barrett McGurn, "WAACs Drop An 'A,'" *Yank, the Army Weekly*, August 20, 1943, 8–9.

*piece generated letters:* McGurn, "WAACs Drop An 'A,'" 8–9.

*featured the navy's WAVES:* "The Navy Takes to the Air Waves," *Yank, the Army Weekly*, August 27, 1943, 16; "WACs at Fort Belvoir, Va.," *Yank, the Army Weekly*, October 8, 1943, 16.

*depicted smiling women:* "The Navy Takes to the Air Waves," 16; "WACs at Fort Belvoir, Va.," 16.

*"feminine propaganda"*: Bob Bowie, "Wacs—Pro and Con," *Yank, the Army Weekly*, February 18, 1944, 14.

150 *"Why we GIs"*: Bob Bowie, "Wacs—Pro and Con," 14.

*"I was disgusted"*: William J. Robinson, "Wacs—Pro and Con," *Yank, the Army Weekly*, February 18, 1944, 14.

*published responses:* "Wacs Hit Back," *Yank, the Army Weekly*, March 31, 1944, 14.

151 *coining the term pinup:* H. L. Mencken, *American Language Treatise, Supplement II* (New York: Alfred A. Knopf, 1948), 781, n. 4.

*"devoted its front cover":* *Yank, the Army Weekly*, June 9, 1944; *see also* "This Week's Cover," *Yank, the Army Weekly*, June 9, 1944, 7.

*"That is worth":* "Pvt. Grace Glocke," *Yank, the Army Weekly*, July 14, 1944, 14.

*recruitment of women:* "WAAC Recruitment Under Expectations," *Battle Creek Enquirer* (Battle Creek, Michigan), March 9, 1943, 5.

*begging for more WACs:* Treadwell, *The Women's Army Corps*, 211.

*"good and faithful":* "Wacs Praised by Military Leaders on Anniversary," *Marshall News Messenger* (Marshall, Texas), May 13, 1945, 9.

*"outstanding performance":* "Wacs Praised by Military Leaders on Anniversary," 9.

152 *WAC magazine kit:* John Jamieson, *Books for the Army: The Army Library Service in the Second World War* (New York: Columbia University Press, 1950), 141.

*ten thousand packages:* Jamieson, *Books for the Army*, 141.

*"Soldiers would grab":* Ray L. Trautman and Adelaide, interview, undated (from after war ended, before RLT left Library Branch), folder 27, RLT Interviews, Speeches, Talks, Ray L. Trautman Materials, The Trautman Museum, New York City.

*covered stories about women: The Service Woman*, September 14, 1945.

*in the European theater: Overseas Woman*, July 1945.

153 *"malicious and untruthful":* "Wacs in Africa Working Hard," *WAC News*, August 7–14, 1944, 4.

*interview with a civilian:* "Wacs in Africa Working Hard," 4.

*army's double standards:* "Pin-Up Boy," *WAC News*, December 4, 1943, 1.

*a congratulatory cartoon:* "WAC News Celebrates 2nd Birthday," *WAC News*, October 7, 1944, 1.

*an ingenious ploy:* "WAC News One Year Old—October 5th," *WAC News*, October 2–9, 1944, 1.

*male attitudes toward:* Treadwell, *The Women's Army Corps*, 448 (chart).

## 10. NOW—WHERE WERE WE?

169   *"Please send us":* Kaplan, "A 92nd Seabee's Yuletide Prayer," *92nd Island X Press*, December 23, 1944, 3.

170   *Alexander Woollcott:* Samuel Hopkins Adams, A. Woollcott: His Life and His World (New York: Reynal & Hitchcock, 1945), 92.

     "in a corner": Adams, *A. Woollcott*, 92.

171   *redeployed to the Pacific:* Sidney Shalett, "Army to Return 3,100,000 in Year; 400,000 Will Remain in Europe," *New York Times*, May 10, 1945.

     *"like asking a child":* L. "Buckshot" Beebe, "Hi 'N Low," *Yankee Doodler*, May 13, 1945, 4.

     *"beneficial to you":* "What Do You Think?" *Alhambra Echo*, July 14, 1946, 2.

172   *"The spirit which":* "Society Could Insure Defense," *Railsplitter*, May 18, 1945, 8.

     *summer and fall:* "Publish Book of Addresses," *Railsplitter*, December 23, 1945, 1.

173   *In December 1945:* "Division Going Home," *Railsplitter*, December 2, 1945, 1.

     *"rocket ships":* "Thanks Anyway," *Leonitic*, July 2, 1945, 1.

     *provided a road map:* "Here's a Play by Play on That Trip Home," *Railsplitter*, December 5, 1945, 1.

     *"Many qualities make":* "Division Commander Inspired His Men," *Railsplitter*, December 25, 1945, 1.

174   *set sail from Le Havre:* "Final Pass Totals Are Over 10,000," *Railsplitter*, December 2, 1945, 1.

     *first postwar Railsplitter: Railsplitter*, July 29, 1946.

*printing its own:* "A Soldier's Guide to the United States of America," *Home Run*, November 10, 1945, 4.

*guidebook informed readers:* "A Soldier's Guide to the United States of America," *Home Run*, November 10, 1945, 4.

175   *an unspoken understanding:* Ernie Pyle, Brave Men (Lincoln and London: University of Nebraska Press, 2001), 287.

*"We salute you":* Jasper Jones, "To the Unknown," *Skunk Hollow News*, V. E. Edition, 7.

177   *"Your mess kit":* James W. Currie, "Farewell from the Chaplain, *Alhambra Echo*, July 14, 1946, 1, 3.

*ports of debarkation:* "Navy Separation Centers Open for Business," *Skyscrapers*, US Naval Air Station, Floyd Bennett Field, August 23, 1945, 1.

*appointed US ambassador:* Forrest C. Pogue, *George C. Marshall: Statesman* (New York: Viking Penguin, Inc., 1987), 26; "Marshall to China," *New York Times*, December 16, 1945, 2E.

*adopted new regulations:* Circular no. 103, 6 April 1946, War Department.

178   *no longer needed:* C. P. Trussell, "Draft Opposition Rising in Congress," *New York Times*, August 15, 1945, 13.

*would cease publication:* "Fall Out!" *Outfit*, December 31, 1945 (cover).

*final issue featured:* Yank the Army Weekly, December 30, 1945 (cover).

*readers still lamented:* "Last Issue," *Yank, the Army Weekly*, December 30, 1945, 20.

*"You lightened many":* Robert C. Harvey, *Meanwhile...: A Biography of Milton Caniff* (Seattle, Washington: Fantagraphics Books, 2007), 493.

179   *cartoon depicts Lace:* "Now—Where Were We?" *Pennant Parade*, November 6, 1945, 1.

## AFTERWORD

181   *"War is a stupid":* "Editorial," *Sea Devil Sentinel* II, no. XVI (undated), Farewell Issue, 2.

182 *magazine circulation rates:* Theodore Peterson, *Magazines in the Twentieth Century* (Urbana, Illinois: The University of Illinois Press, 1956), 54.

*continue to climb:* Peterson, *Magazines in the Twentieth Century*, 55, 58 (table 3).

*over fifty-two million:* Frank Luther Mott, *American Journalism: A History: 1690–1960* (Toronto, Canada: Macmillan, 1962), 784.

*was reading newspapers:* "Vital Statistics of the United States 1949" (Washington, DC: United States Printing Office, 1951), 37 (table XVII).

183 *a dozen books:* Andy Rooney, *My War* (New York: Times Books, 1995).

*Bill Mauldin returned:* "Mauldin Insists the Soldier's Newspaper Is 'the One Thing That Should Be Left Free,'" *New York Times*, June 12, 1945, 9.

*his drawing pencil:* Richard Severo, "Bill Mauldin, Newspaper Cartoonist, Dies at 81," *New York Times*, January 22, 2003.

*became a novelist:* John Monaghan, "Scott Corbett Dies, Author and Educator," *Providence Journal*, March 6, 2006.

# SELECTED BIBLIOGRAPHY

## OFFICIAL GOVERNMENT PUBLICATIONS

*Army Editors' Manual*. New York: War Department, undated.

*Army Newspaper Editors' Manual*. New York: Information and Education Division, Headquarters, Army Special Forces, September 1944.

*Biennial Reports of Gen. George C. Marshall, Chief of Staff of the US Army July 1, 1939 to June 30, 1943 to the Secretary of War*. Washington, DC: The Infantry Journal, 1943.

*The Bluejackets Manual*. Annapolis, Maryland: United States Naval Institute, 1940.

*A Book of Facts about the WAC*. Booklet. War Department, 1944.

*Code of Wartime Practices for the American Press*. Booklet. Washington, DC: US Government Printing Office, 1942.

*French Language Guide*, TM 30-302. Washington, DC: War Department, 1943.

*Military Intelligence Military Censorship*, FM 30-28. Washington, DC: Government Printing Office, 1944.

*North African Arabic Language Guide*, TM 30-321. Washington, DC: War Department, 1943.

*Pocket Guide to North Africa*. Washington, DC: War and Navy Departments.

*The Special Service Company*, FM 28-105. Washington, DC: War Department, January 5, 1944.

War Department. Memorandum, 7 September 1942, no. W210-6-42. re: publication of post, camp, and unit newspapers.

War Department. Pamphlet, 16 May 1944, no. 21-7, "If you should be CAPTURED these are your rights."

## ARCHIVES, MUSEUMS, AND PERSONAL PAPERS

Arthur Hays Sulzberger papers. New York Times Company Records. Manuscripts and Archives Division. New York Public Library. Astor, Lenox, and Tilden Foundations.

Byron Price Papers, 1901–1976. Archives Division, State Historical Society of Wisconsin, Madison.

Council on Books in Wartime Records, 1942–1947. Coll. no. MC038. 20th Century Public Policy Papers. Seeley G. Mudd Manuscript Library, Department of Rare Books and Special Collections, Princeton University Library.

Frederick Osborn Papers. American Philosophical Society Archives.

General Correspondence of the Office of the Stars and Stripes, 1917–1919. National Archives identifier 6634103, entry number NM-91 236. National Archives Building, Washington, DC.

George C. Marshall Papers. Pentagon Office Collection, Selected Materials. George C. Marshall Research Library, Lexington, Virginia.

*GI Galley*, 1942–1945. Army Service Forces. Camp Newspaper Service. US Army Heritage and Education Center, Carlisle, Pennsylvania.

*New Yorker* records. Manuscripts and Archives Division, New York Public Library. Astor, Lenox, and Tilden Foundations.

Ray L. Trautman Materials. World War II Papers, 1940–1945. The Trautman Museum, New York.

Roosevelt, Franklin D. Papers as President. Franklin D. Roosevelt Presidential Library, Hyde Park, New York.


## PAMPHLETS AND LEAFLETS

"Good Luck! 1945." Propaganda leaflet, 374/12.

*Home Telegram*. Propaganda newspaper.

"I fought in Italy too . . . Your dead pal speaking . . ." Propaganda leaflet, A1-067-5-44.

"If you should be CAPTURED you will be safe." Propaganda leaflet, SKJ 2004.

"My Africa Souvenir." Propaganda leaflet, series A, no. 4.

"Paved With Skulls!" Propaganda leaflet, A1-061-4-44.

"THE P.O.W. WILL SAFELY RETURN!" Propaganda leaflet.

"Two Ways to End the Maneuver." Propaganda leaflet, to the "Men of the 84th."

"Why are you still fighting in Italy?" Propaganda leaflet, T 37.

"Words Are Weapons." Pamphlet. US Office of War Information Psychological Warfare Team, APO 465.


## SELECTED ARTICLES

Dornbusch, C. E. *Stars and Stripes: Check List of the Several Editions*. New York: New York Public Library, 1948.

Dornbusch, C. E. *Yank, The Army Weekly*. New York: New York Public Library, 1950.

Mehler, Barry Alan. "A History of the American Eugenics Society, 1921–1940." PhD diss., University of Illinois, Urbana, 1988.

Morgan, Thomas D. "Native Americans in World War II." *Army History*,

US Army Center of Military History (Fall 1995).

Sergio, Lisa. "The Importance of Interpreting America." *American Library Association Bulletin* 35, no. 9 (October 1, 1941).

## NEWSPAPERS AND PERIODICALS PRINTED IN THE UNITED STATES

*Adrian (MI) Daily Telegram*

*Akron (OH) Beacon Journal*

*Arizona Republic*

*Atlanta Constitution*

*Baltimore Sun*

*Battle Creek (MI) Enquirer*

*Boston Herald*

*Burlington (VT) Free Press*

*Capital (WI) Times*

*Charlotte (NC) News*

*Courier-Journal (KY)*

*Daily Mirror (NY)*

*El Paso (TX) Herald-Post*

*Facts in Review* (New York: German Library Association)

*Furniture Worker*

*Gallup (NM) Independent*

*Greenville (SC) News*

*Hartford Courant*

*Hawaii Tribune Herald*

*Herald and Review (IL)*

*Journal Herald (OH)*

*Kilgore (TX) News Herald*

*Life*

*Lincoln (NE) Sunday Journal and Star*

*Los Angeles Times*

*Marshall (TX) News Messenger*

*Medford (OR) Mail Tribune*

*National Geographic*

*New-Journal (OH)*

*New London (CT) Evening Day*

*New York Daily News*

*New York Times*

*New Yorker*

*Newsweek*

*Oregonian*

*Pittsburgh Press*

*Press and Sun-Bulletin (NY)*

*Providence Journal*

*Salem (OH) News*

*San Francisco Examiner*

*Sunday Herald-Leader (KY)*

*Sunday Providence (RI) Sunday Journal*

*Time*

*United States News*

## MILITARY NEWSPAPERS AND PERIODICALS

*42d Rainbow Infantry Division World News*

*45th Division News*

*49er's Buzzin' Briefs*

*59th Latrineogram*

*92nd Island X Press*

*Alhambra Echo*

*All Hands*

*Bamboo Bulletin*

*Beachmaster*

*Blue Bonnet*

*Bonjour*

*Brief*

*Camp Claiborne News*

*Camp Howze Howitzer*

*Camp Newspaper Clip Sheet*

*The Chronicle*

*Engineerful*

*Fighter Post*

*GI Galley*

*Home Run*

*Hornet Tales*

*Invasion Bulletin*

*Leonitic*

*Oflag 64 Item*

*The Otter News*

*Outfit*

*Overseas Woman*

*Pennant Parade*

*The Railsplitter*

*Rainbow Reveille*

*Sandfly*

*Sea Devil Sentinel*

*Service Woman*

*Skunk Hollow News*

*Skyscrapers*

*Sortie*

*The Spectator*

*Stars and Stripes*

*SWPA Maptalk*

*Tale Spinner*

*This is It!*

*Tough Sheet*

*U.S.A.T.*

*WAC News*

*Weekly 127 Seabreeze*

*Yank, the Army Weekly*

*Yankee Doodler*

## BOOKS CITED

Adams, Samuel Hopkins. *A. Woollcott: His Life and His World*. New York: Reynal & Hitchcock, 1945.

Ambrose, Stephen E. *D-Day, June 6, 1944: The Climatic Battle of World War II*. New York: Simon & Schuster, 1994.

Applebaum, Harold. *Solo and Other Poems*. New York: Creative Age Press, 1947.

Atkinson, Rick. *The Day of Battle*: *The War in Sicily and Italy, 1943–1944*. New York: Henry Holt and Co., 2007.

*The Best from Yank, the Army Weekly*. New York: E. O. Dutton & Co., Inc., 1945.

Bland, Larry I., Sharon R. Ritenour, and Clarence E. Wunderlin Jr., eds. *The Papers of George Catlett Marshall*. Baltimore, Maryland: Johns Hopkins University Press, 1986.

Blumenson, Martin, ed. *The Patton Papers 1940–1945*. Boston: Houghton Mifflin, 1974.

Blumenson, Martin. *Patton: The Man Behind the Legend, 1885–1945*. New York: William Morrow & Co., 1985.

Blunt Jr., Roscoe C. *Foot Soldier: A Combat Infantryman's War in Europe*. Rockville Centre, New York: Sarpedon, 2001.

Bolling, A. R. *The 84th Infantry Division in The Battle of the Ardennes, December 1944–January 1945*. Historical Section, 84th Infantry Division. Société d'Impression et d'Edition Société Coopérative, Liége, April 1945.

Bolte, Charles G. *The New Veteran*. New York: Reynal & Hitchcock, 1945.

Brome, Vincent. *Europe's Free Press*. London: Feature Books Limited, undated.

Chatlain, Dean F. *With Pen and Sword*. Cuyahoga Falls, Ohio: F. W. Orth Company, 1945.

Daly, Hugh C., *42nd "Rainbow" Infantry Division: A Combat History of World War II*. Baton Rouge, Louisiana: Army and Navy Publishing Company, 1946.

Dann, Sam, ed. *Dachau 29 April 1945: The Rainbow Liberation Memoirs*. Texas: Texas Tech University Press, 1998.

Eisenhower, Dwight D. *Crusade in Europe*. New York: Doubleday & Company, 1948.

Erdmann, James M. *Leaflet Operations in the Second World War*. Privately published, 1969.

Fahey, James J. *Pacific War Diary*. New York: Kensington Publishing Corp., 1963.

Frye, William. *Marshall: Citizen Soldier*. New York: Bobbs-Merrill Company, 1947.

Fussell, Paul. *Wartime: Understanding and Behavior in the Second World War*. New York: Oxford University Press, 1989.

Goodwin, Doris Kearns. *No Ordinary Time*. New York: Simon & Schuster, 1994.

Hardy, Alexander G. *Hitler's Secret Weapon: The "Managed" Press and Propaganda Machine of Nazi Germany*. New York: Vantage Press, 1967.

Hargrove, Marion. *See Here, Private Hargrove*. New York: Pocket Books, 1942.

Harvey, Robert C. *Meanwhile . . . : A Biography of Milton Caniff*. Seattle, Washington: Fantagraphics Books, 1982.

Howard, Clive, and Joe Whitley. *One Damned Island after Another*. Chapel Hill: University of North Carolina Press, 1946.

Hutton, Bud, and Andy Rooney. *The Story of the Stars and Stripes: A Paper for Joe*. New York: Farrar & Rinehart, Inc., 1946.

Jamieson, John. *Books for the Army: The Army Library Service in the Second World War*. New York: Columbia University Press, 1950.

Kaye, Harvey J. *The Fight for the Four Freedoms: What Made FDR and the Greatest Generation Truly Great*. New York: Simon & Schuster, 2014.

Knightley, Phillip. *The First Casualty, from the Crimea to Vietnam: The War Correspondent as Hero, Propagandist, and Myth Maker*. New York: Harcourt Brace Jovanovich, 1975.

Koch, Theodore Wesley. *War Libraries and Allied Studies*. New York: G. E. Stechert & Co., 1918.

Koop, Theodore F. *Weapon of Silence*. Chicago: University of Chicago Press, 1946.

Lorimer, Frank, and Frederick Osborn. *Dynamics of Population*. New York: The Macmillan Company, 1934.

Lucas, Richard. *Axis Sally*. Philadelphia and Newbury: Casemate Publishing, 2010.

MacGregor Jr., Morris J. *Integration of the Armed Forces 1940–1965*. Washington, DC: Center of Military History, US Army, 1981.

Mauldin, Bill. *The Brass Ring*. New York: W. W. Norton & Co., Inc., 1971.

McDavid, O.C. *My Name Is O.C.* Gene McDavid, 2003.

McGurn, Barrett. *Yank, the Army Weekly: Reporting the Greatest Generation*. Golden, Colorado: Fulcrum Publishing, 2004.

Mencken, H. L. *The American Language: Supplement II*. New York: Alfred A. Knopf, 1948.

Morehouse, Maggi M. *Fighting in the Jim Crow Army: Black Men and Women Remember World War II*. Lanham, Maryland: Rowman & Littlefield Publishers, Inc. 2000.

Motley, Mary Penick. *The Invisible Soldier: The Experience of the Black Soldier, World War II*. Detroit: Wayne State University Press, 1987.

Mott, Frank Luther. *American Journalism A History: 1690–1960*. Toronto, Canada: Macmillan, 1962.

Norquist, Ernest O. *Our Paradise: A GI's War Diary*. Hancock, Wisconsin: Pearl-Win Publishing Co., 1989.

O'Brien, Francis A. *Battling for Saipan*. New York: Ballantine Books, 2003.

Perret, Geoffrey. *Old Soldiers Never Die: The Life of Douglas MacArthur*. New York: Random House, 1996.

Peterson, Theodore. *Magazines in the Twentieth Century*. Urbana, Illinois: University of Illinois, 1956.

Pogue, Forrest C. *George C. Marshall: Education of a General 1880–1939*. New York: Viking Press, 1963.

Pogue, Forrest C. *George C. Marshall: Ordeal and Hope 1939–1942*. New York: Viking Press, 1966.

Pogue, Forrest C. *George C. Marshall: Statesman*. New York: Viking Penguin, 1987.

Pyle, Ernie. *Brave Men*. Lincoln and London: University of Nebraska Press, 2001.

Pyle, Ernie. *Here Is Your War*. New York: Pocket Books, 1944.

Rampersad, Arnold, and David Roessel, eds. "Let America Be America Again." In *The Collected Poems of Langston Hughes*. New York: Vintage Classics, 1994.

Robinson, Don. *News of the 45th*. New York: Grosset & Dunlap, 1944.

Rooney, Andy. *My War*. New York: Random House Times Books, 1995.

Roosevelt, James. *My Parents*. Chicago: Playboy Press, 1976.

Sansone, Leonard. *The Wolf*. New York: United Publishers, 1945.

Sayers, Michael, and Albert E. Kahn. *Sabotage*. New York: Harper & Bros. Publishers, 1942.

Sledge, E. B. *With the Old Breed at Peleliu and Okinawa*. New York: Ballantine Books, 2007.

Stouffer, Samuel A., Edward A. Suchman, Leland C. DeVinney, Shirley A. Star, and Robin M. Williams Jr. *The American Soldier: Adjustment During Army Life* (vol. 1). Princeton, New Jersey: Princeton University Press, 1949.

Sweeney, Michael S. *Secrets of Victory*. Chapel Hill, North Carolina: University of North Carolina Press, 2001.

Taylor, Edmond. *The Strategy of Terror*, revised ed. New York: Pocket Books, 1942.

Treadwell, Mattie E. *United States Army in World War II Special Studies: The Women's Army Corps*. Washington, DC: Office of the Chief of Military History Department of the Army, 1954.

Unsworth, Michael E., ed. *Military Periodicals*. New York: Greenwood Press, 1990.

Van Doren, Mark. *Man's Right to Knowledge and the Free Use Thereof.* New York: Columbia University, 1954.

Whitlock, Flint. *The Rock of Anzio*. Boulder, Colorado: Westview Press, 1998.

Winkler, Allan M. *The Politics of Propaganda: The Office of War Information 1942–1945*. New Haven, Connecticut: Yale University Press, 1978.

Woollcott, Alexander. *The Command Is Forward: Tales of the A.E.F. Battlefields as They Appeared in the Stars and Stripes*. New York: The Century Co., 1919.

# INDEX

**SYMBOLS**

Four Freedoms  5, 12, 60

**A**

Adams, Franklin Pierce  26, 58

Algeria  82

*Alhamabra Echo*  163

*American*  75

American Library Association  27

anticartoon crusade  88

"Approved by Censor" (poem)  44

*Arizona Republic*  142

Army Library Service  73, 75, 152

Atkinson, Rick  91

**B**

Baker, George  38, 58

Baldwin, Hanson  15

*Barbarian, The*  41

Bartholomew Building (Fort
    Bartholomew) (New York City)  58

*Baseball*  75

Basinger, Henry C.  63

Bastian, Fred  151

"Battle Baby"  75

Battle of Saipan  126

Battle of the Bulge  96, 98

Beasley, P.  141

Belgium  97, 103

Berg, Dave  38, 131

*Bi-Monthly Bitch*  41

Black Americans  137, 138

*Blue Bonnet*  29

Blunt, Roscoe  97, 98, 99

Bolling, Alexander R.  102, 105, 159,
    160

Bolte, Charles G.  64

bombs  35, 87

*Bonjour*  78

*Boston Herald*  70, 102

Bowie, Bob  150

*Brief*  132

Britain  8, 13

*Broadcaster, The*  33

*Bull Sheet*  41

**C**

*Camp Barkeley News*  41

Camp Blanding, Florida  18

Camp Butner  39

*Camp Claiborne News* 97

Camp Edwards *News* 33

*Camp Howze Howitzer* 97

Camp Newspaper Service (CNS) 36, 164

*Camp Parks Log* 41

Caniff, Milton 37

*Cannoneers, The* 33

Carnegie Corporation 27

cartoons 37, 58, 63, 81, 88, 129, 153, 164, 169

casualties 86, 93, 94, 97, 99, 100, 109, 111

censorship 13, 36, 62, 96, 100

Châtillon 119

Chatlain, Dean 2

Chavez, Alex 63

*Chicago Tribune* 71

*Chronicle, The* 92

Civilian Conservation Corps 72

Civil Rights Movement 145

Civil War 26

Clark, Mark 88, 152

*Clip Sheet* 36, 92, 164

*Cobra Chronicle* 33

*Cocktail, The* 92

Code of Censorship 15

"Codes of Wartime Practices for the American Press" 14

*Collier's* 75

Collins, Harry J. 110

combat 68, 116. *See also specific battles*

concentration camps 111, 114, 117

Corbett, Scott 106, 108, 110, 113, 169

Corps Public Relations Office 110

country guides 66

*Courier-Journal* 71

Cowling, William K., III 109

C rations 68

Creasman, James 110

Criminal Investigation Division (CID) 87

*Crisis, The* 138

"Cursified Advertising" 48

**D**

Dachau 110

*Daily Mirror* 70

Dann, Sam 94

"Death of Private Jones, The" 59

*Del Valle News* 39

*Detective Story* 75

*Devil's Digest* 41

discharge 157, 163

"Don't Send Me In" 125

donuts 127

Downs, William 100

draft, military 21

*Drum* 35

*Duck Board* 39

**E**

Early, Stephen 26

Editorial Control Law 6, 168

Edwards, Raymond 109

Eighty-Fourth 97, 158

Eighty-Second Airborne Division 84

Eisenhower, Dwight 56, 88, 93, 94, 124, 152

*Engineerful* 78

Erdmann, James 93

*Esquire* 75

Estoff, Bill 52

ETO 123, 124

eugenics 117

Executive Order 8985 14

*Extractor, The* 41

**F**

*Facts in Review* 11

field kits, recreational 30

Fifteenth Air Force 92

*59th Latrineogram* 41

*Fighter Post* 131

"Fighting Faces" 63

*Flying* 75

fog of the soul 156

food 68

*Fore n' Aft* 39

Fort Belvoir 39

Fort Huachuca 142

Fort McClellan, Alabama 18

Fort Niagara 35

Fort Sill 23

*45th Division News* 80, 83, 87, 91

Forty-Fifth Infantry Division (Thunderbirds) 82

*42d Rainbow Infantry Division World News* 110

Forty-Second 96, 106

Foxhole Press 34

France 8, 9, 10, 22, 94, 97

freedom of expression 167

Freeman, Don 38

friendship 36, 157

*FUBAR* ("'Fouled' Up Beyond All Recognition,") 41, 115

Furst, Peter 109

**G**

*Gangplank Gazette* 41

German Library of Information 11

Germany

    attacks from 90, 98

    Editorial Control Law of 6, 168

    falsehoods from 5

    mental warfare of 9

    military power of 21

    newspaper sales of 6

    Press Division within 7

    propaganda from 66, 77, 79, 80, 91, 99

    surrender of 114

    whispering campaigns of 9

*GI Galley* 31, 34, 35, 139, 164

Gill, Brendan 77

GI slang 33

Givens, Howard 63

Glocke, Grace 151

Goebbels, Joseph 139

*Gooney Tales* 41

Grant, Jane 76

grief 161

group living 46

"Guys Who Miss Their Buddies" 63

**H**

H. A. Moos Bookstore 72

Hardy, Alexander 8

Hargrove, Marion 17, 19

*Harper's Bazaar* 152

Harrison, Walter M. 80

Hastie, William H. 137

"Hate Your Enemies" 42

*Hawk's Cry* 139

Hazard, William 110, 113

Hazell, Watson and Viney 51

*Hellcat News* 41

*Hell on Wheels* 41

"Heroes Don't Win Wars." 132

Higgins, Marguerite 109

Hitler, Adolf 5, 6, 7, 8, 9, 65, 117

HMS *Malaya* 13

Holocaust 117

*Home Crier* 41

homesickness 47, 55, 70, 156

*Home Telegram* 101

*Home-Wrecker* 41

Hopkins, Harry 29

*Hospital Gauzette* 41

hospitals, publication for 62

House Appropriations Committee 22

Houston, Herbert S. 11

Hughes, Langston 136

Hutton, Bud 52

**I**

ideologies, as war cause 167

*Infantry Journal* 75

Information and Education Division 93

Intelligence Division (AEF) 25

internment camps 136

*Invasion Bulletin* 95

Italy 82, 86, 90

Iwo Jima 129, 130

*Iwo Jima Inquirer* 41

**J**

Jackson, Andrew 26

Japan 116, 126

Japanese Americans 136

Jefferson, Thomas 6

Jim Crow laws 138

Jordan Marsh department store 70

*Journal Herald* 70

journalists. *See also specific persons*

   combat of 53

   innovations by 96

   recruiting of 51

   tenacity of 4

   tension regarding 53

   travels of 14

   war coverage by 52

Julius Caesar 50

**K**

Kaplan, Arthur 144

Keppel, Frank 53

King, Ernest 15

Knightley, Phillip 120

Knox, Frank 12

Krock, Arthur 14

**L**

Lace (comic strip character) 38, 165

*Ladies' Home Journal* 152

*La Libre Belgique* 103

Lambiotte, E. J. 59

"Lament of a Private" 46

*La Métropole* 103

*L'Chaim* 41

Library War Service 27

Liebling, A. J. 77

*Life* 23, 75

Linden, Henning 109

Linotype machine 86

"A Little Story for the Nazis"
   (*45th Division News*) 91

Llewellyn, Ensley 50

Lockhart, Elmer 142

London, Helen 150

*Look* 75

*Love Nest* 169

**M**

MacArthur, Douglas 118, 152

MacKechnie, Ted 110

*Mademoiselle* 152

magazine kit 152

magazines 57, 72, 73, 75, 169.
   *See also specific publications*

mail 99

"Mail Call" 59

*Male Call* 38, 108, 164

Mankin, Douglas 146

*Marauder* 39

Marshall, George

Frederick Osborn and 122

leadership of 20, 38, 50, 62

letter from 54

newspaper expansion plan of 30

popularity of 48

quote of 77, 118

retirement and appointment of 163

Mattick, H. W. 56

Mauldin, Bill 38, 81, 83, 87, 169

*McCall's* 152

McGlamery, Mildred 150

McGurn, Barrett 60

McIntyre, Marvin H. 38

*Mein Kampf* (Hitler) 7

Mencken, H. L. 41

mental warfare 9. *See also* propaganda

"Men We Won't Forget" 104

Military Intelligence Branch (US
   Army) 93

mimeograph machine 31, 33, 34, 40, 85

*Modern Screen* 75

Moldauer, H. 60

Monroe, Marilyn 169

Moora, Bob 52

morale 93, 95, 121

motion picture field kit 31

*MP Blotter* 41

music field kit 31

Mussolini, Benito 87

"My Girl and Me" 45

**N**

NAACP 138

Napoleon 50

National Guard 22

Native Americans 137

natural disasters 35

Nazis. *See* Germany

Negro Artillery Unit 142

Nelson, Earl 132

New Deal 11

Newmark, Bill 108

newspapers.

   *See also specific publications*

   Adolf Hitler's control of 6

   as published abroad 33

   challenges of 33, 36, 95

   characteristics of 40

   field kit for 31, 77

   French 9

   growth of 16

   guides for 31

   headline errors within 100

   headlines, German 8

   inaccuracy of 130

   in the Southwest Pacific 123

   morale and 25

   power of 5

   regulation of 163

   requirements for 71

   resistance 10

   secrecy within 12

   sentimental preservation of 48

   statistics regarding 136

   unit-based origin of 30, 40

*Newsweek* 74, 75, 76

*New York Daily News* 147

*New Yorker* 75, 76, 77, 145

Ninety-First Air Service Group 127

*"A 92nd Seabee's Yuletide Prayer"* 155

Normandy 95

Norquist, Ernest 70

North Africa 65

Nugent, Jane 150

**O**

Office of Censorship 14, 28, 148

Office of the Chief of Military History 147

Office of War Information (OWI) 92

officers, military 24

O'Hara, John 77

*Ohio Rainbow Reveille* 106

Omaha Beach 97

*Omnibook* 75

"One Damned Island After Another" 135

105th Infantry Division 18

Operation Husky 82

*Oregonian* 70

Osborn, Frederick 117

*Outfit* 62, 164

*Overseas Woman* 153

**P**

*Palace Guard* 92

paper rationing 71, 73

Parker, Dorothy 77

Patton, George 85, 88

Pearl Harbor 14, 15, 73

"'Perfect' Paper, A" 139

Perret, Geoffrey 120, 122

Pershing, John J. 25, 54, 69

pinups 129

*Pocket Guide to North Africa, A* 66

poetry 59. *See also specific poems*

Poland 8

"Pony Edition" 75

*Popular Mechanics* 75

*Popular Photography* 75

*Post Review* 33

Press Division (German Reich) 7

Price, Byron 14

printing facilities 103

prisoners of war (POWs) 101, 102

"Problem Hour" 129

propaganda

    fighting against 167

    from Germany 66, 77, 79, 80, 91, 99

    German spending for 11

    Japanese 126

    susceptibility to 101

    US Army 92

    within the United States 11

*Prop Wash* 33

*Providence Sunday Journal* 70

publishing

    challenges of 33

    friendship within 36

    process of 5, 31, 85, 170

publishing house, liberation of 87

Pyle, Ernie 67, 69, 121

**R**

racial intermingling 137

radio 101

*Radio News* 75

*Railsplitter* 97, 102, 158

*Rainbow Reveille* 106

*Ramp-Age, The* 41

Ramsey, Claude 30

*Reader's Digest* 73, 75

recreation 118

redeployment 157

Reese, Montana 128

resistance newspapers 10

Rice, Grantland 26, 58

Roberts, Orville 127, 130

Robinson, Don 83, 87

Robinson, William J. 150

Rogers, Edith Nourse 146

Rooney, Andy 52, 53, 57, 169

Roosevelt, Eleanor 23

Roosevelt, Franklin 5, 11, 14, 21, 28, 60, 67

Roosevelt, Theodore, Jr. 88

Ross, Harold 26, 58, 75

**S**

"Sad Sack" cartoon 58

San Antonio Aviation Cadet Center 42

Sandler, Gilbert 30, 76

Sansone, Leonard 39

Santiago, Gustave 144

*Saturday Evening Post* 27, 75

*SBAD News* 41

*Scars and Gripes* 41

*Screamer, The* 41

*Sea Devil Sentinel* 167

secrecy 12, 15

*See Here, Private Hargrove*
    (Hargrove) 19

segregation 136, 137, 138, 145

Selective Training and Service Act
    22, 137

Senate Military Affairs Committee 146

*Service Woman* 153

*S.H.A.E.F.* 95

Sicily, battle for 82

*615th Bakery Weekly* 41

slang, GI 33

Sledge, E. B. 116

Smith, Gaddis 28

*SNAFU* ("Situation Normal: All
    'Fouled' Up") 41

*Snarkyville Gazette* 41

soldiers. *See also specific persons*
    characteristics of 17
    combat challenges of 68
    deployment of 65
    diet of 68
    discharge of 114, 157, 163
    discontent of 124, 132
    emotions of 156, 161
    expectations for 88
    fog of the soul of 156
    group living of 46
    nostalgia of 158
    recreational needs of 118
    supplies of 82, 95

training for 43
    women's magazines and 152
"A Soldier's Guide to the United States
    of America" 160

Solomon Islands 15

*Sorryburg Gazette* 41

*Sortie* 92

*South Pacific Daily News* 41

Southwest Pacific 118, 122

"So You Wanna go Home, Eh?" 55

Spear and Company furniture store 70

Special Service Division 30, 31, 54,
    60, 69, 72, 95, 117, 122

*Spectator, The* 92

*Sponge City Splash* 35

sports and games field kit 31

*Stars and Stripes* 26, 51, 81, 88, 141,
    149, 168, 169

Stewart Field 33

Stimson, Henry 117, 137

"Strictly GI" 47

suicide 126

Sulzberger, Arthur 13, 15, 28

*Sunday Mud & Mildew* 41

*Superman* 75

Surdan, Herman 56

survivor's guilt 161

*SWPA Maptalk* 123

synthetic lemonade 68

**T**

*Tale Spinner* 42

*TARFU* ("Things Are Really 'Fouled'
    Up") 41

*Terry and the Pirates* 37

Third Army 142

*Third Strike, The* 34

*This Is It!* 127

Thunderbirds (Forty-Fifth Infantry Division) 82

Thurber, James 77

*Time* 23, 48, 75, 76

"To The Unknown" 161

*Tough Sheet* 34, 35, 124

*Trail Blazer* 35

training 19, 68

Trautman, Ray 72, 152

Trimmingham, Rupert 142

troops. *See* soldiers

Truman, Harry S. 145

Twenty-First Engineers 92

*24th Hi-Lites* 38

typewriters 31

typhoons 35

**U**

underground newspapers 10, 103

*United States News* 118

United States Seventh Army 109

US Air Force 22

US Army

    conditions of 22

    decline of 21

    facilities conditions of 18

    funding for 21

    Japanese Americans within 136

    morale of 25

    propaganda from 92

    rewards within 24

    service terms of 20

    training within 19

    weapons of 18

US military, demographics of 137

US Navy 15, 28

USS *Alcyone* 76

**V**

V-E Day 157

*Vigilante, The* 41

V-J Day 157

V-mail technology 74

**W**

"WAACs Drop An 'A'" 149

*WAC News* 153

Wadsworth, James 3

war correspondents. *See* journalists

War Department 148, 151, 163

War of 1812 26

War Production Board (WPB) 71, 73

Washington, George 25

Watson, Mark 58

weaponry 18, 91, 167

*Western Trails* 75

whispering campaigns 9. *See also* propaganda

White, E. B. 77

Whitman, William 60

Wilson, Wesley G. 56

Wilson, Woodrow 11

*With Pen and Sword* (Chatlain) 3

*Wolf, The* 39, 92, 108

*Woman's Home Companion* 44, 152

women, as volunteers 146

Women's Army Auxiliary Corps
(WAAC) 146

Women's Army Corps (WACs) 147

Woollcott, Alexander 26, 58, 156

Wooten, Henry S., Jr. 143

World War I 25, 28

World War II, opinion polls regarding
22


**X**

*X-Isle, The* 41


**Y**

*Yankee Doodler* 157

*Yank, the Army Weekly* 57, 139, 143,
146, 149, 164, 168